·Bartholomew·

GLASGOW
Streetfinder
COLOUR ATLAS

Contents

Bartholomew
An Imprint of HarperCollins*Publishers*

ISBN 0 7028 2710 X   GI 7716 ANB

Key to map symbols

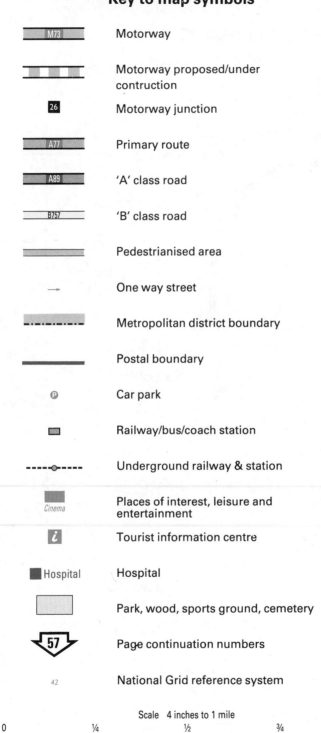

M73	Motorway
	Motorway proposed/under contruction
26	Motorway junction
A77	Primary route
A89	'A' class road
B757	'B' class road
	Pedestrianised area
→	One way street
	Metropolitan district boundary
	Postal boundary
Ⓟ	Car park
	Railway/bus/coach station
---○---	Underground railway & station
Cinema	Places of interest, leisure and entertainment
i	Tourist information centre
Hospital	Hospital
	Park, wood, sports ground, cemetery
57	Page continuation numbers
42	National Grid reference system

Scale 4 inches to 1 mile

0	¼	½	¾	1 mile
0	500	1000	1500	metres

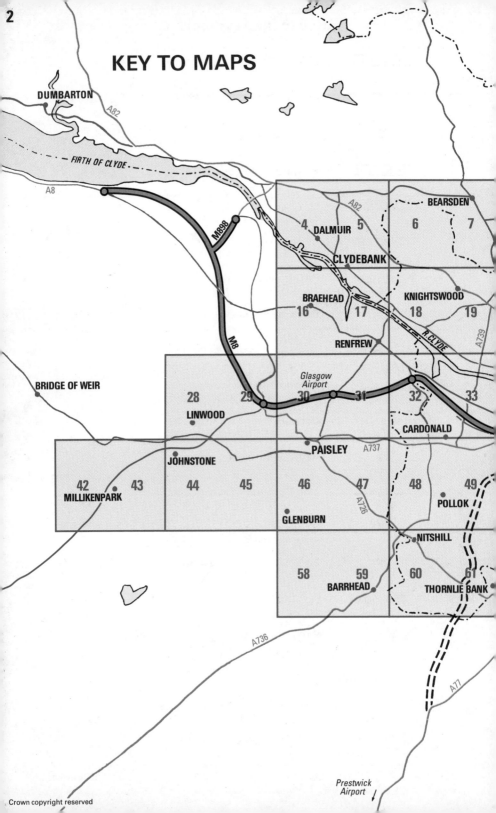

2

KEY TO MAPS

DUMBARTON

A82

FIRTH OF CLYDE

A8

M998

M8

BRIDGE OF WEIR

BEARSDEN

A82

4 DALMUIR 5 6 7

CLYDEBANK

KNIGHTSWOOD

BRAEHEAD

16 17 18 19

RENFREW

R. CLYDE

A739

Glasgow Airport

28 29 30 31 32 33

LINWOOD

CARDONALD

JOHNSTONE PAISLEY *A737*

42 43 44 45 46 47 48 49

MILLIKENPARK

POLLOK

GLENBURN

A726

NITSHILL

58 59 60 61

BARRHEAD THORNLIEBANK

A736

A77

Prestwick Airport

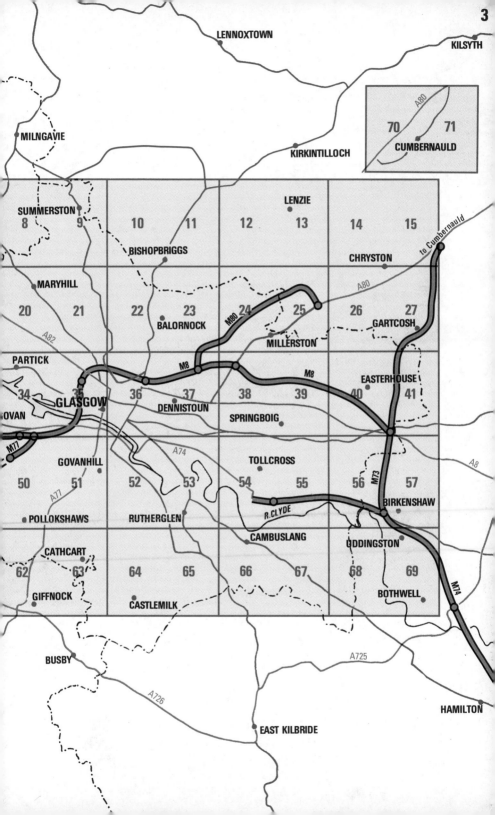

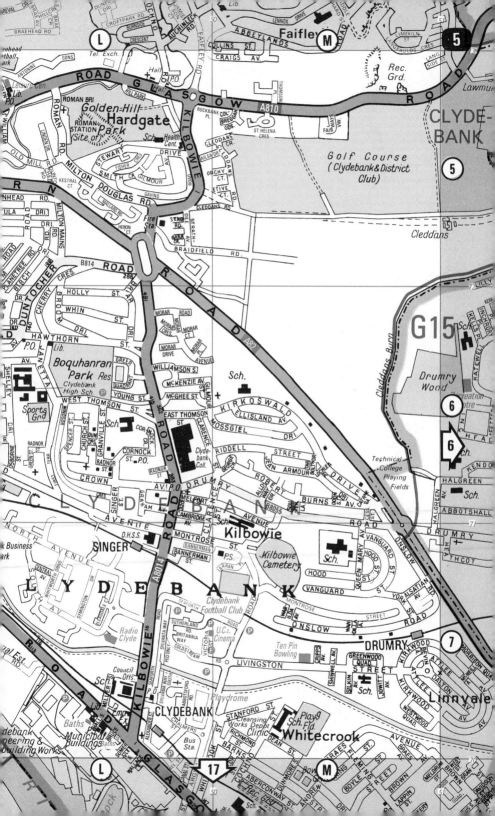

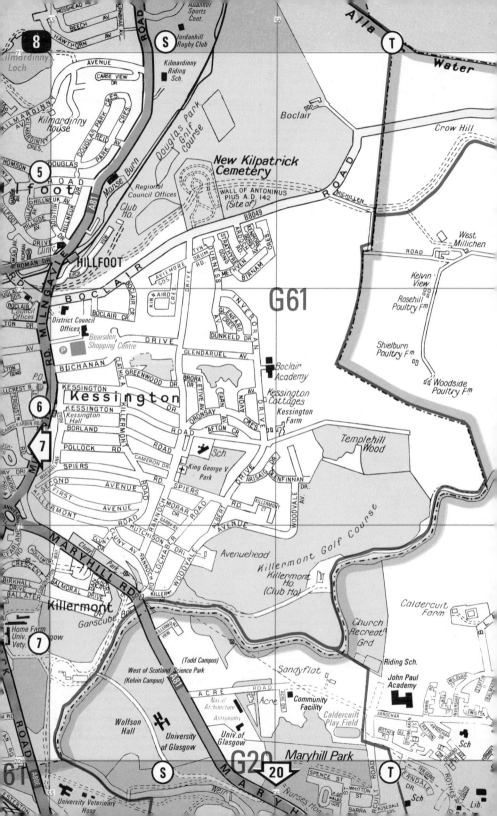

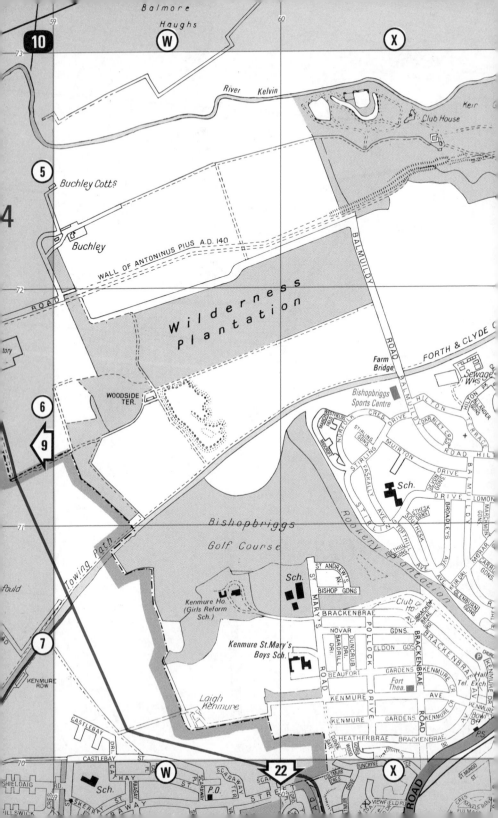

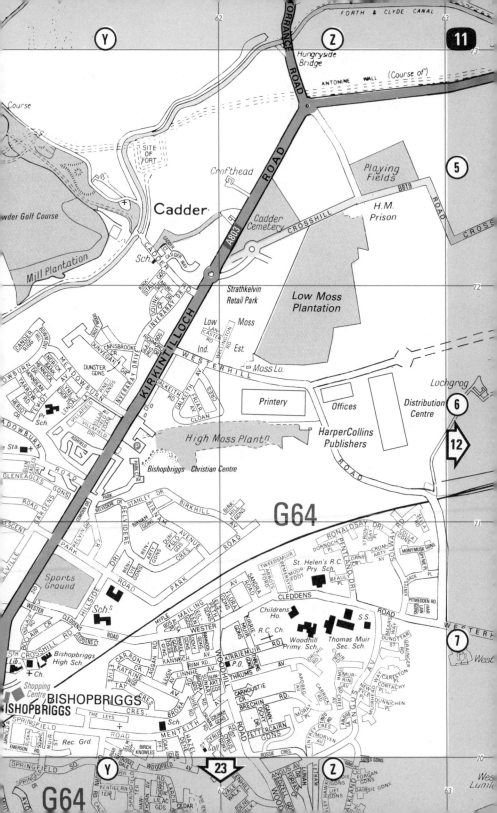

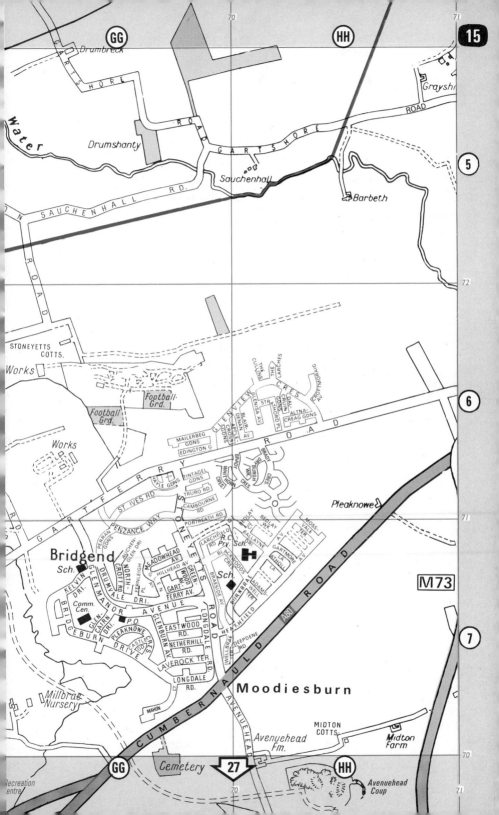

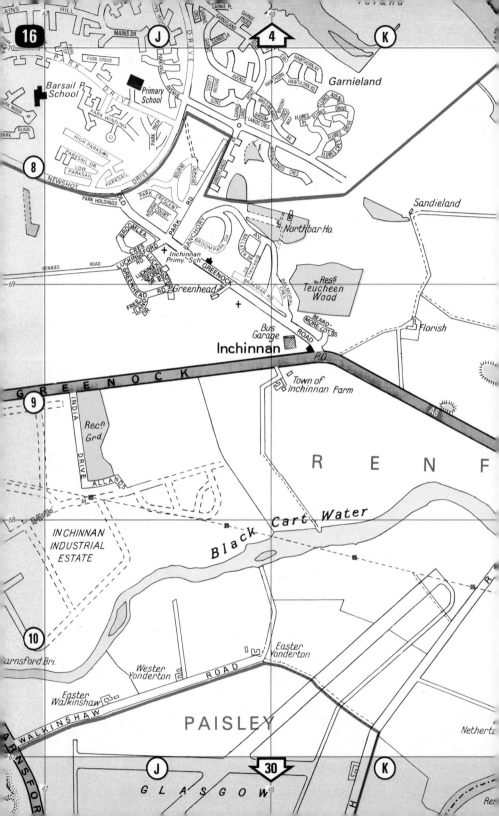

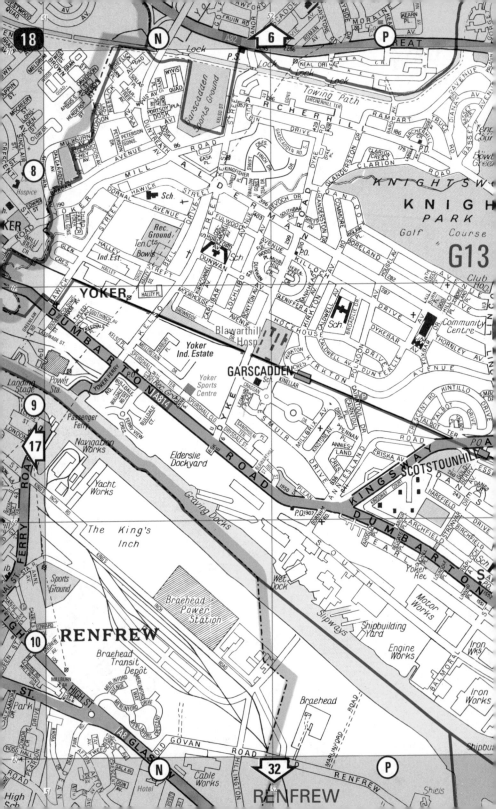

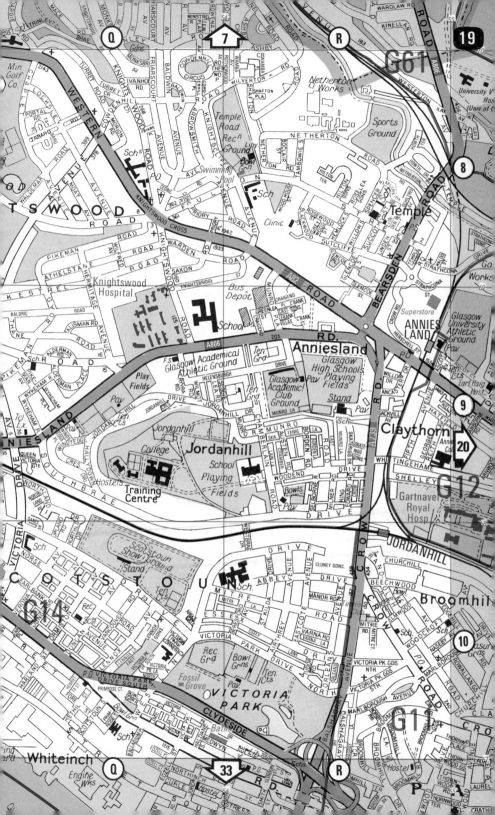

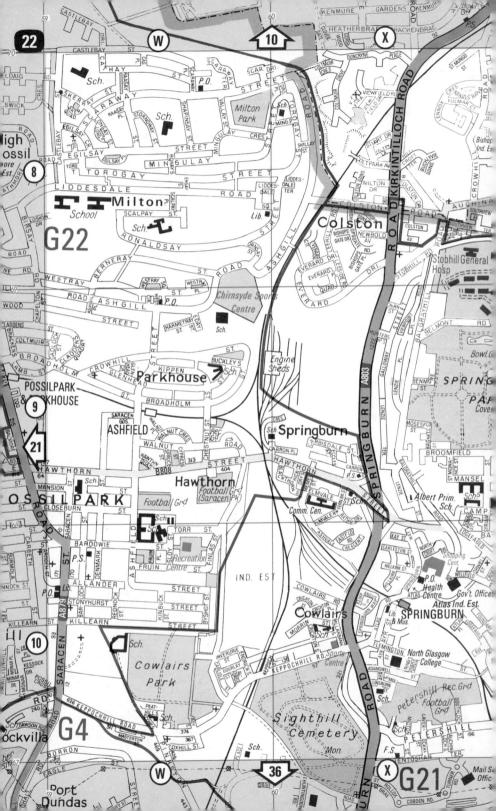

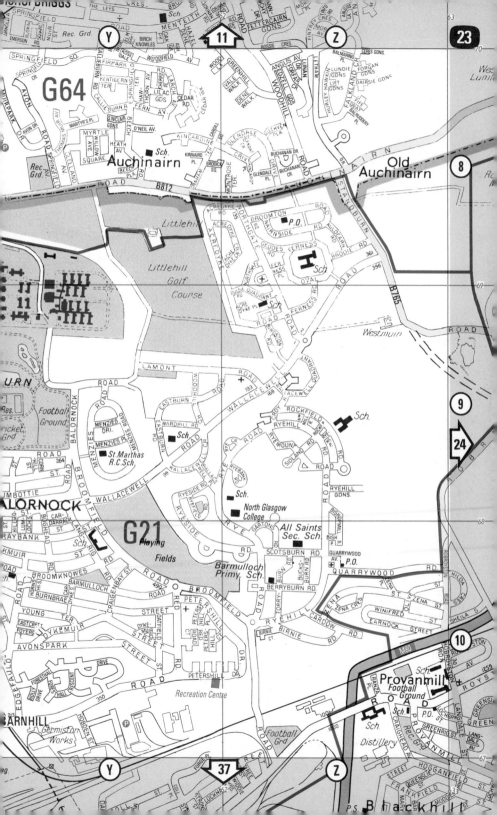

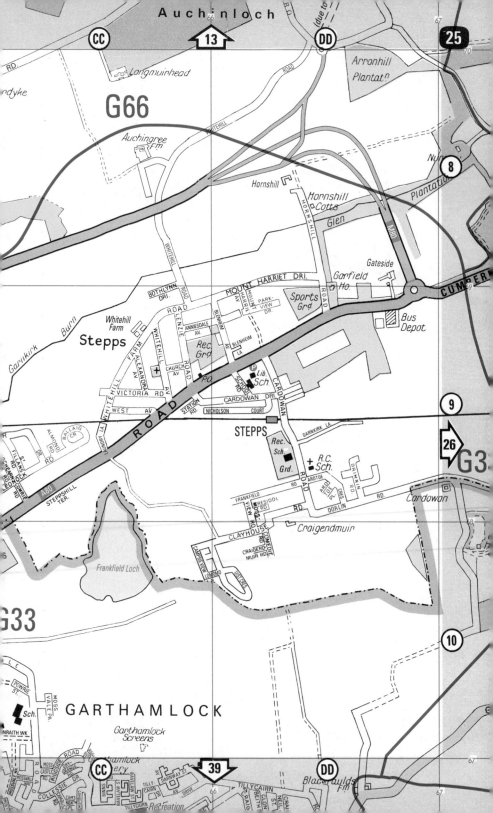

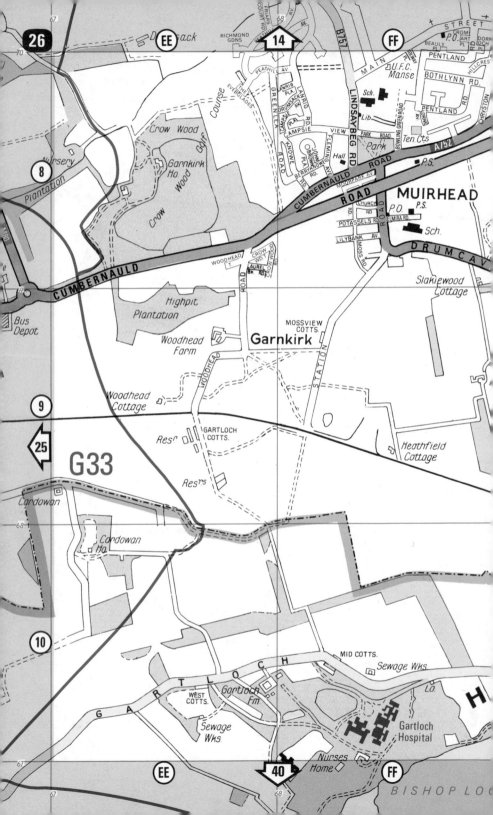

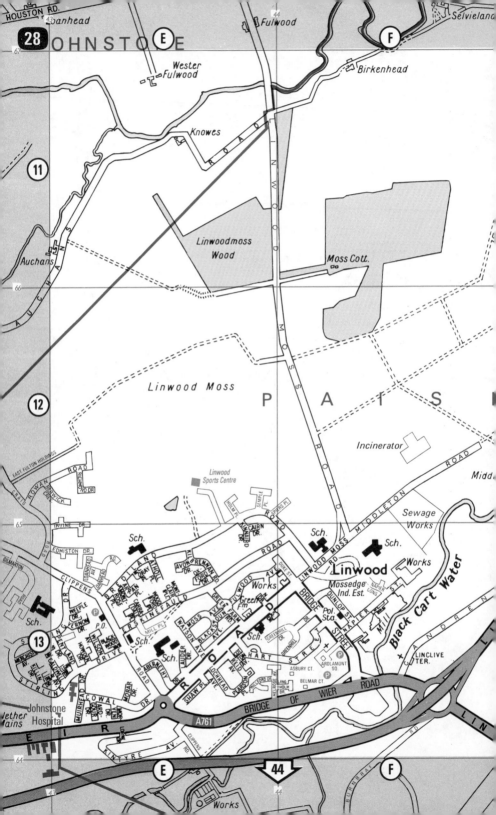

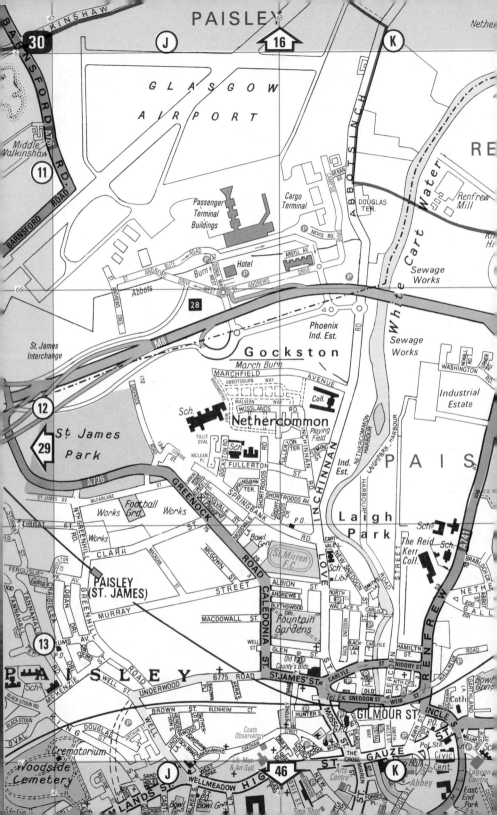

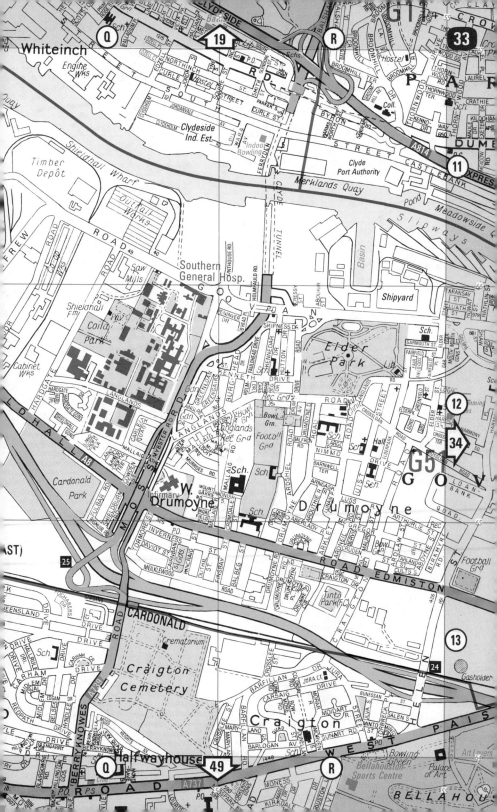

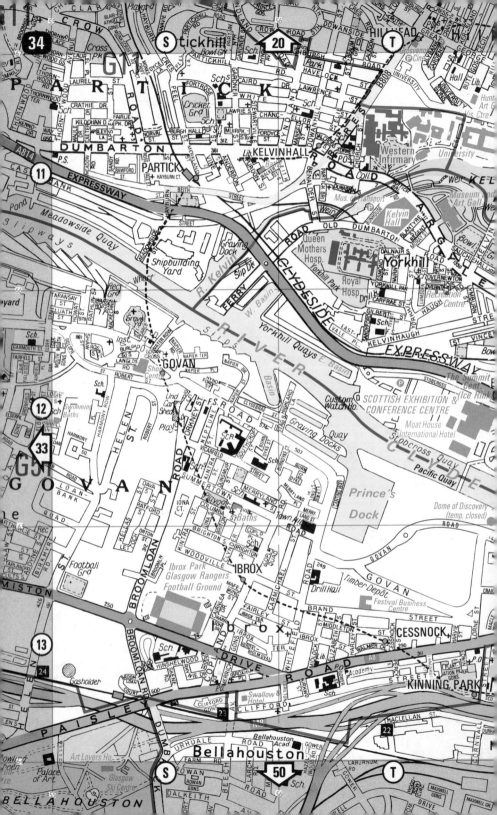

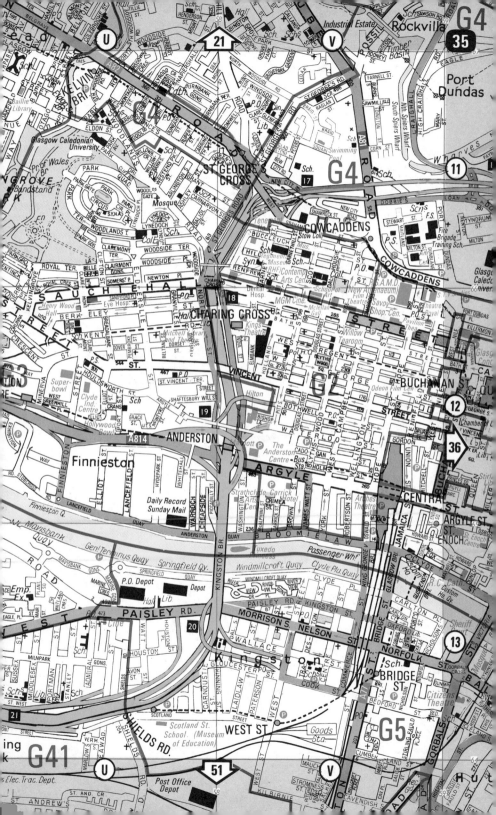

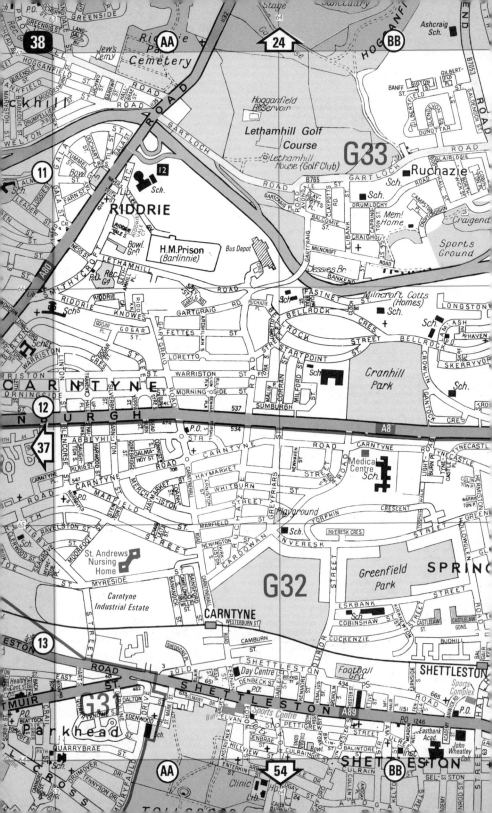

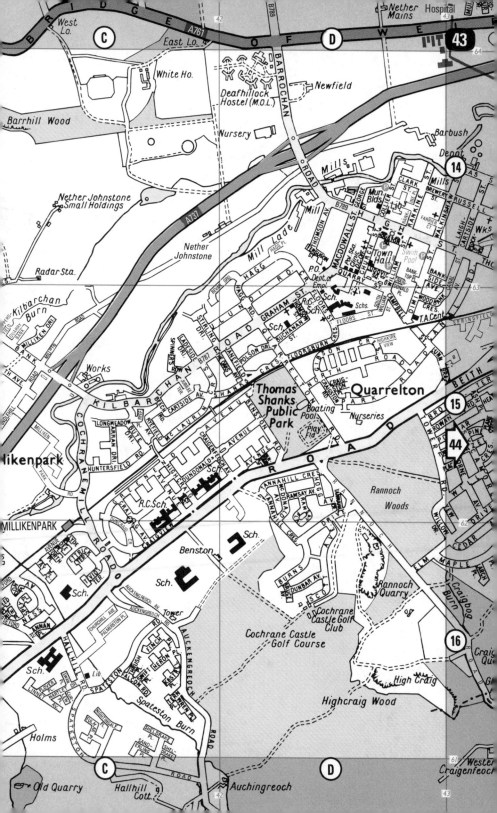

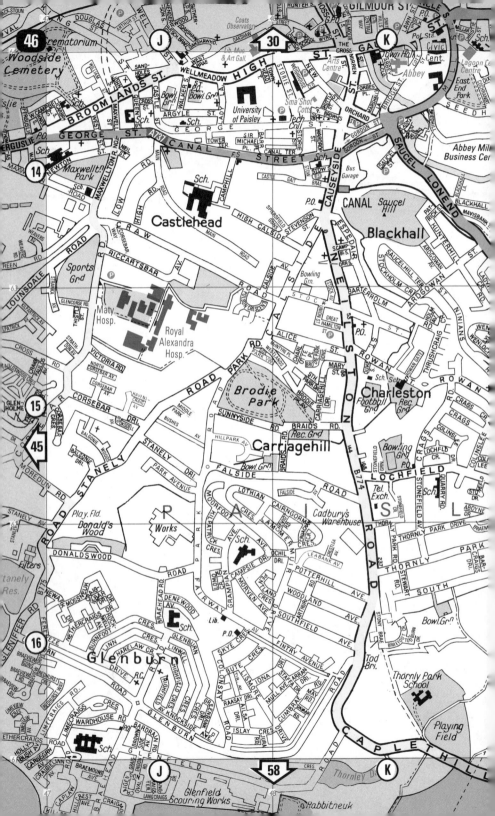

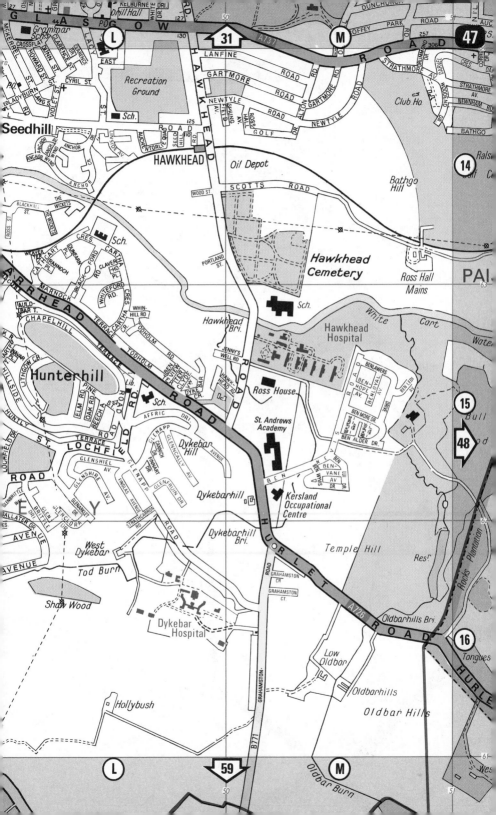

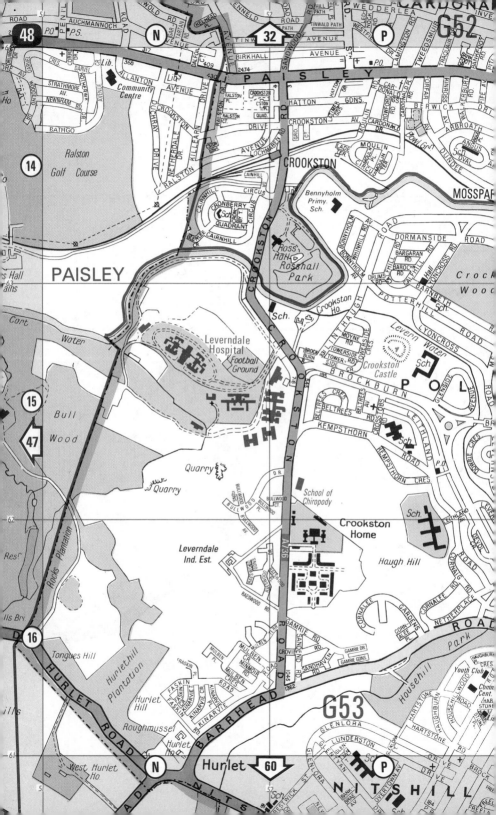

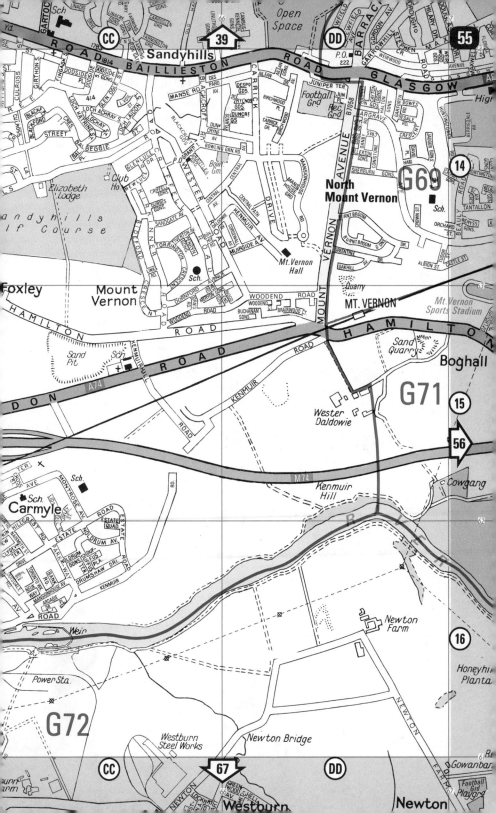

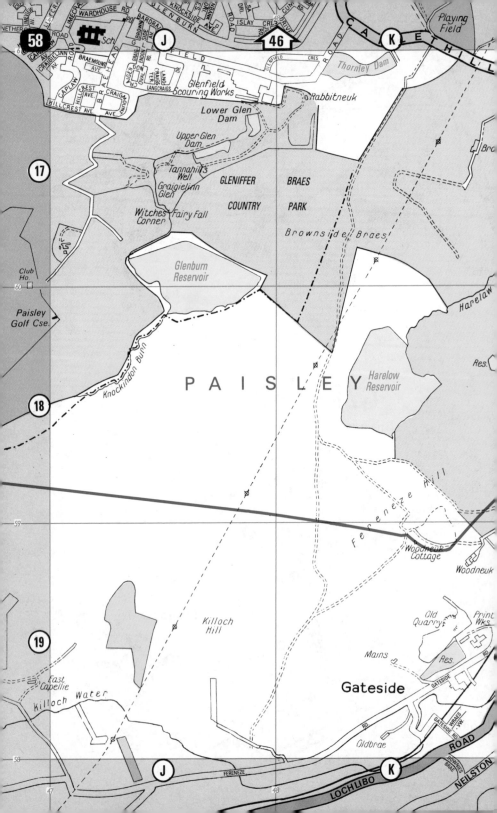

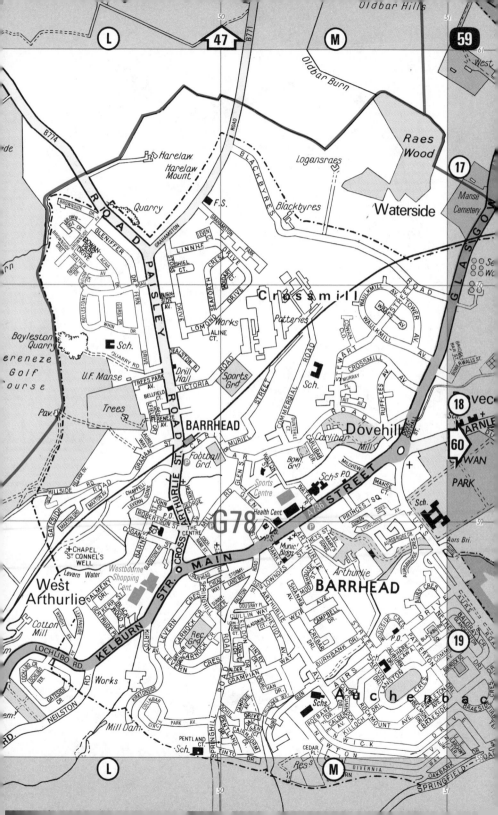

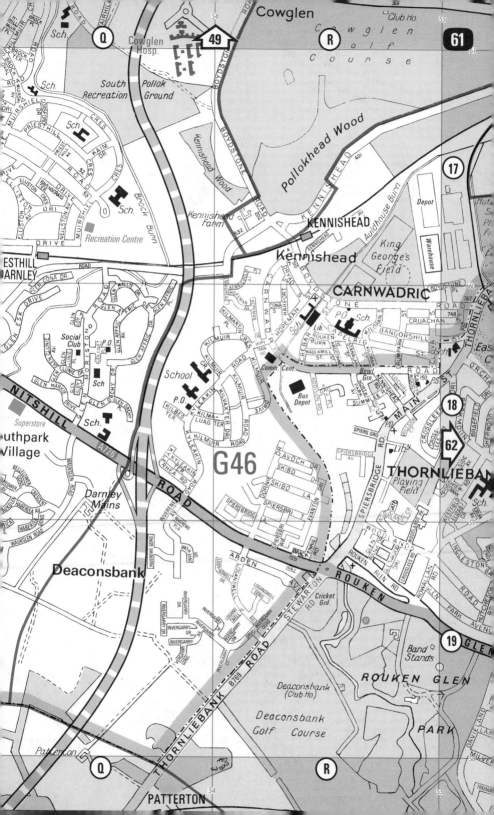

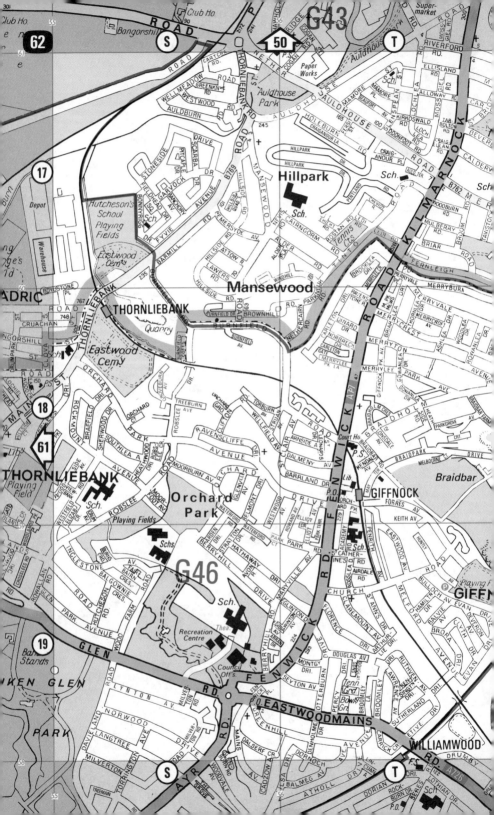

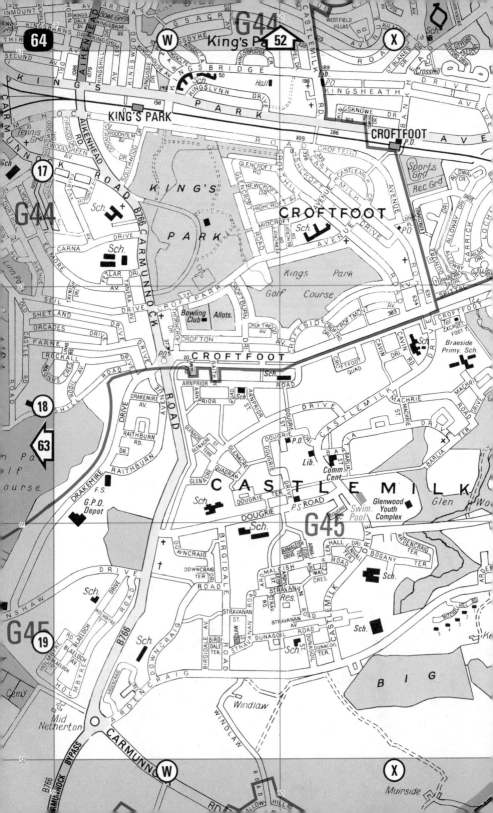

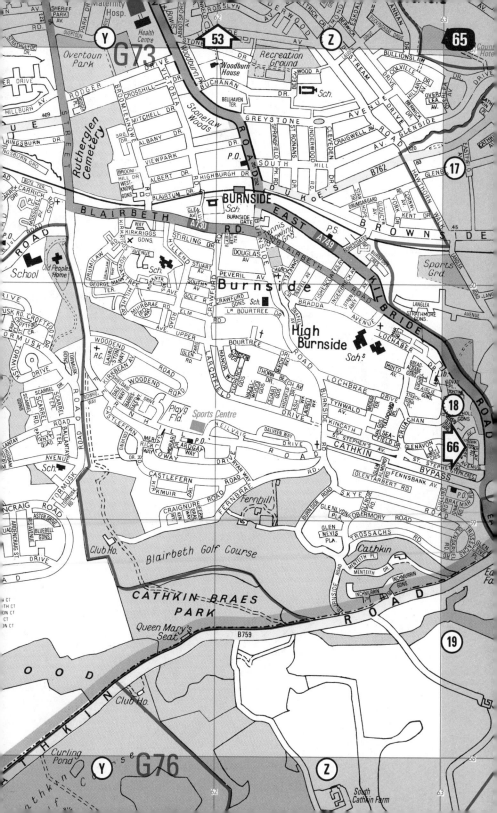

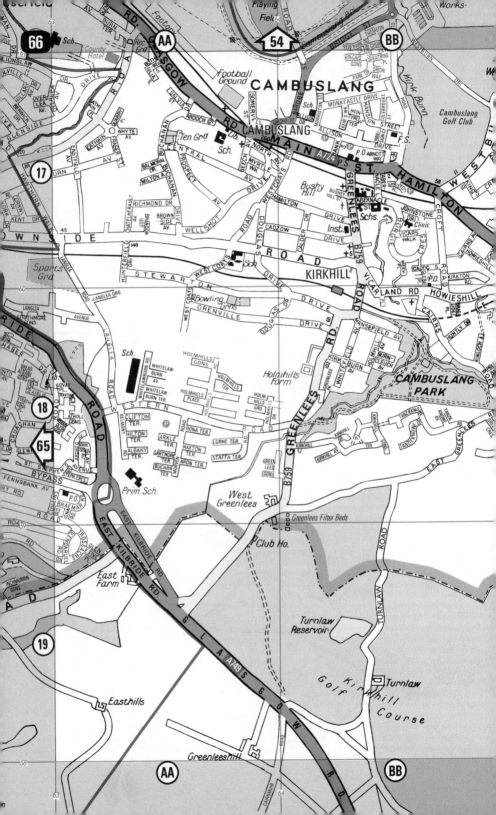

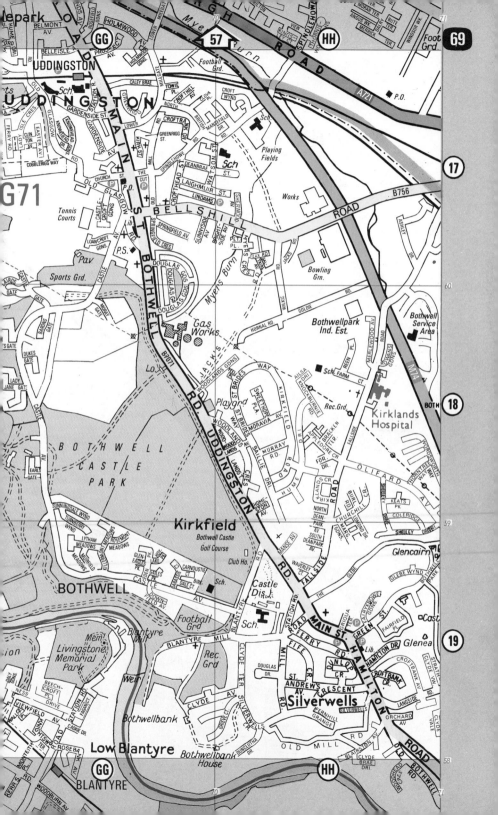

Glasgow

Information

Contents

History & Development

The City of Glasgow began life as a makeshift hamlet of huts huddled round a 6thC church, built by St. Mungo on the banks of a little salmon river - the Clyde. It was called Gleschow, meaning 'beloved green place' in Celtic. The cathedral was founded in 1136; the university, the second oldest in Scotland, was established in the 15thC; and in 1454 the flourishing medieval city wedged between the cathedral and the river was made a Royal burgh. The city's commercial prosperity dates from the 17thC when the lucrative tobacco, sugar and cotton trade with the New World flourished. The River Clyde, Glasgow's gateway to the Americas, was dredged, deepened and widened in the 18thC to make it navigable to the city's heart.

By the 19thC, Glasgow was the greatest shipbuilding centre in the world. From the 1820s onwards, it grew in leaps and bounds westwards along a steep ridge of land running parallel with the river. The hillside became encased in an undulating grid of streets and squares. Gradually the individualism, expressed in one-off set pieces characteristic of the 18thC and early 19thC, gave way to a remarkable coherent series of terraced squares and crescents of epic proportions - making Glasgow one of the finest of Victorian cities. But the price paid for such rapid industrialisation, the tremendous social problems manifest in the squalor of some of the worst of 19thC slums, was high. Today the city is still the commercial and industrial capita of the West of Scotland. The most notorious of the slums have been cleared but the new buildings lack that sparkling clenchfisted Glaswegian character of the 19thC. Ironically, this character was partially destroyed when the slums were cleared for it wasn't the architecture that had failed, only the bureaucrats, who designated such areas as working class ghettos.

Districts
Little remains of medieval Glasgow,

which stood on the wedge of land squeezed between the cathedral and the River Clyde. Its business centre was The Cross, a space formed by the junction of several streets - the tall, square Tolbooth Steeple, 1626, in the middle. Opposite is Trongate, an arch astride a footpath, complete with tower and steeple salvaged from 17thC St. Mary's Church - destroyed by fire in 1793. The centre of 20thC Glasgow is George Square, a tree-lined piazza planned in 1781 and pinned down by more than a dozen statues including an 80 foot high Doric column built in 1837 to carry a statue of Sir Walter Scott. Buildings of interest: the monumental neo-Baroque City Chambers 1883-88 which takes up the east side and the Merchants' House 1874, on the west. To the south of the square, in a huddle of narrow streets, is the old Merchant City. Of interest here is the elegant Trades House, 85 Glassford Street, built by Robert Adam in 1794. An elegant Ionic portico stands on a rusticated ground storey flanked by domed towers. Hutcheson's Hospital, 158 Ingram Street, is an handsome Italianate building designed by David Hamilton in 1805. Nearby is Stirling's Library, originally an 18thC private residence, it became the Royal Exchange in 1827 when the Corinthian portico was added. To the north west is Kelvingrove, Victorian Glasgow at its best. Built around a steep saddle of land, landscaped by Paxton in 1850 and lined along its edge with handsome terraces.

Last but not least are the banks of the River Clyde. From Clyde Walkway on the north bank you can see: the Suspension Bridge of 1871 with its pylons in the form of triumphal arches; 17thC Merchants' Steeple; the Gothic Revival St. Andrew's R.C. Cathedral of 1816; the church, built 1739, in nearby St. Andrew's Square is a typical copy of London's St. Martin-in-the-Fields.

City of Glasgow Local Information Guide

Useful Information

Area of City 79 sq. miles (approx)

Population (Glasgow City)
(1993 estimate) 681,470

Early Closing Days
Tuesday with alternative of Saturday. Most of the shops in the central area operate six-day trading.

Electricity 240 volts A.C.

Emergency Services
Police, Fire and Ambulance. Dial 999 on any telephone.

Licensing Hours
Public Houses
Daily (except Sundays) 11 a.m. to 2.30 p.m. and 5 to 11 p.m. (many open continuously 11 a.m. to 11 p.m.) Sundays, 12.30 to 2.30 p.m. and 6.30 to 10.30 p.m.
Restaurants, Hotels and Public Houses with catering facilities; same as above but can be extended for drinks with meals.

Information Bureau

Tourist Information Centres:
35 St. Vincent Place
Glasgow. 0141 204 4400

Town Hall, Abbey Close
Paisley. 0141 889 0711

Glasgow Airport (Abbotsinch)
Paisley. 0141 848 4440

Pier Head, Gourock
(Summer only)
01475 639467

Help & Advice

British Broadcasting Corporation
Queen Margaret Drive, G12 8DQ.
0141 339 8844

British Council
6 Belmont Crescent, G12 8ES.
0141 339 8651

British Telecom Scotland
Glasgow Area
Westergate Chambers, 11 Hope Street, Glasgow, G2 6AB. All Enquiries 0141 220 1234 or dial 100 and ask for FREEFONE BT GLASGOW.

Chamber of Commerce
30 George Square, G2 1EG.
0141 204 2121

Citizens Advice Bureau
87 Bath Street, Glasgow, G2 4HW
0141 331 2345/6/7/8
119 Main Street, Glasgow, G40 1HA
0141 554 0336
27 Dougrie Drive, Castlemilk, Glasgow, G45 9AD 0141 634 0338

139 Main Street (Town Hall),
Rutherglen, G73 2JJ 0141 647 5100
216 Main Street, Barrhead, G78 1SN
0141 881 2032
1145 Maryhill Road, Glasgow, G20 9AZ
0141 946 6373/4
46 Township Centre, Easterhouse,
Glasgow, G34 9DS 0141 771 2328

Consumer Advice Centre
St. Enoch House, 1 St. Enoch Square,
Glasgow, G1 4BH 0141 204 0262

Customs and Excise
21 India Street, G2 4PZ 0141 221 3828

H.M. Immigration Office
Admin Block D, Argyll Avenue, Glasgow
Airport 0141 887 4115

Housing Aid and Advice
Shelter, 53 St. Vincent Crescent,
Glasgow, G3 8NQ 0141 221 8895/6

Legal Aid and Advice
Castlemilk Advice and Law Centre
27 Dougrie Drive, Glasgow, G45 9AD
0141 634 0338

Law Centre
30 Dougrie Drive, G45 9AG
0141 634 0313

Lost Property
Strathclyde Passenger Transport
Executive
Glasgow Central Station 0141 335 4362
(Scotrail Trains)
Glasgow Queen Street Station 0141 335
3276 (Scotrail Trains and Underground)
Buses - Office of bus company
Trains - Station of arrival.
Elsewhere in City - Strathclyde Police.
Lost Property Department, 173 Pitt
Street, G2 0141 204 1468

Passport Office
Northgate 96 Milton Street, Glasgow,
G4 0BT 0141 332 0271

**Registrar of Births, Deaths and
Marriages**
1 Martha Street, G1 4PF 0141 225 7677
Hours - Monday to Friday 9.15 a.m. to
4.00 p.m.

Births must be registered within twenty-
one days, deaths within eight days and
marriages within three days. The
Registrar should be consulted at least
one month before intended date of
marriage.

**Royal Scottish Society for the
Prevention of Cruelty to Children**
15 Annfield Place, G31 2XE
0141 556 1156

**RNID - Royal National Institute for
the Deaf**
9 Clairmont Gardens, Glasgow, G3
7LW 0141 332 0343

Samaritans
218 West Regent Street, Glasgow, G2
4DQ 0141 248 4488

**Scottish Society for the Mentally
Handicapped**
13 Elmbank Street, Glasgow, G2 4QA
0141 226 4541

Scottish Television
Cowcaddens, G2   0141 332 9999

**Society for the Prevention of Cruelty
to Animals**
15 Royal Terrace, G3 7NY   (Business
Hours) 0141 332 0716

Newspapers

Morning Daily
Daily Record
Anderston Quay, G3 8DA.
0141 248 7000

The Herald
195 Albion Street, G1 0141 552 6255

Scottish Daily Express
Park Circus Place, G3 0141 332 9600

The Scotsman
181 - 195 West George Street, G2 2LB
0141 221 6485

Evening Daily
Evening Times
195 Albion Street, G1 0141 552 6255

Weekly
Scottish Sunday Express
Park Circus Place, G3 0141 332 9600

Sunday Mail
Anderston Quay, G3 8DA
0141 248 7000

Sunday Post
144 Port Dundas Road, G4 0HF
0141 332 9933

Parking

Car Parking in the central area of Glasgow is controlled. Parking meters are used extensively and signs indicating restrictions are displayed at kerbsides and on entry to the central area. Traffic Wardens are on duty.

British Rail Car Parks
(Open 24 hours)
Central Station
Queen Street Station

Multi-Storey Car Parks
(Open 24 hours)
Anderston Cross: Cambridge Street: George Street: Mitchell Street: Port Dundas Road: Waterloo Street.

(Limited Opening)
Charing Cross: Cowcaddens Road: St. Enoch Centre:Sauchiehall Street Centre

Surface Car Parks
Cathedral Street (Concert Hall):Dunlop Street: High Street: Ingram Street: King Street: McAlpine Street: Oswald Street: Shuttle Street:

Post Offices

Head Post Office
George Square, G2 0141 248 2882
Open Monday to Thursday 9 a.m. to 5.30 p.m. Fridays 9.30 a.m. to 5.30 p.m. Saturdays 9 a.m. to 12.30 p.m. Closed Sunday.

Taxis

Glasgow has over 1400 traditional London type taxis, all licensed by the Glasgow District Council and all fitted with meters sealed and approved by the Council. A fare card stating the current tariff is displayed in a prominent position within each taxi. At the time of publishing a three mile journey costs £3.10 and waiting time is charged at 12½p per minute. The total price of each journey is shown on the meter. Fares are normally reviewed annually by the council. Each taxi can carry a maximum of five passengers.

The major taxi companies in the city offer City tours at fixed prices, listing the places of interest to be visited, leaflets are available at all major hotel reception areas. Tours vary from 2 to 3 hours and in price between £20 and £28. A tour "Glasgow by Night" is also available.

Any passenger wishing to travel to a destination outside the Glasgow District Boundary should ascertain from the driver the fare to be charged or the method of calculating the fare PRIOR to making the journey.

Complaints
Any complaints regarding the conduct of a taxi driver should be addressed to the Senior Enforcement Officer, Town Clerk's Office, City Chambers, Glasgow. 0141 227 4535

Local Government

Strathclyde Regional Council
Strathclyde House, 20 India Street
Glasgow, G2 4PF
0141 204 2900

District Councils:

Argyll & Bute
District Council Headquarters
Kilmory, Lochgilphead PA31 8RT
01546 602127

Bearsden & Milngavie
Municipal Building, Boclair
Bearsden G61 2TQ
0141 942 2262

Clydebank
Council Offices, Rosebery Place
Clydebank G81 1TG
0141 941 1331

Clydesdale
Clydesdale District Offices
Lanark ML11 7JT
01555 661331

Cumbernauld & Kilsyth
Council Offices, Bron Way
Cumbernauld G67 1DZ
01236 722131

Cummock & Doon Valley
Council Offices, Lugar
Cummock KA18 3JQ
01290 22111

Cunninghame
Cunninghame House
Irvine KA12 8EE
01294 74166

Dumbarton
Crosslet House
Dumbarton G82 3NS
01389 65100

East Kilbride
Civic Centre
East Kilbride G74 1AB
01355 271200

Eastwood
Council Offices
Eastwood Park, Rouken Glen Road
Rouken Glen, Giffnock
Glasgow G46 6UG
0141 638 6511
0141 638 1101

Glasgow City
City Chambers
Glasgow G2 1DU
0141 221 9600

Hamilton
Town House
102 Cadzow Street
Hamilton ML3 6HH
01698 282323

Inverclyde
Municipal Buildings
Greenock PA15 1LY
01475 724400

Kilmarnock & Loudoun
Civic Centre
Kilmarnock KA1 1BY
01563 21140

Kyle & Carrick
Burns House
Burns Statue Square
Ayr KA7 1UT
01292 281511

Monklands
Municipal Buildings
Dunbeth Road
Coatbridge ML5 3LF
01236 441200

Motherwell
P.O. Box 14
Civic Centre
Motherwell ML1 1TW
01698 266166

Renfrew
Municipal Buildings
Cotton Street
Paisley PA1 1BU
0141 889 5400

Strathkelvin
Tom Johnston House
Civic Way
Kirkintilloch
Glasgow G66 4TJ
0141 776 7171

Buildings & Shops

Interesting Buildings

Victorian Glasgow was extremely eclectic architecturally. Good examples of the Greek Revival style are Royal College of Physicians 1845, by W.H. Playfair and the Custom House 1840, by G.L. Taylor. The Queen's Room 1857, by Charles Wilson, is a handsome temple used now as a Christian Science church. The Gothic style is seen at its most exotic in the Stock Exchange 1877, by J. Burnet. The new Victorian materials and techniques with glass, wrought and cast iron were also ably demonstrated in the buildings of the time. Typical are: Gardener's Stores 1856, by J. Baird; the Buck's Head, Argyle Street, an amalgam of glass and cast iron; and the Egyptian Halls of 1873, in Union Street, which has a masonry framework. Both are by Alexander Thomson. The Templeton Carpet Factory 1889, Glasgow Green, by William Leiper, is a Venetian Gothic building complete with battlemented parapet.

Glasgow University

The great genius of Scottish architecture is Charles Rennie Mackintosh whose major buildings are in Glasgow. In the Scotland Street School 1904-6, he punctuated a 3-storey central block with flanking staircase towers in projecting glazed bays. His most famous building - Glasgow School of Art 1897-9 - is a magnificent Art Nouveau building of taut stone and glass; the handsome library, with its gabled facade, was added later in 1907-9.

Stirling's Library

Galleries & museums

Scotland's largest tourist attraction, The Burrell Collection, is situated in Pollok Country Park, Haggs Road and has more than 8,000 objects, housed in an award winning gallery. The Museum and Art Gallery, Kelvingrove Park, Argyle Street, a palatial sandstone building with glazed central court, has one of the best municipal collections in Britain; superb Flemish, Dutch and French paintings, drawings, prints, also ceramics, silver, costumes and armour, as well as a natural history section. The recently refurbished McLellan Galleries in Sauchiehall Street provide an important venue for touring and temporary art exhibitions. Provand's Lordship c1471, in Castle Street, is Glasgow's oldest house and now a museum of 17th-18thC furniture and household articles. Pollok House, Pollok Country Park, a handsome house designed by William Adam in 1752, has paintings by William Blake and a notable collection of Spanish paintings, including works by El Greco. The Museum of Transport, housed in Kelvin Hall, Bunhouse Road, has a magnificent collection of trams, cars, ships models, bicycles, horse-drawn carriages and 7 steam locos. The People's Palace, The Green built 1898 with a huge glazed Winter Garden, has a lively illustrated history of the city. But the oldest museum in Glasgow is the Hunterian Museum, University of Glasgow, University Avenue, opened in 1807, it has a fascinating collection of manuscripts, early painted books, as well as some fine archaeological and geological exhibits. 400-year old Haggs Castle, St. Andrew's Drive, is now a children's museum with practical demonstrations and exhibits showing how everyday life has changed over the centuries.

Streets & shopping

The Oxford Street of Glasgow is Sauchiehall (meaning 'willow meadow') Street. This together with Buchanan Street, Argyle Street, Princes Square and St. Enoch Centre form the main shopping area. Here you will find the department stores, boutiques and

Old Sheriff Court

general shops. All three streets are partly pedestrianised, but the most exhilarating is undoubtedly Buchanan Street. Of particular interest is the spatially elegant Argyll Arcade 1828, the Venetian Gothic-style Stock Exchange 1877, the picturesque Dutch gabled Buchanan Street Bank building 1896 and the Glasgow Royal Concert Hall (opened 1990). In Glasgow Green is The Barras, the city's famous street market, formed by the junction of London Road and Kent Street. The Market is open weekends. Some parts of the city have EC Tue.

Museum & Art Gallery Kelvingrove

Places of Worship.

Glasgow Cathedral is a perfect example of pre-Reformation Gothic architecture. Begun in 1238, it has a magnificent choir and handsome nave with shallow projecting transepts. On a windy hill to the east is the Necropolis, a cemetery with a spiky skyline of Victoriana consisting of pillars, temples and obelisks, dominated by an 1825 Doric column carrying the statue of John Knox. Other churches of interest: Landsdowne Church built by J. Honeyman in 1863; St. George's Tron Church by William Stark 1807; Caledonian Road Church, a temple and tower atop a storey-high base, designed by Alexander Thomson in 1857; a similar design is to be found at the United Presbyterian Church, St. Vincent Street, 1858, but on a more highly articulated ground storey; Queen's Cross Church 1897 is an amalgam of Art Nouveau and Gothic Revival by the brilliant Charles Rennie Mackintosh.

Places of worship within the central Glasgow area are:

Church of Scotland
Glasgow Cathedral
Castle Street
Renfield St. Stephen's Church
262 Bath Street
St. George's Tron Church
165 Buchanan Street
St. Columba Church (Gaelic)
300 St. Vincent Street

Baptist
Adelaide Place Church
209 Bath Street

Congregational
Hillhead Centre
1 University Avenue

Episcopal Church in Scotland
Cathedral Church of St. Mary
300 Great Western Road

First Church of Christ Scientist
1 La Bell Place, Clifton Street
(off Sauchiehall Street)

Free Church of Scotland
265 St. Vincent Street

German Speaking Congregation
Services held at 7 Hughenden Terrace

Greek Orthodox Cathedral
St. Luke's, 27 Dundonald Road

Jewish Orthodox Synagogue
Garnethill, 29 Garnet Street

Methodist
Woodlands Church
229 Woodlands Road

Roman Catholic
St. Andrew's Cathedral
190 Clyde Street
St. Aloysius' Church
25 Rose Street

Unitarian Church
72 Berkeley Street

United Free
Wynd Church
427 Crown Street

Entertainment

As Scotland's commercial and industrial capital, Glasgow offers a good choice of leisure activities. The city now has many theatres where productions ranging from serious drama to pantomime, pop and musicals are performed. The Theatre Royal, Hope Street is Scotland's only opera house and has been completely restored to its full Victorian splendour. The Royal Scottish National Orchestra gives concerts at the Glasgow Royal Concert Hall every Saturday night in winter and is the venue for the proms in June. Cinemas are still thriving in Glasgow, as are the many public houses, some of which provide meals and live entertainment. In the city centre and Byres Road, West End, there is a fair number of restaurants where traditional home cooking, as well as international cuisines, can be sampled. More night life can be found at the city's discos and dance halls.

Outdoors, apart from the many parks and nature trails, there is Calderpark Zoological Gardens, situated 6 miles from the centre between Mount Vernon and Uddingston. Here you may see white rhinos, black panthers and iguanas among many species. Departing from Stobcross Quay, you can also cruise down the Clyde in 'P.S. Waverley' - the last sea-going paddle-steamer in the world.

Cinemas

Cannon Cinema, 380 Clarkston Road
0141 637 2641
MGM Film Centre
326 Sauchiehall Street 0141 332 9513
(Admin Dept), 326 Sauchiehall Street
0141 332 1592
326 Sauchiehall Street
0141 332 1593
Caledonian Associated Cinemas Ltd
Regent House, 72 Renfield Street
0141 332 0606
Glasgow Film Theatre
12 Rose Street (Box Off)
0141 332 6535
Grosvenor Cinema
Ashton Lane
0141 339 4298

Kelburne Cinema
(Manager), Glasgow Road, Paisley. 0141 889 3612
Odeon Film Centre
56 Renfield Street 0141 332 8701

Halls

City Halls, Candleriggs
Couper Institute
86 Clarkston Road
Dixon Halls, 650 Cathcart Road
Glasgow Royal Concert Hall
2 Sauchiehall Street
Govan Hall, Summertown Road
Kelvin Hall, Argyle Street,
Langside Hall, 5 Langside Avenue
Partick Burgh Hall, 9 Burgh Hall Street,
Pollokshaws Hall
2025 Pollokshaws Road,
Woodside Hall, Glenfarg Street
(More information about the above G.D.C. halls and others from the Director, Halls and Theatres Department, Candleriggs 0141 552 1202).

Theatres

Arches Theatre
Midland Street 0141 221 9736
Citizens' Theatre
Gorbals Street 0141 429 0022
King's Theatre
Bath Street 0141 227 5511
Mitchell Theatre and Moir Hall
Granville Street 0141 227 5511
New Athenaeum Theatre
Renfrew Street 0141 332 5057
Old Athenaeum Theatre
Buchanan Street 0141 332 2333
Pavilion Theatre
Renfield Street 0141 332 1846
Theatre Royal
Hope Street 0141 332 9000
Tramway
Albert Drive 0141 227 5511
Tron Theatre
38 Parnie Street. 0141 552 4267
The Ticket Centre
Glasgow's Central Box Office for Arches Theatre, Centre for Contemporary Arts, Citizens' Theatre, City Hall at Candleriggs, G1, Kelvin Hall, King's Theatre, Mitchell Theatre, New Athenaeum Theatre, Old Athenaeum Theatre, Theatre Royal, Tron Theatre.
Open Monday to Saturday 10 a.m. to 6.30 p.m. Sunday 12 to 5 p.m.
0141 227 5511

Sport & Recreation

For both spectator and participant, football is Glasgow's favourite sport. Both Celtic and Rangers, Scotland's most famous rival teams, have their grounds within the City. Glasgow houses Scotland's national football stadium at Hampden Park.

Badminton

Scottish Badminton Union's Cockburn Centre, Bogmoor Place, G51 4TQ.
0141 445 1218

Bowling Greens

There are greens in all the main Parks. Information about clubs from the Scottish Bowling Association: 50 Wellington Street, G2. 0141 221 8999

Cricket Grounds

Cartha Haggs Road, G41.
Clydesdale Beaton Road, G41.
Huntershill Crowhill Road, Bishopbriggs.
Poloc 'Shawholm', 2060 Pollokshaws Road, G43.
West of Scotland Peel Street, G11.

Football Grounds

Broadwood (Clyde F.C.) Cumbernauld
Celtic Park (Celtic F.C.) 95 Kerrydale Street, G40
Firhill Park (Partick Thistle F.C.) Firhill Road, G20
Hampden Park (Queen's Park F.C.) Somerville Drive, G42
Ibrox Stadium (Rangers F.C.) Edmiston Drive, G51
Kilbowie Park (Clydebank F.C.) Argyll Road, Clydebank
St. Mirren Park (St. Mirren F.C.) Love Street, Paisley

Golf Courses

Glasgow District Council
9 holes
Alexandra Park, Cumbernauld Road, G31
Cambuslang, Westburn Drive, Cambuslang.
King's Park, Carmunnock Road, Croftfoot, G44
Knightswood, Lincoln Avenue, G13

Ruchill, Brassey Street, G20

18 holes
Barshaw, Glasgow Road, Paisley.
Douglaston, Strathblane Road, Milngavie. (Five miles from Glasgow).
Elderslie, Main Road, Johnstone.
Lethamhill, Cumbernauld Road, G33
Littlehill, Auchinairn Road, G64.
Linn Park, Simshill Road, G44
Pollok, Barrhead Road, Pollokshaws, G43

Putting Greens
There are putting greens in some of the main parks.

Pitch & Putt
Courses at Bellahouston Park, Queen's Park, Rouken Glen and several others.

Rugby Grounds

Auldhouse (Hutchesons'/Aloysians) Thornliebank

Garscadden (Glasgow University) Garscadden Road South, G15.

Hughenden (Hillhead High School) Hughenden Road, G12.

New Anniesland (Glasgow Acad.) Helensburgh Drive, G13.

Old Anniesland (Glasgow High School F.P. & Kelvinside Academicals) Crow Road, G11.

Westerlands (Glasgow University) Ascot Avenue, G12.

Sports Centres

Barrhead, Main Street, Barrhead. 0141 881 1049
Bellahouston Bellahouston Drive, G52. 0141 427 5454

Burnhill Toryglen Road, Rutherglen, G73.
0141 643 0327

Crownpoint Crownpoint Road, Bridgeton, G40.
0141 554 8274

Helenvale Park Outdoor Sports Complex, Helenvale Street, G31. 0141 554 4109

James Murray Caledonia Road, Baillieston, G69.
0141 773 0881

Linwood, Brediland Road, Linwood. 01505 329461

Springburn Springburn Way, Springburn, G21.
0141 558 2666

Tryst, Town Centre, Cumbernauld. 01236 728138

Swimming Pools

Drumchapel, 199 Drumry Road East, G15. 0141 944 5812
Easterhouse, Bogbain Road, G34. 0141 771 7978
Elderslie, Stoddard Square, Elderslie. 01505 328133
Govan, Harhill Street, G51.
0141 445 1899
Lagoon Leisure Centre, Mill St., Paisley. 0141 889 4000
North Woodside, Braid Square, G4. 0141 332 8192
Pollok Leisure Pool, Cowglen Road, G53. 0141 881 3313
Renfrew, Inchinnan Road, Renfrew. 0141 886 2088
Temple, 354 Netherton Road, G13. 0141 954 6537
Whiteinch, Medwyn Street, G14. 0141 959 2465

Hours
Monday to Friday 9 a.m. to 9 p.m.
Saturday 9 a.m. to 1 p.m.

Charges
Admission charges are minimal. OAPs free at certain times.

Tennis

There are courts in some of
the main parks. Information
about clubs from the Secretary
of the West of Scotland Lawn
Tennis Association: Mr N.
Floyd, 1 Boclair Road,
Bearsden 0141 942 0162.

Weather

The City of Glasgow is on the same
latitude as the City of Moscow, but
because of its close proximity to the
warm Atlantic Shores, and the
prevailing westerly winds, it enjoys a
more moderate climate. Summers are
generally cool and winters mostly mild,
this gives Glasgow fairly consistent
summer and winter temperatures.
Despite considerable cloud the City is
sheltered by hills to the south-west and
north and the average rainfall for
Glasgow is usually less than 40 inches
per year. The following table shows the
approximate average figures for
sunshine, rainfall and temperatures to
be expected in Glasgow throughout the
year.

Weather Forecasts
For the Glasgow Area including Loch
Lomond and the Clyde Coast:
Weatherline
01898 500421 (Recording)
The Glasgow Weather Centre
(Meteorological Office), 33 Bothwell
Street, G2 0141 248 3451

Month	Hours of Sunshine	Inches of Rainfall	Temperature °C		
			Ave. Max.	Ave. Min.	High/Low
Jan	36	3.8	5.5	0.8	−18
Feb	62	2.8	6.3	0.8	−15
Mar	94	2.4	8.8	2.2	21
Apr	147	2.4	11.9	3.9	22
May	185	2.7	15.1	6.2	26
June	181	2.4	17.9	9.3	30
July	159	2.9	18.6	10.8	29
Aug	143	3.5	18.5	10.6	31
Sept	106	4.1	16.3	9.1	−4
Oct	76	4.1	13.0	6.8	−8
Nov	47	3.7	8.7	3.3	−11
Dec	30	4.2	6.5	1.9	−12

Parks & Gardens

There are over 70 public parks within the city. The most famous is Glasgow Green. Abutting the north bank of the River Clyde, it was acquired in 1662. Of interest are the Winter Gardens attached to the People's Palace. Kelvingrove Park is an 85-acre park laid out by Sir Joseph Paxton in 1852. On the south side of the city is the 148-acre Queen's Park, Victoria Road, established 1857 - 94. Also of interest: Rouken Glen, Thornliebank, with a spectacular waterfall, walled garden, nature trail and boating facilities; Victoria Park, Victoria Park Drive, with its famous Fossil Grove flower gardens and yachting pond. In Great Western Road are the Botanic Gardens. Founded in 1817, the gardens' 42 acres are crammed with natural attractions, including the celebrated Kibble Palace glasshouse with its fabulous tree ferns, exotic plants and white marble Victorian statues.

The main public parks are;
Alexandra
671 Alexandra Parade, G31.

Barshaw
Glasgow Road, Paisley

Bellahouston
Paisley Road West, G52.

Botanic Gardens
730 Gt. Western Road, G12.

Hogganfield Loch
Cumbernauld Road, G33.

Kelvingrove
Sauchiehall Street, G3.

King's
325 Carmunnock Road, G44.

Linn
Clarkston Road at Netherlee Road, G44.

Pollok Country Park
Pollokshaws Road, G43

Queen's
Victoria Road, G42.

Rouken Glen
Rouken Glen Road, G46.

Springburn
Broomfield Road, G21.

Tollcross
461 Tollcross Road, G32.

Victoria
Victoria Park Drive North, G14.

Kibble Palace

Public Transport

The City of Glasgow has one of the most advanced, fully integrated public transport systems in the whole of Europe. The Strathclyde Transport network consists of; the local British Rail network, the local bus services and the fully modernised Glasgow Underground, with links to Glasgow Airport and the Steamer and Car Ferry Services
For information contact:
Strathclyde Transport Travel Centre
St. Enoch Square
Open Monday - Saturday 9.30 a.m. to 5.30 p.m. 0141 226 4826 (Monday to Saturday 7 a.m. to 9 p.m., Sunday 9 a.m. to 7.30 p.m.) for City services, ferry services, local airlines, train and express services. Free timetables are available.

Bus Services and Tours

Long Distance Coach Service
Buchanan Bus Station 0141 332 9191
Scottish Citylink Coaches Ltd and National Express provide express services to London and most parts of Scotland including Campbeltown, Tarbert, Ardrishaig, Inverary, Oban, Fort William, Skye, Stirling, Perth, Dundee, Arbroath, Montrose, Aberdeen, Aviemore, Inverness and Edinburgh.

Local Bus Services
A comprehensive network of local bus services is provided by a variety of operators within the City of Glasgow and also direct to the following destinations:
Airdrie, Ardrossan, Ayr, Balfron, Barrhead, Bearsden, Beith, Bellshill, Bishopbriggs, Bishopton, Blantyre, Bo'ness, Caldercruix, Cambuslang, Campsie Glen, Carluke, Clydebank, Coatbridge, Cumbernauld, Denny, Drymen, Dunfermline, Duntocher, Eaglesham, East Kilbride, Erskine, Falkirk, Glenrothes, Grangemouth, Hamilton, Irvine, Johnstone, Kilbarchan, Kilbirnie, Killearn, Kilmarnock, Kilsyth, Kirkintilloch, Kirkcaldy, Lanark, Largs, Larkhall, Lennoxtown, Lochwinnoch, Motherwell, Milngavie, Newton Mearns, Old Kilpatrick, Paisley, Prestwick, Renfrew, Saltcoats,
Shotts, Stirling, Strathblane, Strathaven, Uddingston, Wishaw.
These services depart from City Centre bus stops or from Buchanan Bus Station.

Coach Hire and Day, Half Day and Extended Tours
Scottish City Link Coaches Ltd
Buchanan Bus Station
0141 332 9191
Private hire and seasonal tours
0141 332 8055

Haldane's of Cathcart
Delvin Road, G44 0141 637 2234
Private Hire

Strathclyde Buses Ltd.
197 Victoria Road, G42 7AD
0141 636 3190
Private hire and seasonal tours

British Rail

Passenger enquiries: 0141 204 2844
Sleeper reservations: 0141 221 2305

Local Strathclyde Transport trains serve over 170 stations in Glasgow and Strathclyde (see map). ScotRail services operate to most destinations in Scotland. InterCity services operate to England.

Glasgow Queen Street Station
for services to Cumbernauld, Edinburgh, Falkirk, Stirling, Perth, Dundee, Arbroath, Montrose, Aberdeen, Pitlochry, Aviemore, Inverness, Dumbarton, Balloch, Helensburgh, Oban, Fort William, Mallaig, Coatbridge, Airdrie.

Glasgow Central Station
for services to Gourock (ferry connection to Dunoon), Greenock, Wemyss Bay (ferry connection to Rothesay), Paisley, Johnstone, Largs, Ardrossan (ferry connection to Brodick), Irvine, Ayr, Girvan, Stranraer, East Kilbride, Kilmarnock, Dumfries, Motherwell, Hamilton, Lanark, Carlisle, Shotts, Edinburgh, Berwick, Newcastle.
London and destinations on West and East Coast Main Lines.

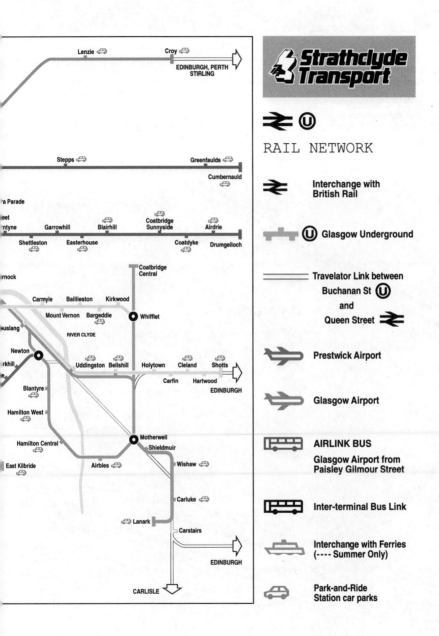

Lenzie

Croy

EDINBURGH, PERTH
STIRLING

Stepps

Greenfaulds

Cumbernauld

a Parade

eet
ntyne   Garrowhill   Blairhill   Coatbridge   Airdrie
                                                       Sunnyside

Shettleston   Easterhouse   Coatdyke   Drumgelloch

Coatbridge
Central

rnock

Carmyle   Baillieston   Kirkwood

Mount Vernon   Bargeddie   Whifflet

RIVER CLYDE

uslang

Newton

rkhill   Uddingston Bellshill   Holytown   Cleland   Shotts
e

Blantyre   Carfin   Hartwood

                                                          EDINBURGH

Hamilton West

                Motherwell

Hamilton Central   Shieldmuir

East Kilbride   Airbles   Wishaw

Carluke

Lanark   Carstairs

                            EDINBURGH

CARLISLE

Strathclyde Transport

RAIL NETWORK

Interchange with
British Rail

Glasgow Underground

Travelator Link between
Buchanan St
and
Queen Street

Prestwick Airport

Glasgow Airport

AIRLINK BUS
Glasgow Airport from
Paisley Gilmour Street

Inter-terminal Bus Link

Interchange with Ferries
(---- Summer Only)

Park-and-Ride
Station car parks

Glasgow *(Abbotsinch)* Airport

Glasgow Airport is located eight miles west of Glasgow alongside the M8 motorway at Junction 28. It is linked by a bus service to Anderston Cross Bus Station, the journey time is 25 minutes and buses leave at 30 minute intervals. There is a frequent coach service linking the Airport with all major bus and rail terminals in the City and a Coach/Air link to and from Prestwick Airport.

The Airport Terminal has a restaurant, grill, buffet, three bars, lounges, shop, post office and banking facilities.

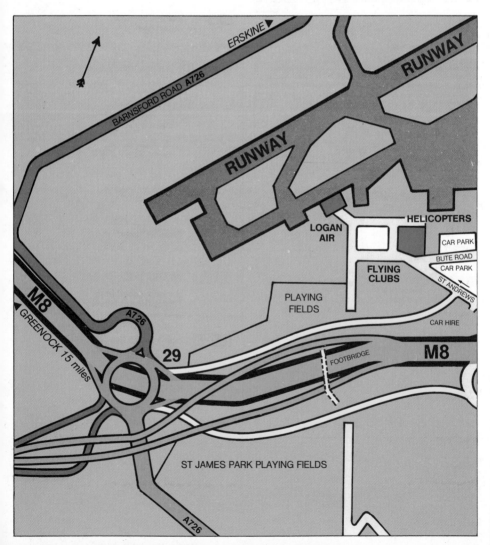

Car parking is available with a graduated scale of charges.
The Airport telephone no is 0141 887 1111.

Airlines

(Domestic Routes)
Air U.K.
Reservations 01345 666777

British Airways
66 Gordon Street
Glasgow, G1 3RS
Reservations 01345 222111

British Midland
Merlin House, Mossland Road,
Hillington, Glasgow. G54 4XZ
Reservations 01345 554554

Loganair Ltd.
Glasgow Airport (administration)
0141 889 3181
Trident House, Renfrew Road, Paisley.

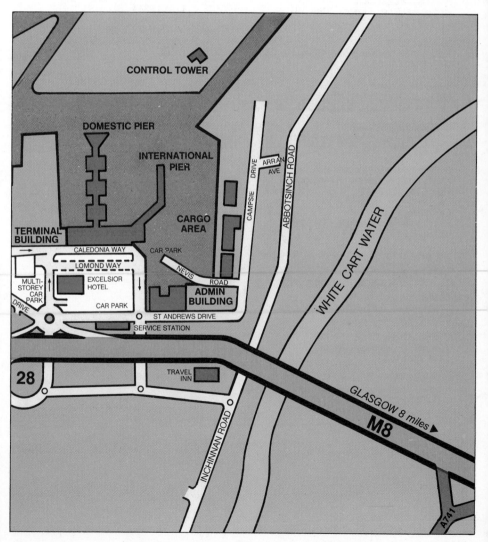

Hospitals

**Greater Glasgow Health Board
(Administration)
112 Ingram Street, Glasgow, G1 1ET.
0141 201 4444**

Acorn Street Psychiatric Day Hospital
23 Acorn Street, Bridgeton, Glasgow, G40
4AA. 0141 556 4789

Baillieston Health Centre
20 Muirside Road, Glasgow, G69 7AD.
0141 771 0871

Belvidere Hospital
1362 - 1452 London Road, Glasgow, G31
4PG. 0141 211 8500

Blawarthill Hospital
129 Holehouse Drive, Knightswood,
Glasgow, G13 3TG. 0141 954 9547

Bridgeton Health Centre
201 Abercromby Street, Glasgow, G40
2AD 0141 554 1866

Broomhill & Lanfine Hospitals
Kilsyth Road, Kirkintilloch, Glasgow, G60
1RR. 0141 776 5141

Canniesburn Hospital
Switchback Road, Bearsden, Glasgow,
G61 1QL. 0141 942 2255

Carsewell House (Psychiatric Outpatient)
5 Oakley Terrace, Glasgow, G31 2HX.
0141 554 6267

Castlemilk Health Centre
Dougrie Drive, Castlemilk, Glasgow, G45
9AW 0141 634 3434

Charing Cross Clinic
8 Woodside Crescent, Glasgow, G3 7UL.
0141 332 5463

Clydebank Health Centre
Kilbowie Road, Clydebank, G81 2TQ.
0141 952 2080

Cowglen Hospital
Boydstone Road, Glasgow, G53 6XJ.
0141 632 9106

Douglas Inch Centre
2 Woodside Terrace, Glasgow, G3 7UY.
0141 332 3844

Drumchapel Hospital
129 Drumchapel Road, Glasgow, G15
6PX. 0141 944 2344

Easterhouse Health Centre
9 Auchinlea Road, Glasgow, G34 9QU.
0141 771 0781

Gartloch Hospital,
Gartloch Road, Glasgow, G69 8EJ
0141 771 0771

Gartnavel General Hospital
1053 Great Western Road, Glasgow, G12
0YN. 0141 211 3000

Gartnavel Royal Hospital
1055 Great Western Road, Glasgow, G12
0XH. 0141 211 3600

Glasgow Caledonian University,
The Division of Occupational Therapy,
Crawford Building, South Brae Campus,
Glasgow, G13 1PP 0141 337 4725

Glasgow Dental Hospital and School
378 Sauchiehall Street, Glasgow, G2 3JZ.
0141 332 7020

Glasgow Eye Infirmary
3 Sandyford Place, Glasgow, G3 7NB.
0141 204 0721

Glasgow Homeopathic Hospital
1000 Great Western Road, Glasgow, G12
0AA. 0141 339 0382

Glasgow Royal Infirmary
84 Castle Street, Glasgow, G4 0NA
0141 552 3535

Glasgow Royal Maternity Hospital
Rottenrow, Glasgow, G4 0NA.
0141 552 3400

Glasgow School of Paediatry,
1345 Govan Road, Glasgow, G51 4TS
0141 883 0418

Gorbals Health Centre
45 Pine Place, Glasgow, G5 0BQ.
0141 429 6291

Govan Health Centre
5 Drumoyne Road, Glasgow G51 4BJ.
0141 440 1212

Govanhill Health Centre
233 Calder Street, Glasgow, G42 7DR.
0141 424 3003

Knightswood Hospital
125 Knightswood Road, Glasgow, G13
2XG. 0141 954 9641

Lennox Castle Hospital
Lennoxtown, Glasgow, G65 7LB.
01360 329200

Lenzie Hospital
Auchinloch Road, Kirkintilloch, Glasgow,
G66 5DF. 0141 776 1208

Leverndale Hospital
510 Crookston Road, Glasgow, G53 7TU.
0141 211 6400

Lightburn Clinic
966 Carntyne Road, Glasgow, G32 6ND
0141 774 5102

Maryhill Health Centre
41 Shawpark Street, Glasgow, G20 9DR.
0141 946 7151

Mearnskirk Hospital
Newton Mearns, Glasgow, G77 5RZ.
0141 639 2251

Parkhead Health Centre
101 Salamanca Street, Glasgow, G31
5NA 0141 556 5232

Parkhead Hospital
81 Salamanca Street, Glasgow, G31
5ES. 0141 554 7951

Pollock Health Centre
21 Cowglen Road, Glasgow, G53 6EQ.
0141 880 8899

Possilpark Health Centre
85 Denmark Street, Glasgow, G22 5EG.
0141 336 5311

Queen Mother's Hospital
Yorkhill, Glasgow, G3 8SH. 0141 201 0550

Royal Hospital for Sick Children
Yorkhill, Glasgow, G3 8SJ. 0141 201 0000

Ruchill Hospital
Bilsland Drive, Glasgow, G20 9NB.
0141 946 7120

Rutherglen Health Centre
130 Stonelaw Road, Rutherglen, Glasgow,
G73 2PQ. 0141 647 7171

Rutherglen Maternity Hospital
120 Stonelaw Road, Rutherglen, Glasgow,
G73 2PG. 0141 207 6060

Shettleston Health Centre
420 Old Shettleston Road, Glasgow, G32
7JZ. 0141 550 2199

Southern General Hospital
1345 Govan Road, Glasgow, G51 4TF.
0141 201 1100

Springburn Health Centre
200 Springburn Way, Glasgow, G21 1TR.
0141 554 1464

Stobhill General Hospital
133 Balornock Road, Glasgow, G21 3UW.
0141 558 0111

Thornliebank Health Centre
20 Kennishead Road, Glasgow, G46 8NY.
0141 620 2222

Townhead Health Centre
16 Alexandra Parade, Glasgow, G31 2ES.
0141 552 3477

Victoria Geriatric Unit
100 Mansionhouse Road, Glasgow, G41
3DX. 0141 201 6167

Victoria Infirmary
Langside Road, Glasgow, G42 9TY.
0141 201 6161

Western Infirmary
Dumbarton Road, Glasgow, G11 6NT.
0141 211 2000

Woodilee Hospital
Lenzie, Glasgow, G66 3UG
0141 777 8000

Woodside Health Centre
Barr Street, Glasgow, G20 7LR.
0141 332 9977

Strathclyde Further Education

Anniesland College
Hatfield Drive, Glasgow, G12 0YE.
0141 357 3969

Ayr College
Dam Park, Ayr, KA8 0EU. 01292 265184

Bell College of Technology
Almada Street, Hamilton, Lanarkshire,
ML3 0JB. 01698 283100

Cambuslang College
Hamilton Road, Cambuslang, Glasgow,
G72 7BS. 0141 641 6600

**Cardonald College of Further
Education**
690 Mosspark Drive, Glasgow, G52
3AY. 0141 883 6151

Central College of Commerce
300 Cathedral Street, G1 2TA.
0141 552 3941

Clydebank College
Kilbowie Road, Clydebank,
Dunbartonshire, G81 2AA.
0141 952 7771

Coatbridge College
Kildonan Street, Coatbridge,
Lanarkshire, ML5 3LS. 01236 422316

Cumbernauld College
Town Centre, Cumbernauld, Glasgow,
G67 1HU. 01236 731811

Glasgow Caledonian University
Cowcaddens Road, Glasgow G4 0BA
0141 331 3000

**Glasgow College of Building and
Printing**
60 North Hanover Street, Glasgow, G1
2BP. 0141 332 9969

**Glasgow College of Food
Technology**
230 Cathedral Street, Glasgow, G1
2TG. 0141 552 3751

Glasgow College of Nautical Studies
21 Thistle Street, Glasgow, G5 9XB.
0141 429 3201

James Watt College
Finnart Street, Greenock, Renfrewshire,
PA16 8HF. 01475 24433

John Wheatley College
1346-1364 Shettleston Road, Glasgow,
G32 9AT. 0141 778 2426

Kilmarnock College
Holehouse Road, Kilmarnock, Ayrshire,
KA3 7AT. 01563 23501

Langside College
50 Prospecthill Road, Glasgow, G42
9LB. 0141 649 4991

Motherwell College
Dalzell Drive, Motherwell, Lanarkshire,
ML4 2DD. 01698 59641

North Glasgow College
110 Flemington Street, Glasgow, G21
4BX. 0141 558 9001

Reid Kerr College, The
Renfrew Road, Paisley, Renfrewshire,
PA13 4DR. 0141 889 4225

Stow College
43 Shamrock Street, Glasgow, G4 9LD.
0141 332 1786

University of Glasgow
University Avenue, Glasgow.
0141 339 8855

University of Paisley
High St, Paisley
0141 848 3000

University of Strathclyde
George Street, Glasgow, G1 1XQ.
0141 552 4400

Renfrew District

A selection of leisure, recreational and cultural attractions in Renfrew District:

Barrhead Sports' Centre
The Centre contains swimming pools, sports halls, activity rooms and sauna suite. Bar and restaurant facilities add to the wide range of sporting and leisure activities available.

Barshaw Park, Glasgow Road, Paisley
The park is extensive with formal and informal areas. It adjoins the public golf course and incorporates a boating pond, playgrounds, model "ride-on" railway and a nature corner.

Castle Semple Country Park, Lochwinnoch
Castle Semple Loch is a popular feature for sailing and fishing. Canoes, rowing boats and sailing boards for hire. Fishing permits available. 01505 842882

Coats Observatory
The Observatory has traditionally recorded astronomical and meteorological information since 1882. Now installed with a satellite picture receiver, it is one of the best equipped Observatories in the country. Monday, Tuesday, Thursday 2 -8 p.m., Wednesday, Friday, Saturday 10 a.m. - 5 p.m. 0141 889 3151

Erskine Bridge (Toll)
The bridge is an impressive high level structure opened by HRH Princess Anne in 1971 and provides a direct link from Renfrew District to Loch Lomond and the Trossachs. The bridge replaced the Erskine Ferry and affords extensive views up and down river to pedestrian users.

Finlaystone Estate
Off the A8 at Langbank. The Estate is now a garden centre with woodland walks. The house has connections with John Knox and Robert Burns and is open April to August on Sundays from 2.30 - 4.30 p.m. At other times groups by appointment. Estate open all year round. 0147 554 285

Formakin Estate, By Bishopton
A group of buildings and landscaped grounds designed in the Arts and Crafts style at the turn of the century. The estate has a visitor centre, tea room and offers walks, trails, picnic areas and play areas. Open 7 days 11 a.m. - 6 p.m. 01505 863400

Gleniffer Braes Country Park, Glenfield Road, Paisley
1,000 breathtaking acres including Glen Park nature trail, picnic and children's play areas. Open dawn till dusk, the park affords extensive walks and spectacular views from this elevated moorland area, and contains an area reserved for model aero flying. 0141 884 3794

Houston Village
Houston was developed in the 18th century as an estate village. The traditional smiddy building, village pubs and terraced houses combine to create a quiet, sleepy atmosphere which has successfully survived the development of extensive modern housing on its periphery.

Inchinnan Bridges
Early 19th century stone bridges over the White Cart and Black Cart rivers close to St. Conval's stone, and the site of the Inchinnan Church which houses the graves of the Knights Templar, whose order was introduced to Scotland in 1153 by King David I.

Johnstone Castle
The remnants of a 1700 building formerly a much larger structure but demolished in the 1950's. The castle has significant historical links with the Cochrane and Houston families, major landowners who were instrumental in the development of the Burgh of Johnstone.

Kilbarchan Village
A good example of an 18th Century weaving village with many original buildings still fronting the narrow streets. A focal point is the steeple building in the square, originally a school and meal market and now used as public meeting rooms. A cycle route/footpath system links it to Glasgow and the Clyde Coast.

Lagoon Leisure Centre, Paisley
Ultra-modern complex housing superb ice rink and extensive "fun" pool featuring artificial wave machine and water slides. Also has cafe/bar facilities. Unique within the area, the complex is easily reached by public transport and has ample parking. Monday - Friday 10 a.m. - 10 p.m., Saturday and Sunday 10 a.m. - 5.00 p.m. 0141 889 4000

Laigh Kirk, Paisley

Originally built in 1738, the Laigh Kirk has been converted to an Arts Centre, with a theatre, workshop, bistro and bar open daily 10 a.m. - 11 p.m. For further information 0141 887 1010

Linwood Sports Centre

A wide range of indoor and outdoor sporting activities include football and rugby pitches, games hall, squash courts, BMX track, fitness trail, tennis courts and conditioning suite.

Lochwinnoch Village

An attractive rural village close to the Castle Semple Water Park, Muirshiel Country Park and the R.S.P.B. nature reserve, Lochwinnoch contains a small local museum with displays reflecting agricultural, social and industrial aspects of village life. Museum open Monday, Wednesday and Friday 10 a.m. - 1 p.m., 2 - 5 p.m. and 6 - 8 p.m. Tuesday and Saturday 10 a.m. - 1 p.m. and 2 - 5 p.m. Open most days throughout the year, visitors should telephone 01505 842615

Muirshiel Country Park

Four miles north of Lochwinnoch, the park features trails of varying length radiating from the Information Centre. Open daily 9 a.m. - 4.30 p.m. (Winter), 9 a.m. - 7.30 p.m. (Summer). 01505 842803

Paisley Abbey

Birthplace of the Stewart Dynasty, the Abbey dates, in part, to the 12th century and features regimental flags, relics, the Barochan Cross and beautiful stained glass windows. Monday - Saturday 10 a.m. - 12.30 p.m., 1.30 - 3.30 p.m. 0141 889 3630

Paisley Arts Centre

Converted 18th century church. Performing arts, works by local artists and participatory events and includes bar and bistro. Box office open 7 days 10 a.m. - 8 p.m. Further information 0141 887 1007

Paisley Museum and Art Gallery, High Street, Paisley

In addition to the world famous collection of Paisley shawls, the Museum traces the history of the Paisley pattern, the development of weaving techniques and houses collections of local and natural history, ceramics and paintings. Monday - Saturday 10 a.m - 5 p.m. 0141 889 3151

Paisley Town Hall

A Renaissance style building by the River Cart in the heart of Paisley, it features a slim clock tower and houses a Tourist Information Centre. It accommodates many exhibitions during the year and is also available for conferences and functions. Monday - Saturday 9 a.m. - 5 p.m. 0141 887 1007

Paisley Town Trail

An easy-to-follow route taking in the town's historic and architecturally significant buildings. Visitors can spend an hour or two walking round the trail and referring to a printed guide and wall plaques on the main buildings.

Renfrew Town Hall

The Town Hall has a "fairy-tale" style to its 105 feet high spire and was the administrative centre of the Royal Burgh of Renfrew. Originally the principal town in the area, Renfrew was strategically placed on the River Clyde, and a passenger ferry continues to operate daily.

Robert Tannahill, Weaver Poet

The works of Tannahill ranks with those of Burns. Born 1774 he took his own life in 1810 and is buried in a nearby graveyard. Visitors can visit his early home, site of his death, and his grave, and read his works in Paisley Library.

Royal Society for Protection of Birds, Lochwinnoch

An interesting visitor centre with observation tower, hides, displays and gift shop. Thursday, Friday, Saturday and Sunday 10 a.m. - 5 p.m. Shop open 7 days. 01505 842663

Sma' Shot Cottages, Paisley

Fully restored and furnished artisan's house of the Victorian era; exhibition room displaying photographs plus artefacts of local interest. 18th Century weaver's loomshop with combined living quarters. Open Wednesday & Saturday May - September 1 - 5 p.m. Group visits arranged by appointment. Tel: 0141 812 2513 or 0141 889 0530

The Clyde Estuary

Visitors travelling along the rural route to the Old Greenock Road above Langbank village at the western end of the District are able to take advantage of extensive views of the upper and lower Clyde Estuary, the Gareloch and the mountains beyond.

Thomas Coats Memorial Church

Open Monday - Friday 9 a.m. - 12 noon. Visitors should check in advance. Another gift from the Coats family to Paisley, the church was built in 1894 and constructed of red sandstone, is one of the finest Baptist Churches in the country. Tel: 0141 889 9980

Wallace Monument, Elderslie

The monument was erected in 1912 and marks the birthplace of the Scottish Patriot, Sir William Wallace. It stands adjacent to the reconstructed foundation plan of the adjacent Wallace Buildings which dated from the 17th Century.

Weaver's Cottage, Kilbarchan

This cottage, built in 1723, houses the last of the village's 800 looms and demonstrations are still given. It contains displays of weaving and domestic utensils, with Cottage garden and refreshments. Open Monday, Tuesday, Thursday, Friday 2 - 5 p.m., Saturday 10 a.m. - 1 p.m. and 2 - 5 p.m.

INDEX TO STREETS

General Abbreviations

Arc.	Arcade	Dr.	Drive	Mans.	Mansions	Sta.	Station
Av.	Avenue	E.	East	Ms.	Mews	Ter.	Terrace
Bk.	Bank	Est.	Estate	N.	North	Twr.	Tower
Bldgs.	Buildings	Ex.	Exchange	Par.	Parade	Vill.	Villa
Boul.	Boulevard	Fm.	Farm	Pas.	Passage	Vills.	Villas
Bri.	Bridge	Gdns.	Gardens	Pk.	Park	Vw.	View
Cen.	Centre, Central	Gra.	Grange	Pl.	Place	W.	West
Cft.	Croft	Grn.	Green	Quad.	Quadrant	Wd.	Wood
Circ.	Circus	Gro.	Grove	Rd.	Road	Wds.	Woods
Clo.	Close	Ho.	House	Ri.	Rise	Wf.	Wharf
Cor.	Corner	Ind.	Industrial	S.	South	Wk.	Walk
Cotts.	Cottages	La.	Lane	Sch.	School		
Cres.	Crescent	Ln.	Loan	Sq.	Square		
Ct.	Court	Lo.	Lodge	St.	Street/Saint		

Postal District Abbreviations

Clyde.	Clydebank	Ersk.	Erskine	Pais.	Paisley
Coat.	Coatbridge	John.	Johnstone	Renf.	Renfrew

NOTES

This index contains some street names in standard text which are followed by another street named in italics. In these cases the street in standard text does not actually appear on the map due to insufficient space but can be located close to the street named in italics.

For streets outwith the Glasgow post town area, the appropriate post town abbreviation is used. Thus the post town for Abbey Close is Paisley and it will be found on page 46 in square K14.

Street	Page	Sq.
Abbey Clo., Pais.	46	K14
Abbey Dr. G14	19	R10
Abbey Rd., John.	44	F15
Abbeycraig Rd. G34	40	FF11
Abbeydale Way G73	65	Z18
Neilvaig Dr.		
Abbeyhill St. G32	38	AA12
Abbot St. G41	51	U15
Frankfort St.		
Abbot St., Pais.	30	K13
Abbotsburn Way, Pais.	30	J12
Abbotsford G64	11	Z7
Abbotsford Av. G73	53	Y16
Abbotsford Ct. G67	70	NN4
Abbotsford Cres., Pais.	44	F16
Abbotsford La. G5	51	V14
Cumberland St.		
Abbotsford Pl. G5	51	V14
Abbotsford Pl. G67	70	NN4
Abbotsford Rd. G61	7	Q5
Abbotsford Rd. G67	70	NN4
Abbotsford Rd., Clyde.	5	L7
Abbotshall Av. G15	6	N6
Abbotsinch Rd., Pais.	30	K11
Abbotsinch Rd., Renf.	30	K11
Abbott Cres., Clyde.	17	M8
Aberconway St., Clyde.	17	M8
Abercorn Av. G52	32	N12
Abercorn Pl. G23	9	U7
Abercorn St., Pais.	30	K13
Abercrombie Cres. G69	41	GG13
Abercromby Dr. G40	36	X13
Abercromby Sq. G40	36	X13
Abercromby St. G40	36	X13
Aberdalgie Path G34	40	EE12
Aberdalgie Rd. G34	40	EE12
Aberdour St. G31	37	Z12
Aberfeldy St. G31	37	Z12
Aberfoyle St. G31	37	Z12
Aberlady Rd. G51	33	R12
Abernethy Dr., Pais.	28	E13
Abernethy St. G31	37	Z12
Aberuthven Dr. G32	54	BB14
Abiegail Pl. G72	68	FF19
Abington St. G20	21	V10
Aboukir St. G51	33	R12
Aboyne Dr., Pais.	46	K15
Aboyne St. G51	33	R13
Acacia Dr. G78	59	L17

Street	Page	Sq.
Acacia Dr., Pais.	45	H15
Acacia Pl., John.	44	E16
Academy Rd. G46	62	T19
Academy St. G32	54	BB14
Acer Cres., Pais.	45	H15
Achamore Pl. G15	6	N6
Achamore Rd.		
Achamore Rd. G15	6	N6
Achray Dr., Pais.	45	H15
Acorn Ct. G40	52	X14
Acorn St.		
Acorn St. G40	52	X14
Acre Dr. G20	8	T7
Acre Rd. G20	8	S7
Acredyke Cres. G21	23	Z8
Acredyke Pl. G21	23	Z9
Acredyke Rd. G21	23	Y8
Acredyke Rd. G73	52	X16
Acrehill St. G33	37	Z11
Adams Ct. La. G2	35	V12
Howard St.		
Adamswell St. G21	22	X10
Adamswell Ter. G69	15	HH7
Addiewell St. G32	38	BB12
Addison Gro. G46	61	R18
Addison Pl. G46	61	R18
Addison Rd. G12	20	T10
Addison Rd. G46	61	R18
Adelphi St. G5	36	W13
Admiral St. G41	35	U13
Advie Pl. G42	51	V16
Prospecthill Rd.		
Affric Dr., Pais.	47	L15
Afton Cres. G61	8	S6
Afton Dr., Renf.	18	N10
Afton Rd. G67	71	PP2
Afton St. G41	51	U16
Agamemnon St., Clyde.	4	K7
Aigas Cotts. G13	19	R9
Crow Rd.		
Aikenhead Rd. G42	51	V14
Aikenhead Rd. G44	64	W17
Ailean Dr. G32	55	DD14
Ailean Gdns. G32	55	DD14
Ailort Av. G44	63	V17
Lochinver Dr.		
Ailsa Dr. G42	51	U16
Ailsa Dr. G71	69	HH18

Street	Page	Sq.
Ailsa Dr. G73	64	X17
Ailsa Dr., Clyde.	5	M5
Ailsa Dr., Pais.	46	J16
Ailsa Rd. G64	11	Y7
Ailsa Rd., Renf.	31	M11
Ainslie Rd. G52	32	P12
Ainslie Rd. G67	71	QQ2
Airdale Rd. G46	62	T19
Aird's La. G1	36	W13
Bridgegate		
Airgold Dr. G15	6	N6
Airgold Pl. G15	6	N6
Airlie Gdns. G73	65	Z18
Airlie Rd. G69	56	EE14
Airlie St. G12	20	S10
Airlour Rd. G43	63	U17
Airth Dr. G52	49	R14
Airth La. G52	49	R14
Airth Pl. G52	49	R14
Airthrey Av. G14	19	R10
Aitken St. G31	37	Z12
Aitkenhead Av., Coat.	57	HH14
Aitkenhead Rd. G71	57	HH16
Alasdair Ct. G78	59	M19
Albany Av. G32	39	CC13
Albany Cotts. G13	19	R9
Crow Rd.		
Albany Dr. G73	65	Y17
Albany Pl. G71	69	HH19
Marguerite Gdns.		
Albany Quad. G32	39	CC13
Mansionhouse Dr.		
Albany St. G40	53	Y14
Albany Ter. G72	66	AA18
Albany Way, Pais.	30	K12
Abbotsburn Way		
Albert Av. G42	51	U15
Albert Bri. G1	36	W13
Albert Bri. G5	36	W13
Albert Ct. G41	51	U14
Albert Dr.		
Albert Cross G41	51	U14
Albert Dr. G41	50	T15
Albert Dr. G61	8	S7
Albert Dr. G73	65	Y17
Albert Rd. G42	51	V15
Albert Rd. G66	13	CC6
Albert Rd., Clyde.	5	L6
Albert Rd., Renf.	17	M10

95

Alberta Ter. G12	20	T10
Saltoun St.		
Albion St. G1	36	W12
Albion St. G69	55	DD14
Albion St., Pais.	30	K13
Alcaig Rd. G52	49	R15
Alder Av. G66	12	BB5
Alder Ct. G78	59	M19
Alder Pl. G43	62	T17
Alder Pl., John.	44	E15
Alder Rd. G43	62	T17
Alder Rd. G67	71	QQ3
Alder Rd., Clyde.	4	K5
Alderman Pl. G13	19	Q9
Alderman Rd. G13	18	N8
Aldersdyke Pl. G72	68	FF19
Alderside Dr. G71	57	GG16
Alexander St., Clyde.	5	L7
Alexandra Av. G33	25	CC9
Alexandra Av. G66	13	CC6
Alexandra Ct. G31	37	Y12
Roebank St.		
Alexandra Cross G31	37	Y12
Duke St.		
Alexandra Dr., Pais.	45	H14
Alexandra Dr., Renf.	17	M10
Alexandra Gdns. G66	13	CC6
Alexandra Par. G31	37	Y12
Alexandra Pk. St. G31	37	Y12
Alexandra Rd. G66	13	CC6
Alford St. G21	22	W10
Alfred Ter. G12	20	T10
Cecil St.		
Algie St. G41	51	U16
Alice St., Pais.	46	K15
Aline Ct. G78	59	L18
Allan Av., Renf.	32	N11
Allan Pl. G40	53	Y14
Allan St. G40	53	Y15
Allander Gdns. G64	10	X6
Allander Rd. G61	7	Q6
Allander St. G22	22	W10
Allands Av., Renf.	16	J9
Allanfauld Rd. G67	70	NN2
Allanton Av., Pais.	48	N14
Allanton Dr. G52	32	P13
Allerton Gdns. G69	55	DD14
Alleysbank Rd. G73	53	Y15
Allison Dr. G72	66	BB17
Allison Pl. G42	51	V15
Prince Edward St.		
Allison Pl. G69	27	GG10
Allison St. G42	51	V15
Allnach Pl. G34	41	GG12
Alloway Cres. G73	64	X17
Alloway Dr. G73	64	X17
Alloway Dr., Clyde.	5	M6
Alloway Rd. G43	62	T17
Alma St. G40	37	Y13
Almond Av., Renf.	32	N11
Almond Bk. G61	7	Q7
Almond Rd.		
Almond Cres., Pais.	45	G15
Almond Dr. G66	12	BB5
Almond Rd. G33	25	CC9
Almond Rd. G61	7	Q7
Almond St. G33	37	Z11
Almond Vale G71	57	HH16
Hamilton Vw.		
Alness Cres. G52	49	R14
Alpatrick Gdns., John.	44	E14
Alpine Gro. G71	57	GG16
Alsatian Av., Clyde.	5	M7
Alston La. G40	36	X13
Claythorn St.		
Altnacreag Gdns. G69	15	HH6
Alton Gdns. G12	20	T10
Great George St.		
Alton Rd., Pais.	47	M14
Altyre St. G32	54	AA14
Alva Gdns. G52	49	R15
Alva Gate G52	49	R15
Alva Pl. G66	13	DD6

Alyth Gdns. G52	49	R14
Ambassador Way, Renf.	31	M11
Cockels Ln.		
Amisfield St. G20	21	U9
Amochrie Dr., Pais.	45	H16
Amochrie Rd., Pais.	45	G15
Amulree Pl. G32	54	BB14
Amulree St. G32	38	BB13
Ancaster Dr. G13	19	R9
Ancaster La. G13	19	Q8
Great Western Rd.		
Anchor Av., Pais.	47	L14
Anchor Cres., Pais.	47	L14
Anchor Dr., Pais.	47	L14
Anchor Wynd, Pais.	47	L14
Ancroft St. G20	21	V10
Anderson Dr., Renf.	17	M10
Anderson Gdns. G72	69	GG19
Station Rd.		
Anderson Quay G3	35	U13
Anderson St. G11	34	S11
Anderston Cross Cen. G2	35	V12
Anderston Quay G3	35	U13
Andrew Av. G66	13	CC6
Andrew Av., Renf.	18	N10
Andrew Dr., Clyde.	17	M8
Andrew Sillars Av. G72	67	CC17
Andrews St., Pais.	30	K13
Angle Gate G14	19	Q10
Angus Av. G52	48	P14
Angus Av. G64	23	Z8
Angus Gdns. G71	57	GG16
Angus La. G64	11	Z7
Angus Oval G52	48	P14
Angus Pl. G52	48	P14
Angus St. G21	22	X10
Angus St., Clyde.	18	N8
Angus Wk. G71	57	HH16
Annan Dr. G61	7	Q6
Annan Dr. G73	53	Z16
Annan Dr., Pais.	45	G15
Annan Pl., John.	43	C16
Annan St. G42	51	V16
Annandale St. G42	51	V14
Annbank St. G31	36	X13
Anne Av., Renf.	17	M10
Anne Cres. G66	13	CC6
Annette St. G42	51	V15
Annfield Gdns. G72	68	FF19
Annfield Pl. G31	36	X12
Annick Dr. G61	7	Q7
Annick St. G32	38	BB13
Annick St. G72	67	CC17
Anniesdale Av. G33	25	CC9
Anniesland Cres. G14	18	P9
Anniesland Mans. G13	19	R9
Ancaster Dr.		
Anniesland Rd. G13	19	Q9
Anniesland Rd. G14	18	P9
Anson St. G40	52	X14
Anson Way, Renf.	31	M11
Britannia Way		
Anstruther St. G32	38	AA13
Anthony St. G2	35	V12
Cadogan St.		
Antonine Gdns.,	5	L5
Clyde.		
Antonine Rd. G61	6	P5
Anwoth St. G32	54	BB14
Appin Rd. G31	37	Y12
Appin Ter. G73	65	Z18
Lochaber Dr.		
Appin Way G71	69	HH18
Bracken Ter.		
Appleby St. G22	21	V10
Applecross Gdns. G69	15	GG6
Applecross St. G22	21	V10
Appledore Cres. G71	69	HH18
Apsley La. G11	34	S11
Apsley St. G11	34	S11
Aranthrue Cres., Renf.	17	M10
Aranthrue Dr., Renf.	17	M10
Aray St. G20	20	T9

Arbroath Av. G52	48	P14
Arcadia St. G40	36	X13
Arcan Cres. G15	6	P7
Archerfield Av. G32	54	BB15
Archerfield Cres. G32	54	BB15
Archerfield Dr. G32	54	BB15
Archerfield Gro. G32	54	BB15
Archerhill Av. G13	18	N8
Archerhill Cotts. G13	18	P8
Archerhill Rd.		
Archerhill Cres. G13	18	P8
Archerhill Gdns. G13	18	P8
Archerhill Rd.		
Archerhill Rd. G13	18	P8
Archerhill Sq. G13	18	N8
Kelso St.		
Archerhill St. G13	18	P8
Archerhill Rd.		
Archerhill Ter. G13	18	P8
Archerhill Rd.		
Ard Rd., Renf.	17	L10
Ard St. G32	54	BB14
Ardagie Dr. G32	55	CC16
Ardagie Pl. G32	55	CC16
Ardbeg Av. G64	11	Z7
Ardbeg Av. G73	66	AA18
Ardbeg St. G42	51	V15
Ardconnel St. G46	61	R18
Arden Av. G46	61	R19
Arden Dr. G46	62	S19
Arden Pl. G46	61	R19
Stewarton Rd.		
Ardencraig Cres. G45	64	W19
Ardencraig Dr. G45	64	X19
Ardencraig La. G45	64	W19
Ardencraig Rd.		
Ardencraig Quad. G45	64	X19
Ardencraig Rd. G45	64	W19
Ardencraig St. G45	65	Y19
Ardencraig Ter. G45	64	X19
Ardenlea Rd. G71	57	GG16
Ardenlea St. G40	53	Y14
Ardery St. G11	34	S11
Apsley St.		
Ardessie Pl. G20	20	T9
Ardessie St. G23	8	T7
Torrin Rd.		
Ardfern St. G32	54	BB14
Ardgay Pl. G32	54	BB14
Ardgay St. G32	54	BB14
Ardgay Way G73	65	Y18
Ardgour Dr., Pais.	28	E13
Ardgowan Av., Pais.	46	K14
Ardgowan Dr. G71	57	GG16
Ardgowan St., Pais.	46	K15
Ardholm St. G32	38	BB13
Ardhu Pl. G15	6	N6
Ardlamont Sq., Pais.	28	F13
Ardlaw St. G51	33	R13
Ardle Rd. G43	63	U17
Ardlui St. G32	54	AA14
Ardmaleish Cres. G45	64	X19
Ardmaleish Rd. G45	64	W19
Ardmaleish St. G45	64	X19
Ardmaleish Ter. G45	64	X19
Ardmay Cres. G44	52	W16
Ardmillan St. G33	38	AA12
Ardmore Oval, Pais.	29	H13
Ardmory Av. G42	52	W16
Ardmory La. G42	52	X16
Ardmory Pl. G42	52	X16
Ardnacross Dr. G33	39	CC11
Ardnahoe Av. G42	52	W16
Ardnahoe Pl. G42	52	W16
Ardneil Rd. G51	33	R13
Ardnish St. G51	33	R12
Ardo Gdns. G51	34	S13
Ardoch Gro. G72	66	AA17
Ardoch Rd. G61	8	S5
Ardoch St. G22	22	W10
Ardoch Way G69	15	GG7
Braeside Av.		
Ardshiel Rd. G51	33	R12

Name	Page	Grid
Ardsloy La. G14	18	P10
Ardsloy Pl.		
Ardsloy Pl. G14	18	P10
Ardtoe Cres. G33	25	DD9
Ardtoe Pl. G33	25	DD9
Arduthie Rd. G51	33	R12
Ardwell Rd. G52	49	R14
Argosy Way, Renf.	31	M11
Britannia Way		
Argyle St. G2	35	V12
Argyle St. G3	34	T11
Argyle St., Pais.	46	J14
Argyll Arc. G2	35	V12
Argyll Av., Pais.	30	K11
Argyll Av., Renf.	17	L10
Argyll Rd., Clyde.	5	M7
Arisaig Dr. G52	49	R14
Arisaig Pl. G61	8	S6
Arisaig Pl. G52	49	R14
Ark La. G31	36	X12
Arkle Ter. G72	66	AA18
Arkleston Cres., Pais.	31	L12
Arkleston Rd., Pais.	31	L12
Arkleston Rd., Renf.	31	L12
Arklet Rd. G51	33	R13
Arlington St. G3	35	U11
Armadale Ct. G31	37	Y12
Townmill Rd.		
Armadale Path G31	37	Y12
Armadale Pl. G31	37	Y12
Armadale St. G31	37	Y12
Armaleish Dr. G45	64	X19
Armour Pl., John.	44	E14
Armour St. G31	36	X13
Armour St., John.	44	E14
Armstrong Cres. G71	57	HH16
Arngask Rd. G51	33	R12
Arnhall Pl. G52	49	R14
Arnholm Pl. G52	49	R14
Arnisdale Pl. G34	40	EE12
Arnisdale Rd. G34	40	EE12
Arnisdale Way G73	65	Y18
Shieldaig Dr.		
Arniston St. G32	38	AA12
Arnol Pl. G33	39	DD12
Arnold Av. G64	11	Y7
Arnold St. G20	21	V9
Arnott Way G72	66	BB17
Arnprior Gdns. G69	15	GG7
Braeside Av.		
Arnprior Quad. G45	64	W18
Arnprior Rd. G45	64	W18
Arnprior St. G45	64	W18
Arnside Av. G46	62	T18
Arnthern St. G72	67	CC17
Arnwood Dr. G12	20	S9
Aron Ter. G72	66	AA18
Aros Dr. G52	49	R15
Arran Av., Pais.	30	K11
Arran Dr. G46	62	S19
Arran Dr. G52	49	R14
Arran Dr. G67	70	MM4
Arran Dr., John.	43	C15
Arran Dr., Pais.	46	K16
Arran La. G69	15	HH7
Burnbrae Av.		
Arran Pl., Clyde.	5	M7
Arran Pl., Pais.	28	E13
Arran Rd., Renf.	31	M11
Arran Ter. G73	64	X17
Arriochmill Rd. G20	20	T10
Kelvin Dr.		
Arrochar Ct. G23	21	U8
Sunningdale Rd.		
Arrochar Dr. G23	8	T7
Arrochar St. G23	20	T8
Arrol Pl. G40	53	Y14
Arrol St. G52	32	N12
Arrowsmith Av. G13	19	Q8
Arthur Av. G78	59	L19
Arthur Rd., Pais.	46	K16
Arthur St. G3	34	T11
Arthur St., Pais.	30	J13
Arthurlie Av. G78	59	M19
Arthurlie Dr. G46	62	T19
Arthurlie St. G51	33	R12
Arthurlie St. G78	59	M19
Arundel Dr. G42	51	V16
Arundel Dr. G64	11	Y6
Asbury Ct., Pais.	28	F13
Ascaig Cres. G52	49	R15
Ascog Rd. G61	7	R7
Ascog St. G42	51	V15
Ascot Av. G12	19	R9
Ascot Ct. G12	20	S9
Ash Gro. G64	11	Y7
Ash Gro. G66	12	BB5
Ash Gro. G71	57	HH16
Douglas Cres.		
Ash Pl., John.	44	E15
Ash Rd. G67	71	QQ1
Ash Rd. G69	56	EE14
Ash Rd., Clyde.	4	K5
Ash Wk. G73	65	Z18
Ashburton Rd. G12	20	S9
Ashby Cres. G13	7	R7
Ashcroft Dr. G44	64	X17
Ashdale Dr. G52	49	R14
Ashdene Rd. G22	21	V8
Ashfield G64	11	Y6
Ashfield St. G22	22	W10
Ashgill Pl. G22	22	W9
Ashgill Rd. G22	21	V9
Ashgrove G69	41	GG13
Ashgrove St. G40	53	Y15
Ashkirk Dr. G52	49	R14
Ashlea Dr. G46	62	T18
Ashley Dr. G71	69	HH19
Ashley La. G3	35	U11
Woodlands Rd.		
Ashley St. G3	35	U11
Ashmore Rd. G43	63	U17
Ashmore Rd. G44	63	U17
Ashton Gdns. G12	34	T11
Ashton Rd.		
Ashton La. G12	34	T11
University Av.		
Ashton Pl. G12	20	T10
Byres Rd.		
Ashton Rd. G12	34	T11
University Av.		
Ashton Rd. G73	53	Y15
Ashton Ter. G12	34	T11
University Av.		
Ashton Way, Pais.	45	G16
Ashtree Rd. G43	50	T16
Ashvale Cres. G21	22	X10
Aspen Dr. G21	23	Y10
Foresthall Dr.		
Aspen Pl., John.	44	E15
Aster Dr. G45	65	Y18
Aster Gdns. G53	61	Q18
Waukglen Cres.		
Athelstane Dr. G67	70	MM4
Athelstane Rd. G13	19	Q8
Athena Way G71	57	HH16
Athol Av. G52	32	N12
Athol Ter. G71	57	GG15
Athole Gdns. G12	20	T10
Athole La. G12	20	T10
Saltoun St.		
Atholl Cres., Pais.	32	N13
Atholl Gdns. G64	11	Y6
Atholl Gdns. G73	66	AA18
Atholl La. G69	15	HH7
Atholl Pl., Pais.	28	E13
Atlas Pl. G21	22	X10
Atlas Rd. G21	22	X10
Atlas St., Clyde.	17	L8
Attlee Av., Clyde.	5	M7
Attlee Pl., Clyde.	5	M7
Attlee Av.		
Attow Rd. G43	62	S17
Auburn Dr. G78	59	M19
Auburn Pl. G31	37	Z13
Auchans Rd., John.	28	E11
Auchencrow St. G34	40	FF12
Auchendale G66	13	DD5
Auchengeich Rd. G69	14	FF6
Auchenglen Dr. G69	15	GG7
Auchengreoch Av., John.	43	C16
Auchengreoch Rd., John.	43	C16
Auchenlodment Rd., John.	44	E15
Auchentorlie Quad., Pais.	47	L14
Auchentorlie St. G11	33	R11
Dumbarton Rd.		
Auchentoshan Av., Clyde.	4	K5
Auchentoshan Ter. G21	36	X11
Auchentoshen Cotts. G60	4	J5
Auchinairn Rd. G64	22	X8
Auchinbee Way G68	70	MM2
Eastfield Rd.		
Auchingill Path G34	40	FF11
Auchingill Rd.		
Auchingill Pl. G34	40	FF11
Auchingill Rd. G34	40	FF11
Auchinlea Rd. G34	39	DD11
Auchinleck Av. G33	24	AA9
Auchinleck Cres. G33	24	AA9
Auchinleck Dr. G33	24	AA9
Auchinleck Gdns. G33	24	AA9
Auchinleck Rd. G33	24	AA8
Auchinloch Rd. G66	13	CC6
Auchinloch St. G21	22	X10
Auchmannoch Av., Pais.	32	N13
Auckland Pl., Clyde.	4	J6
Auckland St. G22	21	V10
Auld Kirk Rd. G72	67	CC18
Auld Rd., The G67	71	PP2
Auld St., Clyde.	4	K6
Auldbar Rd. G52	49	R14
Auldbar Ter., Pais.	47	L15
Auldburn Pl. G43	62	S17
Auldburn Rd.		
Auldburn Rd. G43	62	S17
Auldearn Rd. G21	23	Z8
Auldgirth Rd. G52	49	R14
Auldhouse Av. G43	62	S17
Harriet St.		
Auldhouse Rd. G43	62	S17
Auldhouse Ter. G43	62	T17
Auldhouse Rd.		
Aultbea St. G22	21	V8
Aultmore Rd. G33	39	DD12
Aurs Cres. G78	59	M19
Aurs Dr. G78	59	M19
Aurs Glen G78	59	M19
Aurs Pl. G78	59	M19
Aurs Rd. G78	59	M18
Aursbridge Cres. G78	59	M19
Aursbridge Dr. G78	59	M19
Austen La. G13	19	R9
Skaterig La.		
Austen Rd. G13	19	R9
Avenel Rd. G13	7	R7
Avenue, The, John.	42	B15
Low Barholm		
Avenue End Rd. G33	24	BB10
Avenue St. G40	37	Y13
Avenue St. G73	53	Y15
Avenuehead Rd. G69	15	GG7
Avenuepark St. G20	21	U10
Aviemore Gdns. G61	8	S5
Aviemore Rd. G52	49	R15
Avoch Dr. G46	61	R18
Avoch St. G34	40	EE11
Avon Av. G61	8	S6
Avon Dr. G64	23	Y8
Avon Dr., Pais.	28	E13
Avon Rd. G46	62	S19
Avon Rd. G64	23	Y8
Avon St. G5	35	U13
Avonbank Rd. G73	52	X16
Avondale Dr., Pais.	31	L13
Avondale St. G33	38	BB11
Avonhead Av. G67	70	MM4
Avonhead Gdns. G67	70	MM4
Avonhead Pl. G67	70	MM4
Avonhead Rd. G67	70	MM4

Name	No.	Ref.
Avonspark St. G21	23	Y10
Aylmer Rd. G43	63	U17
Ayr Rd. G46	62	S19
Ayr St. G21	22	X10
Aytoun Rd. G41	50	T14

B

Name	No.	Ref.
Back Causeway G31	37	Z13
Back Sneddon St., Pais.	30	K13
Backmuir Rd. G15	6	P6
Bagnell St. G21	22	X9
Baillie Dr. G71	69	HH18
Baillie Wynd G71	57	HH16
Baillieston Rd. G32	55	CC14
Baillieston Rd. G71	56	EE14
Bain Sq. G40	36	X13
Bain St.		
Bain St. G40	36	X13
Bainsford St. G32	38	AA13
Baird Av. G52	32	N12
Baird Dr. G61	7	Q5
Baird St. G4	36	W11
Bairdsbrae G4	21	V10
Possil Rd.		
Baker Pl. G22	51	U15
Baker St.		
Baker St. G41	51	U15
Bakewell Rd. G69	40	EE13
Balaclava St. G2	35	V13
McAlpine St.		
Balado Rd. G33	39	DD12
Balbeg St. G51	33	R13
Balbeggie Pl. G32	55	CC14
Balbeggie St. G32	55	CC14
Balblair Rd. G52	49	R15
Balcarres Av. G12	20	T9
Balcomie St. G33	38	BB11
Balcurvie Rd. G34	40	EE11
Baldinnie Rd. G34	40	EE12
Baldorran Cres. G68	70	LL2
Baldovan Cres. G33	39	DD12
Baldovie Rd. G52	49	Q14
Baldragon Rd. G34	40	EE11
Baldric Rd. G13	19	Q9
Baldwin Av. G13	7	Q7
Balerno Dr. G52	49	R14
Balfluig St. G34	39	DD11
Balfour St. G20	20	T9
Balfron Rd. G51	33	R12
Balfron Rd., Pais.	31	M13
Balgair Dr., Pais.	31	L13
Balgair St. G22	21	V9
Balgair Ter. G32	38	BB13
Balglass St. G22	21	V10
Balgonie Av., Pais.	45	H15
Balgonie Dr., Pais.	46	J15
Balgonie Rd. G52	49	R14
Balgonie Wds., Pais.	46	J15
Balgownie Cres. G46	62	S19
Balgray Cres. G78	60	N19
Balgraybank St. G21	23	Y10
Balgrayhill Rd. G21	22	X9
Balintore St. G32	38	BB13
Baliol La. G3	35	U11
Woodlands Rd.		
Baliol St. G3	35	U11
Ballagan Av. G61	7	Q5
Ballaig Cres. G33	25	CC9
Ballantay Quad. G45	65	Y18
Ballantay Rd. G45	65	Y18
Ballantay Ter. G45	65	Y18
Ballantyne Rd. G52	32	P12
Ballater Dr. G61	7	R7
Ballater Dr., Pais.	47	L15
Ballater Dr., Renf.	16	J8
Ballater Pl. G5	52	W14
Ballater St. G5	36	W13
Ballayne Dr. G69	15	HH7
Ballindalloch Dr. G31	37	Y12
Balloch Gdns. G52	49	R14
Balloch Rd. G68	70	MM3
Balloch Vw. G67	70	NN3
Ballochmill Rd. G73	53	Z16
Ballogie Rd. G44	51	V16
Balmarino Pl. G64	11	Z7
Balmartin Rd. G23	8	T7
Balmerino Pl. G64	23	Z8
Angus Av.		
Balmoral Cres. G42	51	V15
Queens Dr.		
Balmoral Cres., Renf.	16	K9
Balmoral Dr. G32	54	BB16
Balmoral Dr. G61	8	S7
Balmoral Dr. G72	66	AA17
Balmoral Gdns. G71	57	GG15
Balmoral Gdns. G72	68	FF19
Balmoral Rd., John.	44	E15
Balmore Pl. G22	21	V9
Balmore Rd.		
Balmore Rd. G22	21	V8
Balmore Rd. G23	9	U7
Balmore Rd. G62	9	U5
Balmore Sq. G22	21	V9
Balmuildy Rd. G23	9	V6
Balmuildy Rd. G64	9	V6
Balornock Rd. G21	23	Y9
Balruddery Pl. G64	23	Z8
Balshagray Av. G11	19	R10
Balshagray Cres. G14	19	R10
Balshagray Dr. G11	19	R10
Balshagray La. G11	19	R10
Balshagray Pl. G11	19	R10
Balshagray Dr.		
Baltic Ct. G40	53	Y14
Baltic St.		
Baltic La. G40	53	Y14
Baltic Pl. G40	52	X14
Baltic St. G40	53	Y14
Balure St. G31	37	Z12
Balvaird Cres. G73	53	Y16
Balvaird Dr. G73	53	Y16
Balveny St. G33	39	CC11
Balvicar Dr. G42	51	U15
Balvicar St. G42	51	U15
Balvie Av. G15	6	P7
Balvie Av. G46	62	T19
Banavie Rd. G11	20	S10
Banchory Av. G43	62	S17
Banchory Av., Renf.	16	J8
Banchory Cres. G61	8	S7
Banff St. G33	38	BB11
Bangorshill St. G46	61	R18
Bank Rd. G32	55	CC16
Bank St. G12	35	U11
Bank St. G72	66	BB17
Bank St. G78	59	M19
Bank St., Pais.	46	K14
Bankbrae Av. G53	60	P17
Bankend St. G33	38	BB11
Bankfoot Dr. G52	48	P14
Bankfoot Rd. G52	48	P14
Bankfoot Rd., Pais.	29	H13
Bankglen Rd. G15	6	P6
Bankhall St. G42	51	V15
Bankhead Av. G13	18	P9
Bankhead Dr. G73	53	Y16
Bankhead Rd. G73	64	X17
Bankier St. G40	36	X13
Banknock St. G32	38	AA13
Bankside Av., John.	43	D14
Banktop Pl., John.	43	D14
Banling Grn. Rd. G44	63	V17
Clarkston Rd.		
Bannatyne Av. G31	37	Y12
Banner Dr. G13	7	Q7
Banner Rd. G13	7	Q7
Bannercross Av. G69	40	EE13
Bannercross Dr. G69	40	EE13
Bannercross Gdns. G69	40	EE13
Bannercross Dr.		
Bannerman Pl., Clyde.	5	M7
Bannerman St., Clyde.	5	L7
Bantaskin St. G20	20	T8
Banton Pl. G33	40	EE12
Barassie Ct. G71	69	GG19
Barassie Cres. G68	70	NN1
Barbae Pl. G71	69	HH18
Hume Dr.		
Barberry Av. G53	60	P19
Barberry Gdns. G53	60	P19
Barberry Av.		
Barberry Pl. G53	60	P19
Barberry Av.		
Barbreck Rd. G42	51	U15
Pollokshaws Rd.		
Barcaldine Av. G69	14	EE7
Barclay Av., John.	44	E15
Barclay Sq., Renf.	31	L11
Barclay St. G21	22	X9
Balgrayhill Rd.		
Barcraigs Dr., Pais.	46	K16
Bard Av. G13	18	P8
Bardowie St. G22	21	V10
Bardrain Av., John.	44	F15
Bardrain Rd., Pais.	46	J16
Bardrill Dr. G64	10	X7
Bardykes Rd. G72	68	FF19
Barfillan Dr. G52	33	R13
Barfillan Rd. G52	33	R13
Bargaran Rd. G53	48	P14
Bargarron Dr., Pais.	31	L12
Bargeddie St. G33	37	Z11
Barhill Cres., John.	42	B15
Barholm Sq. G33	39	CC11
Barke Rd. G67	71	PP2
Barlanark Av. G32	39	CC12
Barlanark Cres. G33	39	CC12
Barlanark Pl. G32	39	CC13
Hallhill Rd.		
Barlanark Pl. G33	39	DD12
Barlanark Rd. G33	39	CC12
Barlia Dr. G45	64	X18
Barlia St. G45	64	X18
Barlia Ter. G45	64	X18
Barloch St. G22	22	W10
Barlogan Av. G52	33	R13
Barlogan Quad. G52	33	R13
Barmill Rd. G43	62	S17
Barmulloch Rd. G21	23	Y10
Barn Grn., John.	42	B14
Barnard Gdns. G64	11	Y6
Barnard Ter. G40	53	Y14
Barnbeth Rd. G53	48	P15
Barnes Rd. G20	21	V9
Barnes St. G78	59	L19
Barnflat St. G73	53	Y15
Barnhill Dr. G21	23	Y10
Foresthall Dr.		
Barnkirk Av. G15	6	P6
Barns St., Clyde.	5	M7
Barnsford Av., Renf.	16	J9
Barnsford Rd., Pais.	29	H12
Barnton St. G32	38	AA12
Barnwell Ter. G51	33	R12
Barochan Cres., Pais.	45	H14
Barochan Rd. G53	48	P14
Baron Rd., Pais.	31	L13
Baron St., Renf.	31	M11
Baronald Dr. G12	20	S9
Baronald Gate G12	20	S9
Baronald St. G73	53	Y15
Baronhill G67	71	PP2
Barons Gate G71	69	GG18
Baronscourt Dr., Pais.	45	G14
Baronscourt Gdns., Pais.	45	G14
Baronscourt Rd., Pais.	45	G14
Barony Dr. G69	40	EE13
Barony Gdns. G69	40	EE13
Barony Dr.		
Barr Cres., Clyde.	5	L5
Barr Gro. G71	57	HH16
Barr Pl., Pais.	46	J14
Barr St. G20	21	V10
Barra Av., Renf.	31	M11
Barra Cres. G60	4	J5
Barra Gdns. G60	4	J5
Barra Rd.		

Street	Page	Grid
Barra Rd. G60	4	J5
Barra St. G20	20	T8
Barrachnie Ct. G69	39	DD13
Barrachnie Cres.		
Barrachnie Cres. G69	39	DD13
Barrachnie Rd. G69	39	DD13
Barrack St. G4	36	X13
Barrhead Rd. G43	49	Q16
Barrhead Rd. G53	48	N16
Barrhead Rd., Pais.	47	L14
Barrie Quad., Clyde.	5	L6
Barrie Rd. G52	32	P12
Barrington Dr. G4	35	U11
Barrisdale Rd. G20	20	T8
Barrisdale Way G73	65	Y18
Barrland Dr. G46	62	T18
Barrland St. G41	51	V14
Barrochan Rd., John.	43	D14
Barrowfield St. G40	37	Y13
Barrwood Pl. G71	57	HH16
Barrwood St. G33	38	AA11
Barscube Ter., Pais.	47	L14
Barshaw Dr., Pais.	31	L13
Barshaw Pl., Pais.	31	M13
Barshaw Rd. G52	32	N13
Barterholm Rd., Pais.	46	K15
Bartholomew St. G40	53	Y14
Bartiebeith Rd. G33	39	DD12
Basset Av. G13	18	P8
Basset Cres. G13	18	P8
Bath La. G2	35	V12
Blythswood St.		
Bath La. W. G3	35	U12
North St.		
Bath St. G2	35	V12
Bathgate St. G31	37	Y13
Bathgo Av., Pais.	48	N14
Batson St. G42	51	V15
Battle Pl. G41	51	U16
Battleburn St. G32	54	BB14
Battlefield Av. G42	51	V16
Battlefield Cres. G42	51	V16
Battlefield Gdns.		
Battlefield Gdns. G42	51	V16
Battlefield Rd. G42	51	V16
Bavelaw St. G33	39	CC11
Bayfield Av. G15	6	P6
Bayfield Ter. G15	6	P6
Beaconsfield Rd. G12	20	S9
Beard Cres. G69	27	GG9
Beardmore Cotts., Renf.	16	K9
Beardmore St., Clyde.	4	J6
Beardmore Way, Clyde.	4	J7
Bearford Dr. G52	32	P13
Bearsden Rd. G13	19	R8
Bearsden Rd. G61	19	R9
Beaton Rd. G41	51	U15
Beatson Wynd G71	57	HH15
Beattock St. G31	37	Z13
Beatty St., Clyde.	4	J6
Beaufort Av. G43	62	T17
Beaufort Gdns. G64	10	X7
Beauly Dr., Pais.	45	G15
Beauly Pl. G20	20	T9
Beauly Pl. G64	11	Z7
Beauly Pl. G69	14	FF7
Beauly Rd. G69	56	EE14
Beaumont Gate G12	34	T11
Bedale Rd. G69	55	DD14
Bedford Av., Clyde.	5	M7
Onslow Rd.		
Bedford La. G5	35	V13
Bedford Row G5	35	V13
Dunmore St.		
Bedford St. G5	35	V13
Bedlay Ct. G69	15	HH6
Bedlay St. G21	22	X10
Petershill Rd.		
Bedlay Wk. G69	15	HH6
Beech Av. G41	50	S14
Beech Av. G69	40	EE13
Beech Av. G72	66	AA17
Beech Av. G73	65	Z18
Beech Av., John.	44	F15
Beech Av., Pais.	47	L15
Beech Dr., Clyde.	5	L5
Beech Gdns. G69	40	EE13
Beech Gro. G78	59	M19
Arthurlie Av.		
Beech Pl. G64	23	Y8
Beech Rd. G64	23	Y8
Beech Rd. G66	13	CC5
Beech Rd., John.	43	C15
Beechcroft Pl. G72	69	GG19
Beeches Av., Clyde.	4	K5
Beeches Rd., Clyde.	4	K5
Beeches Ter., Clyde.	4	K5
Beechgrove St. G40	53	Y15
Beechlands Av. G44	63	U19
Beechmount Cotts. G14	18	N9
Dumbarton Rd.		
Beechmount Rd. G66	13	CC6
Beechwood Av. G11	19	R10
Beechwood Dr.		
Beechwood Av. G73	65	Z17
Beechwood Ct. G61	7	R6
Beechwood Dr. G11	19	R10
Beechwood Dr., Renf.	31	L11
Beechwood Gro. G78	59	M19
Arthurlie Av.		
Beechwood La. G61	7	R6
Beechwood Ct.		
Beechwood Pl. G11	19	R10
Beechwood Dr.		
Beechwood Rd. G67	70	NN3
Beil Dr. G13	18	N8
Beith Rd., John.	42	B16
Beith St. G11	34	S11
Belgrave La. G12	21	U10
Belgrave Ter.		
Belgrave Ter. G12	21	UJ0
Belhaven Cres. La. G12	20	T10
Lorraine Rd.		
Belhaven Ter. G12	20	T10
Belhaven Ter. W. G12	20	T10
Bell St. G1	36	W12
Bell St. G4	36	W13
Bell St., Clyde.	17	M8
Bell St., Renf.	17	M10
Bellahouston Dr. G52	49	R14
Bellahouston La. G52	49	R14
Bellairs Pl. G72	68	FF19
Belleisle Av. G71	57	GG16
Belleisle St. G42	51	V15
Bellevue Pl. G21	36	X11
Bellfield Ct. G78	59	L18
Bellfield Cres. G78	59	L18
Bellfield St. G31	37	Y13
Bellflower Av. G53	61	Q18
Bellflower Gdns. G53	61	Q18
Bellflower Pl. G53	61	Q18
Bellgrove St. G31	36	X13
Bellhaven Ter. G73	65	Z17
Bellrock Cres. G33	38	BB12
Bellrock St. G33	38	BB12
Bellscroft Av. G73	52	X16
Bellshaugh Gdns. G12	20	T9
Bellshaugh La. G12	20	T9
Bellshaugh Pl. G12	20	T9
Bellshaugh Rd. G12	20	T9
Bellshill Rd. G71	69	GG17
Belltrees Cres., Pais.	45	H14
Bellwood St. G41	51	U16
Belmar Ct., Pais.	28	F13
Belmont Av. G71	57	GG16
Belmont Cres. G12	21	U10
Belmont Dr. G46	62	S18
Belmont Dr. G73	53	Y16
Belmont Dr. G78	59	M19
Belmont La. G12	20	T10
Great Western Rd.		
Belmont Rd. G21	22	X9
Belmont Rd. G72	66	AA18
Belmont Rd., Pais.	31	L13
Belmont St. G12	21	U10
Belmont St., Clyde.	17	L8
Belses Dr. G52	33	Q13
Belstane Pl. G71	69	HH18
Appledore Cres.		
Belsyde Av. G15	6	P7
Beltane St. G3	35	U12
Beltrees Av. G53	48	P15
Beltrees Cres. G53	48	P15
Beltrees Rd. G53	48	P15
Belvidere Cres. G64	11	Y6
Bemersyde G64	11	Z7
Bemersyde Av. G43	62	S17
Bemersyde Rd., Pais.	45	G16
Ben Alder Dr., Pais.	47	M15
Ben Buie Way, Pais.	47	M15
Ben Lawers Dr. G68	70	MM3
Balloch Rd.		
Ben Ledi Av., Pais.	47	M15
Ben Lui Dr., Pais.	47	M15
Ben More Dr., Pais.	47	M15
Ben Nevis Rd., Pais.	47	M15
Ben Venue Way, Pais.	47	M15
Ben Wyvis Dr., Pais.	47	M15
Benalder St. G11	34	T11
Benarty Gdns. G64	11	Y7
Bencroft Dr. G44	64	X17
Bengairn St. G31	37	Z12
Bengal Pl. G43	50	T16
Christian St.		
Bengal St. G43	50	T16
Benhar Pl. G33	38	AA12
Benholm St. G32	54	AA14
Benhope Av., Pais.	47	M15
Benlawers Dr., Pais.	47	M15
Benloyal Av., Pais.	47	M15
Benmore St. G21	22	X9
Bennan Sq. G42	52	W15
Benston Pl., John.	43	D15
Benston Rd., John.	43	D15
Benthall St. G5	52	W14
Bentinck St. G3	35	U11
Bents Rd. G69	40	EE13
Benvane Av., Pais.	47	M15
Benvie Gdns. G64	11	Y7
Benview St. G20	21	U10
Benview Ter., Pais.	47	L15
Berelands Cres. G73	52	X16
Berelands Pl. G73	52	X16
Beresford Av. G14	19	R10
Berkeley St. G3	35	U12
Berkeley Ter. La. G3	35	U11
Elderslie St.		
Berkley Dr. G72	68	FF19
Bernard Path G40	53	Y14
Bernard St. G40	53	Y14
Bernard Ter. G40	53	Y14
Berneray St. G22	22	W8
Berridale Av. G44	63	V17
Berriedale Av. G69	56	EE14
Berryburn Rd. G21	23	Z10
Berryhill Dr. G46	62	S19
Berryhill Rd. G46	62	S19
Berryhill Rd. G67	70	NN3
Berryknowes Av. G52	33	Q13
Berryknowes La. G52	33	Q13
Berryknowes Rd. G52	49	Q14
Berryknowes Rd. G69	26	FF8
Bertram St. G41	51	U15
Bertrohill Ter. G33	39	CC12
Stepps Rd.		
Bervie St. G51	33	R13
Berwick Cres., Pais.	28	E12
Berwick Dr. G52	48	P14
Berwick Dr. G73	53	Z16
Betula Dr., Clyde.	5	L5
Bevan Gro., John.	43	C16
Beverley Rd. G43	62	T17
Bevin Av., Clyde.	5	M7
Bideford Cres. G32	55	CC14
Biggar Pl. G31	37	Y13
Biggar St. G31	37	Y13
Bigton St. G33	38	BB11
Bilsland Ct. G20	21	V9
Bilsland Dr.		

Street	Page	Grid
Bilsland Dr. G20	21	U9
Binend Rd. G53	49	Q16
Binnie Pl. G40	36	X13
Binniehill Rd. G68	70	MM2
Binns Rd. G33	39	CC11
Birch Cres., John.	44	E15
Birch Dr. G66	13	CC5
Birch Gro. G71	57	HH16
Burnhead St.		
Birch Knowle G64	11	Y7
Birch Rd., Clyde.	5	L5
Birch Vw. G61	8	S5
Birchfield Dr. G14	18	P10
Birchlea Dr. G46	62	T18
Birchwood Av. G32	55	DD14
Birchwood Dr., Pais.	45	H15
Birchwood Pl. G32	55	DD14
Birdston Rd. G21	23	Z9
Birgidale Av. G45	64	W19
Birgidale Rd. G45	64	W19
Birgidale Ter. G45	64	W19
Birkdale Ct. G71	69	GG19
Birken Rd. G66	13	DD6
Birkenshaw St. G31	37	Y12
Birkenshaw Way, Pais.	30	K12
Abbotsburn Way		
Birkhall Av. G52	48	N14
Birkhall Av., Renf.	16	J8
Birkhall Dr. G61	7	R7
Birkhill Av. G64	11	Y6
Birkhill Gdns. G64	11	Z6
Birkmyre Rd. G51	33	R13
Birks Rd., Renf.	31	L11
Tower Dr.		
Birkwood St. G40	53	Y15
Birmingham Rd., Renf.	31	L11
Birnam Av. G64	11	Y6
Birnam Cres. G61	8	S5
Birnam Gdns. G64	11	Y7
Birnam Rd. G31	53	Z14
Birness Dr. G43	50	T16
Birness St. G43	50	T16
Birnie Ct. G21	23	Z10
Birnie Rd. G21	23	Z10
Birnock Av., Renf.	32	N11
Birsay Rd. G22	21	V8
Bishop Gdns. G64	10	X7
Bishop St. G3	35	V12
Bishopmill Pl. G21	23	Z10
Bishopmill Rd. G21	23	Z10
Bishopsgate Dr. G21	22	X9
Bishopsgate Gdns. G21	22	X9
Bishopsgate Pl. G21	22	X9
Bishopsgate Rd. G21	22	X9
Bisset Cres., Clyde.	4	K5
Black St. G4	36	W11
Blackburn Sq. G78	59	M19
Blackburn St. G51	34	T13
Blackbyres Rd. G78	59	M17
Blackcraig Av. G15	6	P6
Blackcroft Gdns. G32	55	CC14
Blackcroft Rd. G32	55	CC14
Blackfaulds Rd. G73	52	X16
Blackford Cres. G32	55	CC14
Blackford Pl. G32	55	CC14
Blackford Rd., Pais.	47	L14
Blackfriars St. G1	36	W12
Blackhall La., Pais.	46	K14
Blackhall St., Pais.	46	K14
Blackhill Cotts. G23	9	V7
Blackhill Pl. G33	37	Z11
Blackhill Rd. G23	8	T7
Blackie St. G3	34	T11
Blacklands Pl. G66	13	DD6
Blacklaw La., Pais.	30	K13
Blackstone Av. G53	49	Q16
Blackstone Cres. G53	49	Q15
Blackstone Rd., Pais.	29	H12
Blackstoun Av., Pais.	28	E13
Blackstoun Oval, Pais.	29	H13
Blackstoun Rd., Pais.	29	H13
Blackthorn Av. G66	12	BB5
Blackthorn Gro. G66	12	BB5
Blackthorn Rd. G67	71	QQ2
Blackthorn St. G22	22	X9
Blackwood Av., Pais.	28	E13
Blackwood St. G13	19	R8
Blackwood St. G78	59	L19
Blackwoods Cres. G69	15	GG7
Blacurvie Rd. G34	40	EE11
Bladda La., Pais.	46	K14
Blades Ct. G69	27	HH9
Bladnoch Dr. G15	7	Q7
Moraine Av.		
Blaeloch Av. G45	64	W19
Blaeloch Dr. G45	64	W19
Blaeloch Ter. G45	64	W19
Blair Cres. G69	56	EE14
Blair Rd., Pais.	32	N13
Blair St. G32	38	AA13
Blairatholl Av. G11	20	S10
Blairatholl Gdns. G11	20	S10
Blairbeth Dr. G44	51	V16
Blairbeth Rd. G73	65	Y17
Blairbeth Ter. G73	65	Y18
Blairdardie Rd. G13	7	Q7
Blairdardie Rd. G15	6	P7
Blairdenan Av. G69	15	HH6
Blairdenon Dr. G68	70	MM2
Blairgowrie Rd. G52	49	Q14
Blairhall Av. G41	51	U16
Blairhill Av. G66	14	EE5
Blairlogie St. G33	38	BB11
Blairston Av. G71	69	HH19
Blairston Gdns. G71	69	HH19
Blairston Av.		
Blairtum Dr. G73	65	Y17
Blairtummock Rd. G33	39	CC12
Blake Rd. G67	71	PP3
Blane St. G4	36	W11
Blantyre Fm. Rd. G72	68	FF19
Blantyre Mill Rd. G71	69	GG19
Blantyre Rd. G71	69	HH19
Blantyre St. G3	34	T11
Blaven Ct. G69	56	FF14
Bracadale Rd.		
Blawarthill St. G14	18	N9
Blenheim Av. G33	25	CC9
Blenheim Ct. G33	25	DD9
Blenheim Av.		
Blenheim Ct., Pais.	30	J13
Blenheim La. G33	25	DD9
Blesdale Ct., Clyde.	5	L7
Blochairn Rd. G21	37	Y11
Bluebell Gdns. G45	65	Y19
Bluevale St. G31	37	Y13
Blyth Pl. G33	39	CC13
Blyth Rd. G33	39	DD13
Blythswood Av., Renf.	17	M10
Blythswood Ct. G2	35	V12
Cadogan St.		
Blythswood Dr., Pais.	30	K13
Blythswood Rd., Renf.	17	M9
Blythswood Sq. G2	35	V12
Blythswood St. G2	35	V12
Boclair Av. G61	7	R6
Boclair Cres. G61	8	S6
Boclair Cres. G64	11	Y7
Boclair Rd. G61	8	S6
Boclair Rd. G64	11	Y7
Boclair St. G13	19	R8
Boden St. G40	53	Y14
Bodmin Gdns. G69	15	GG6
Gartferry Rd.		
Bogany Ter. G45	64	X19
Bogbain Rd. G34	40	EE12
Boggknowe G71	56	FF16
Old Edinburgh Rd.		
Boghall Rd. G71	56	EE15
Boghall St. G33	38	BB11
Boghead Rd. G21	23	Y10
Boghead Rd. G66	12	BB6
Bogleshole Rd. G72	54	AA16
Bogmoor Rd. G51	33	Q12
Bogside Pl. G69	40	FF12
Whamflet Av.		
Bogside Rd. G33	24	BB9
Bogside St. G40	53	Y14
Bogton Av. G44	63	U18
Bogton Av. La. G44	63	U18
Bogton Av.		
Boleyn Rd. G41	51	U15
Bolivar Ter. G42	52	W16
Bolton Dr. G42	51	V16
Bon Accord Sq., Clyde.	17	L8
Bonawe St. G20	21	U10
Boness St. G40	53	Y14
Bonhill St. G22	21	V10
Bonnar St. G40	53	Y14
Bonnaughton Rd. G61	6	P5
Bonnyholm Av. G53	48	P14
Bonnyrigg Dr. G43	62	S17
Bonyton Av. G13	18	N9
Boon Dr. G15	6	P7
Boquhanran Pl., Clyde.	5	L6
Albert Rd.		
Boquhanran Rd., Clyde.	4	K7
Borden La. G13	19	R9
Borden Rd. G13	19	R9
Boreland Dr. G13	18	P8
Boreland Pl. G13	18	P9
Borgie Cres. G72	66	BB17
Borland Rd. G61	8	S6
Borron St. G4	22	W10
Borthwick St. G33	38	BB11
Boswell Ct. G42	51	U16
Boswell Sq. G52	32	N12
Botanic Cres. G20	20	T10
Bothlyn Cres. G69	27	GG8
Bothlyn Dr. G33	25	CC9
Bothlynn Rd. G69	26	FF8
Bothwell La. G2	35	V12
West Campbell St.		
Bothwell Pk. Rd. G71	69	HH19
Bothwell Rd. G71	69	GG17
Bothwell St. G2	35	V12
Bothwell St. G72	66	AA17
Bothwell Ter. G12	35	U11
Bank St.		
Bothwick Way, Pais.	45	G16
Crosbie Dr.		
Boundary Rd. G73	52	X15
Rutherglen Rd.		
Bourne Ct., Renf.	16	J8
Bourne Cres., Renf.	16	J8
Bourock Sq. G78	60	N19
Bourtree Dr. G73	65	Z18
Bouverie St. G14	18	N9
Bouverie St. G73	52	X16
Bowden Dr. G52	32	P13
Bower St. G12	21	U10
Bowerwalls St. G78	60	N18
Bowes Cres. G69	55	DD14
Bowfield Av. G52	32	N13
Bowfield Cres. G52	32	N13
Bowfield Dr. G52	32	N13
Bowfield Pl. G52	32	N13
Bowfield Ter. G52	32	N13
Bowfield Av.		
Bowhouse Way G73	65	Y18
Bowling Grn. La. G14	19	Q10
Westland Dr.		
Bowling Grn. Rd. G14	19	Q10
Bowling Grn. Rd. G32	55	CC14
Bowling Grn. Rd. G44	63	V17
Bowling Grn. Rd. G69	26	FF8
Bowman St. G42	51	V15
Bowmont Gdns. G12	20	T10
Bowmont Hill G64	11	Y6
Bowmont Ter. G12	20	T10
Bowmore Gdns. G71	57	GG16
Bowmore Gdns. G73	66	AA18
Bowmore Rd. G52	33	R13
Boyd St. G42	51	V15
Boydstone Pl. G46	61	R17
Boydstone Rd. G43	61	R17
Boydstone Rd. G46	61	R17
Boydstone Rd. G53	61	R17
Boyle St., Clyde.	17	M8

Boylestone Rd. G78	59	L18
Boyndie Path G34	40	EE12
Boyndie St. G34	40	EE12
Brabloch Cres., Pais.	30	K13
Bracadale Dr. G69	56	FF14
Bracadale Gdns. G69	56	FF14
Bracadale Gro. G69	56	FF14
Bracadale Rd. G69	56	FF14
Bracken Rd. G78	59	L17
Bracken St. G22	21	V9
Bracken Ter. G71	69	HH18
Brackenbrae Av. G64	10	X7
Brackenbrae Rd. G64	10	X7
Brackenrig Rd. G46	61	R19
Brackla Av. G13	18	N8
Brackla Av., Clyde.	18	N8
Bracora Pl. G20	20	T9
Glenfinnan Dr.		
Bradan Av. G13	18	N8
Bradan Av., Clyde.	18	N8
Bradda Av. G73	65	Z18
Bradfield Av. G12	20	T9
Brady Cres. G69	15	HH6
Braeface Rd. G67	70	NN3
Braefield Dr. G46	62	S18
Braefoot Cres., Pais.	46	K16
Braehead Rd. G67	71	PP2
Braehead Rd., Pais.	58	J17
Braehead St. G5	52	W14
Braemar Av., Clyde.	4	K6
Braemar Cres. G61	7	R7
Braemar Cres., Pais.	46	K16
Braemar Dr., John.	44	E15
Braemar Rd. G73	66	AA18
Braemar Rd., Renf.	16	J8
Braemar St. G42	51	U16
Braemar Vw., Clyde.	4	K5
Braemount Av., Pais.	58	J17
Braes Av., Clyde.	17	M8
Braeside Av. G69	15	GG7
Braeside Av. G73	53	Z16
Braeside Cres. G69	41	GG13
Braeside Cres. G78	60	N19
Braeside Dr. G78	59	M19
Braeside Pl. G72	66	BB18
Braeside St. G20	21	U10
Braeview Av., Pais.	45	H16
Braeview Dr., Pais.	45	H16
Braeview Gdns., Pais.	45	H16
Braeview Rd., Pais.	45	H16
Braid Sq. G4	35	V11
Braid St. G4	35	V11
Braidbar Fm. Rd. G46	62	T18
Braidbar Rd. G46	62	T18
Braidcraft Pl. G53	49	Q16
Braidcraft Rd. G53	49	Q15
Braidfauld Gdns. G32	54	AA14
Braidfauld Pl. G32	54	AA15
Braidfauld St. G32	54	AA15
Braidfield Rd., Clyde.	5	L5
Braidholm Cres. G46	62	T18
Braidholm Rd. G46	62	T18
Braidpark Cres. G46	62	T18
Braidpark Dr. G46	62	T18
Braids Rd., Pais.	46	K15
Bramley Pl. G66	13	DD6
Branchock Av. G72	67	CC18
Brand St. G51	34	T13
Brandon Gdns. G72	66	AA17
Brandon St. G31	36	X13
Branscroft, John.	42	B14
Brassey St. G20	21	U9
Breadalbane Gdns. G73	65	Z18
Breadalbane St. G3	35	U12
Brech Av. G69	41	GG13
Brechin Rd. G64	11	Z7
Brechin St. G3	35	U12
Breck Av., Pais.	44	F16
Brediland Rd., Pais.	45	G15
Brediland Rd.	28	E13
(Linwood), Pais.		
Bredisholm Dr. G69	56	FF14
Bredisholm Rd. G69	56	FF14

Bredisholm Ter. G69	56	FF14
Brenfield Av. G44	63	U18
Brenfield Dr. G44	63	U18
Brenfield Rd. G44	63	U18
Brentwood Av. G53	60	P18
Brentwood Dr. G53	60	P18
Brentwood Sq. G53	60	P18
Brentwood Dr.		
Brereton St. G42	52	W15
Bressey Rd. G33	39	DD13
Brewery St., John.	43	D14
Brewster Av., Pais.	31	L12
Briar Dr., Clyde.	5	L6
Briar Neuk G64	23	Y8
Briar Rd. G43	62	T17
Briarlea Dr. G46	62	T18
Briarwood Ct. G32	55	DD15
Briarwood Gdns. G32	55	DD15
Woodend Rd.		
Brick La., Pais.	30	K13
Bridge of Weir Rd., Pais.	28	E13
Bridge St. G5	35	V13
Bridge St. G72	66	BB17
Bridge St., Clyde.	4	K6
Bridge St., Pais.	46	K14
Bridge St.	28	F13
(Linwood), Pais.		
Bridgeber St. G78	60	N18
Bridgeburn Dr. G69	15	GG7
Bridgegate G1	36	W13
Bridgeton Cross G40	36	X13
Brigham Pl. G23	21	U8
Broughton Rd.		
Brighton Pl. G51	34	S13
Brighton St. G51	34	S13
Brightside Av. G71	69	HH17
Brisbane Ct. G46	62	T18
Braidpark Dr.		
Brisbane St. G42	51	V16
Brisbane St., Clyde.	4	J6
Britannia Way, Clyde.	5	L7
Britannia Way, Renf.	31	M11
Briton St. G51	34	S13
Broad Pl. G40	36	X13
Broad St.		
Broad St. G40	36	X13
Broadford St. G4	36	W11
Harvey St.		
Broadholm St. G22	21	V9
Broadleys Av. G64	10	X6
Broadlie Dr. G13	18	P9
Broadloan, Renf.	31	M11
Broadwood Dr. G44	63	V17
Brock Oval G53	61	Q17
Brock Pl. G53	49	Q16
Brock Rd. G53	49	Q16
Brock Ter. G53	61	Q17
Brock Way G67	71	PP3
North Carbrain Rd.		
Brockburn Rd. G53	48	P15
Brockburn Ter. G53	49	Q16
Brockville St. G32	38	AA13
Brodick Sq. G64	23	Y8
Brodick St. G21	37	Y11
Brodie Pk. Av., Pais.	46	K15
Brodie Pk. Gdns., Pais.	46	K15
Brodie Pl., Renf.	31	L11
Brodie Rd. G21	23	Z8
Brogknowe G71	56	FF16
Glasgow Rd.		
Brook St. G40	36	X13
Brooklands Av. G71	57	GG16
Brooklea Dr. G46	62	T17
Brookside St. G40	37	Y13
Broom Cres. G78	59	L17
Broom Dr., Clyde.	5	L6
Broom Gdns. G66	12	BB5
Broom Path G69	55	DD14
Tudor St.		
Broom Rd. G43	62	T17
Broom Rd. G67	71	QQ1
Broom Ter., John.	44	E15
Broomdyke Way, Pais.	30	J12

Broomfield Av. G21	23	Y10
Broomfield Rd.		
Broomfield Av. G72	53	Z16
Broomfield Pl. G21	22	X9
Broomfield Rd.		
Broomfield Rd. G21	22	X9
Broomfield Ter. G71	57	GG15
Broomhill Av. G11	33	R11
Broomhill Av. G32	54	BB16
Broomhill Cres. G11	19	R10
Broomhill Dr. G11	19	R10
Broomhill Dr. G73	65	Y17
Broomhill Gdns. G11	19	R10
Broomhill La. G11	19	R10
Broomhill Path G11	33	R11
Broomhill Pl. G11	19	R10
Broomhill Rd. G11	33	R11
Broomhill Ter. G11	33	R11
Broomieknowe Dr. G73	65	Y17
Broomieknowe Rd. G73	65	Y17
Broomielaw G1	35	V13
Broomknowe G68	70	MM2
Broomknowe Pl. G66	13	DD6
Broomknowes Rd. G21	23	Y10
Broomlands Av., Ersk.	16	J8
Broomlands Cres., Ersk.	16	J8
Broomlands Gdns.,	16	J8
Ersk.		
Broomlands Rd. G67	71	PP4
Broomlands St., Pais.	46	J14
Broomlands Way, Ersk.	16	K8
Broomlea Cres., Renf.	16	J8
Broomley Dr. G46	62	T19
Broomley La. G46	62	T19
Broomloan Ct. G51	34	S13
Broomloan Pl. G51	34	S13
Broomloan Rd. G51	34	S13
Broompark Circ. G31	36	X12
Broompark Dr. G31	36	X12
Broompark Dr., Renf.	16	J8
Broompark St. G31	36	X12
Broomton Rd. G21	23	Z8
Broomward Dr., John.	44	E14
Brora Dr. G46	62	T19
Brora Dr. G61	8	S6
Brora Dr., Renf.	18	N10
Brora Gdns. G64	11	Y7
Brora La. G33	37	Z11
Brora St.		
Brora Rd. G64	11	Y7
Brora St. G33	37	Z11
Broughton Dr. G23	21	U8
Broughton Gdns. G23	9	U7
Broughton Rd. G23	21	U8
Brown Av., Clyde.	17	M8
Brown Pl. G72	66	BB17
Allison Dr.		
Brown Rd. G67	70	NN3
Brown St. G2	35	V12
Brown St., Pais.	30	J13
Brown St., Renf.	31	L11
Brownhill Rd. G43	62	S18
Brownlie St. G42	51	V16
Browns La., Pais.	46	K14
Brownsdale Rd. G73	52	X16
Brownside Av. G72	66	AA17
Brownside Av. G78	59	L17
Brownside Av., Pais.	46	J16
Brownside Cres. G78	59	L17
Brownside Dr. G13	18	N9
Brownside Dr. G78	59	L17
Brownside Gro. G78	59	L17
Brownside Rd. G72	65	Z17
Brownside Rd. G73	65	Z17
Bruce Av., John.	43	D16
Bruce Av., Pais.	31	L12
Bruce Rd. G41	51	U14
Bruce Rd., Pais.	31	L13
Bruce Rd., Renf.	31	L11
Bruce St., Clyde.	5	L7
Bruce Ter. G72	69	GG19
Brucefield Pl. G34	40	FF12
Brunstane Rd. G34	40	EE11

Street	Map	Grid
Brunswick Ho., Clyde.	4	J5
Perth Cres.		
Brunswick St. G1	36	W12
Brunton St. G44	63	V17
Brunton Ter. G44	63	U18
Bruntsfield Av. G53	60	P18
Bruntsfield Gdns. G53	60	P18
Bruntsfield Av.		
Brydson Pl., Pais.	28	E13
Fulwood Av.		
Buccleuch Av. G52	32	N12
Buccleuch La. G3	35	V11
Scott St.		
Buccleuch St. G3	35	V11
Buchan St. G5	35	V13
Norfolk St.		
Buchan Ter. G72	66	AA18
Buchanan Cres. G64	23	Z8
Buchanan Dr. G61	8	S6
Buchanan Dr. G64	23	Z8
Buchanan Dr. G66	13	CC6
Buchanan Dr. G72	66	AA17
Buchanan Dr. G73	65	Y17
Buchanan Gdns. G32	55	DD15
Buchanan St. G1	35	V12
Buchanan St. G69	56	EE14
Buchanan St., John.	43	D15
Buchley G64	10	W5
Buchlyvie Gdns. G64	22	X8
Buchlyvie Path G34	40	EE12
Buchlyvie Rd., Pais.	32	N13
Buchlyvie St. G34	40	EE12
Buckingham Bldgs. G12	20	T10
Great Western Rd.		
Buckingham Dr. G32	54	BB16
Buckingham Dr. G73	53	Z16
Buckingham St. G12	20	T10
Buckingham Ter. G12	20	T10
Bucklaw Gdns. G52	49	Q14
Bucklaw Pl. G52	49	Q14
Bucklaw Ter. G52	49	Q14
Buckley St. G22	22	W9
Bucksburn Rd. G21	23	Z10
Buckthorne Pl. G53	60	P18
Buddon St. G40	53	Z14
Budhill Av. G32	38	BB13
Bulldale Ct. G14	18	N9
Bulldale Rd. G14	18	N9
Bulldale St. G14	18	N9
Bullionslaw Dr. G73	65	Z17
Bulloch Av. G46	62	T19
Bullwood Av. G53	48	N15
Bullwood Ct. G53	48	N15
Bullwood Dr. G53	48	N15
Bullwood Gdns. G53	48	N15
Bullwood Pl. G53	48	N15
Bunessan St. G52	33	R13
Bunhouse Rd. G3	34	T11
Burgh Hall La. G11	34	S11
Fortrose St.		
Burgh Hall St. G11	34	S11
Burgh La. G12	20	T10
Vinicombe St.		
Burghead Dr. G51	33	R12
Burghead Pl. G51	33	R12
Burgher St. G31	37	Z13
Burleigh Rd. G71	69	HH18
Burleigh St. G51	34	S12
Burlington Av. G12	20	S9
Burmola St. G22	21	V10
Burn Gdns. G72	68	FF19
Burn Pl. G72	54	AA16
Burn Ter.		
Burn Ter. G72	54	AA16
Burn Vw. G67	71	QQ2
Burnacre Gdns. G71	57	GG16
Burnbank Dr. G78	59	M19
Burnbank Gdns. G20	35	U11
Burnbank Pl. G4	36	X12
Drygate		
Burnbank Ter. G20	35	U11
Burnbrae, Clyde.	5	L5
Burnbrae Av. G69	15	HH7
Burnbrae Av., Pais.	28	F13
Bridge St.		
Burnbrae Ct. G66	13	CC6
Auchinloch Rd.		
Burnbrae Dr. G73	65	Z17
East Kilbride Rd.		
Burnbrae Rd. G66	13	DD7
Burnbrae Rd. G69	14	EE7
Burnbrae Rd., Pais.	44	F14
Burnbrae St. G21	23	Y10
Burncleuch Av. G72	66	BB18
Burncrooks Ct., Clyde.	4	K5
Burndyke Ct. G51	34	T12
Burndyke Sq. G51	34	T12
Burndyke St. G51	34	S12
Burnett Rd. G33	39	DD12
Burnfield Av. G46	62	S18
Burnfield Cotts. G46	62	S18
Burnfield Dr. G43	62	S18
Burnfield Gdns. G46	62	T18
Burnfield Rd.		
Burnfield Rd. G43	62	S17
Burnfield Rd. G46	62	S18
Burnfoot Cres. G73	65	Z17
Burnfoot Cres., Pais.	46	J16
Burnfoot Dr. G52	32	P13
Burngreen Ter. G67	71	PP1
Burnham Rd. G14	18	P10
Burnham Ter. G14	18	P10
Burnham Rd.		
Burnhead Rd. G43	63	U17
Burnhead Rd. G68	70	MM3
Burnhead St. G71	57	HH16
Burnhill Quad. G73	52	X16
Burnhill St. G73	52	X16
Burnhouse St. G20	20	T9
Burnmouth Ct. G33	39	DD13
Pendeen Rd.		
Burnmouth Rd. G33	39	DD13
Burnpark Av. G71	56	FF16
Burns Dr., John.	43	D16
Burns Gro. G46	62	S19
Burns Rd. G67	71	PP3
Burns St. G4	35	V11
Burns St., Clyde.	4	K6
Burnside Av. G78	59	L18
Burnside, Clyde.	4	K6
Scott St.		
Burnside Gdns., John.	42	B15
Burnside Gate G73	65	Z17
Burnside Rd. G73	65	Z17
Burnside Rd., John.	44	F15
Burnside Ter. G72	67	DD18
Burntbroom Dr. G69	55	DD14
Burntbroom Gdns. G69	55	DD14
Burntbroom Rd. G71	55	DD14
Burntbroom St. G33	39	CC12
Burntshields Rd., John.	42	A15
Burr Gdns. G64	11	Z6
Solway Rd.		
Burrells La. G4	36	X12
High St.		
Burrelton Rd. G43	63	U17
Burton La. G42	51	V15
Langside Rd.		
Bushes Av., Pais.	46	J15
Busheyhill St. G72	66	BB17
Bute Av., Renf.	31	M11
Bute Cres. G61	7	R7
Bute Cres., Pais.	46	J16
Bute Dr., John.	43	C15
Bute Gdns. G12	34	T11
Bute Gdns. G44	63	U18
Bute Rd., Pais.	30	J11
Bute Ter. G71	57	HH16
Bute Ter. G73	65	Y17
Butterbiggins Rd. G42	51	V14
Butterfield Pl. G41	51	U15
Pollokshaws Rd.		
Byrebush Rd. G53	49	Q15
Byres Av., Pais.	31	L13
Byres Cres.		
Byres Cres., Pais.	31	L13
Byres Rd. G11	34	T11
Byres Rd. G12	34	T11
Byres Rd., John.	44	F15
Byron Ct. G71	69	HH19
Shelley Dr.		
Byron La. G11	33	R11
Sandeman St.		
Byron St. G11	33	R11
Byron St., Clyde.	4	K6
Byshot St. G22	22	W10

C

Street	Map	Grid
Cable Depot Rd., Clyde.	4	K7
Cadder Ct. G64	11	Y5
Cadder Gro. G20	21	U8
Cadder Rd.		
Cadder Pl. G20	21	U8
Cadder Rd. G20	21	U8
Cadder Rd. G23	21	U8
Cadder Rd. G64	11	Y5
Cadder Way G64	11	Y5
Cadoc St. G72	66	BB17
Cadogan St. G2	35	V12
Cadzow Dr. G72	66	AA17
Cadzow St. G2	35	V12
Cadogan St.		
Caird Dr. G11	34	S11
Cairn Av., Renf.	32	N11
Cairn Dr., Pais.	28	E13
Cairn La., Pais.	30	J12
Mosslands Rd.		
Cairn St. G21	22	X9
Cairnban St. G51	33	Q13
Cairnbrook Rd. G34	40	FF12
Cairncraig St. G31	53	Z14
Cairndow Av. G44	63	U18
Cairndow Ct. G44	63	U18
Cairngorm Cres. G61	6	P5
Cairngorm Cres. G78	59	M19
Cairngorm Cres., Pais.	46	K15
Cairngorm Rd. G43	62	T17
Cairnhill Circ. G52	48	N14
Cairnhill Dr. G52	48	N14
Cairnhill Pl. G52	48	N14
Cairnhill Circ.		
Cairnhill Rd. G61	7	R7
Cairnlea Dr. G51	34	S13
Cairnoch Hill G68	70	MM3
Cairns Av. G72	66	BB17
Cairns Rd. G72	66	BB18
Cairnsmore Rd. G15	6	N7
Cairnswell Av. G72	67	CC18
Cairnswell Pl. G72	67	CC18
Cairntoul Ct. G68	70	MM3
Cairntoul Dr. G14	18	P9
Cairntoul Pl. G14	18	P9
Caithness St. G20	21	U10
Calcots Path G34	40	FF11
Auchingill Rd.		
Calcots Pl. G34	40	FF11
Caldarvan St. G22	21	V10
Calder Av. G78	59	M19
Calder Dr. G72	66	BB17
Calder Gate G64	10	X6
Calder Pl. G69	56	EE14
Calder Rd. G71	68	EE17
Calder Rd., Pais.	29	H13
Calder St. G42	51	V15
Calderbank Vw. G69	56	FF14
Calderbraes Av. G71	57	GG16
Caldercuilt Rd. G20	20	T8
Caldercuilt Rd. G23	20	T8
Caldercuilt St. G20	20	T8
Calderpark Av. G71	56	EE15
Calderpark Cres. G71	56	EE15
Caldervale G71	68	FF17
Calderwood Av. G69	56	EE14
Calderwood Dr. G69	56	EE14
Calderwood Gdns. G69	56	EE14
Calderwood Rd. G43	62	T17
Calderwood Rd. G73	53	Z16

Name	Map	Grid
Caldwell Av. G13	18	P9
Caldwell Av., Pais.	28	E13
Caledon La. G12	34	T11
Highburgh Rd.		
Caledon St. G12	34	T11
Caledonia Av. G5	52	W14
Caledonia Av. G73	53	Y16
Caledonia Dr. G69	56	EE14
Caledonia Rd. G5	52	W14
Caledonia Rd. G69	56	EE14
Caledonia St. G5	52	W14
Caledonia St., Clyde.	4	K7
Caledonia St., Pais.	30	J13
Caledonia Way W., Pais.	30	J11
Caledonian Circuit G72	67	CC17
Caledonian Cotts. G71	69	HH19
Caledonian Cres. G12	35	U11
Caledonian Mans. G12	20	T10
Great Western Rd.		
Caledonian Pl. G72	67	DD17
Caley Brae G71	69	GG17
Calfhill Rd. G53	48	P14
Calfmuir Rd. G66	14	EE5
Calfmuir Rd. G69	14	EE5
Calgary St. G4	36	W11
Callander St. G20	21	V10
Callieburn Rd. G64	23	Y8
Cally Av. G15	6	P6
Calside, Pais.	46	K15
Calside Av., Pais.	46	J14
Calton Entry G40	36	X13
Gallowgate		
Calvay Cres. G33	39	CC12
Calvay Pl. G33	39	DD13
Calvay Rd. G33	39	CC12
Cambourne Rd. G69	15	GG6
Cambridge Av., Clyde.	5	L6
Cambridge Dr. G20	20	T9
Glenfinnan Dr.		
Cambridge La. G3	35	V11
Cambridge St.		
Cambridge Rd., Renf.	31	M11
Cambridge St. G2	35	V12
Cambridge St. G3	35	V12
Camburn St. G32	38	AA13
Cambus Pl. G33	39	CC11
Cambusdoon Rd. G33	39	CC11
Cambuskenneth Gdns. G33	39	DD13
Cambuskenneth Pl. G33	39	CC11
Cambuslang Rd. G32	54	AA16
Cambuslang Rd. G72	53	Z16
Cambuslang Rd. G73	53	Y19
Cambusmore Pl. G33	39	CC11
Camden St. G5	52	W14
Camelon St. G32	38	AA13
Cameron Dr. G61	8	S6
Cameron Dr. G71	57	HH16
Cameron Sq., Clyde.	5	M5
Glasgow Rd.		
Cameron St. G20	21	V10
Cameron St. G52	32	N12
Cameron St., Clyde.	17	M8
Camlachie St. G31	37	Y13
Camp Rd. G69	40	EE13
Camp Rd. G73	52	X15
Campbell Cres. G71	69	HH18
Campbell Dr. G61	7	Q5
Campbell Dr. G78	59	M19
Campbell St. G20	20	T8
Campbell St., John.	43	D15
Campbell St., Renf.	17	M10
Camperdown St. G20	21	V10
Garscube Rd.		
Camphill, Pais.	46	J14
Camphill Av. G41	51	U16
Camps Cres., Renf.	32	N11
Campsie Av. G78	59	M19
Campsie Dr., Pais.	46	J16
Campsie Dr., Pais.	30	K11
(Abbotsinch), Pais.		
Campsie Dr., Renf.	31	L12
Campsie Pl. G69	26	FF8
Campsie St. G21	22	X9
Campsie Vw. G33	25	CC10
Campsie Vw. G67	71	PP2
Campsie Vw.	41	GG13
(Baillieston) G69		
Campsie Vw.	26	FF8
(Chryston) G69		
Campsie Vw. G71	57	HH16
Campston Pl. G33	38	BB11
Camstradden Dr. E. G61	7	Q6
Camstradden Dr. W. G61	7	Q6
Camus Pl. G15	6	N6
Canal Av., John.	44	E14
Canal Rd., John.	43	D15
Canal St. G4	36	W11
Canal St., Clyde.	17	L8
Canal St., John.	44	F14
Canal St., Pais.	46	J14
Canal St., Renf.	17	M10
Canal Ter., Pais.	46	K14
Canberra Av., Clyde.	4	J6
Canberra Ct. G46	62	T18
Braidpark Dr.		
Cander Rigg G64	11	Y6
Candleriggs G1	36	W13
Candren Rd., Pais.	45	H14
Candren Rd.	28	F13
(Linwood), Pais.		
Canmore Pl. G31	53	Z14
Canmore St. G31	53	Z14
Cannich Dr., Pais.	47	L15
Canniesburn Rd. G61	7	Q6
Canniesburn Sq. G61	7	R7
Macfarlane Rd.		
Canniesburn Toll G61	7	R6
Canonbie St. G34	40	FF11
Canting Way G51	34	T12
Capelrig St. G46	61	R18
Caplaw Rd., Pais.	58	J17
Caplethill Rd. G78	46	K16
Caplethill Rd., Pais.	46	K16
Caprington St. G33	38	BB11
Cara Dr. G51	33	R12
Caravelle Way, Renf.	31	M11
Friendship Way		
Carberry Rd. G41	50	T15
Carbeth St. G22	21	V10
Carbisdale St. G22	22	X9
Carbost St. G23	8	T7
Torgyle St.		
Carbrook Dr. G21	37	Y11
Carbrook St., Pais.	46	J14
Cardarrach St. G21	23	Y10
Cardell Av., Pais.	45	H14
Cardell Dr., Pais.	45	H14
Cardell Rd., Pais.	45	H14
Carding La. G3	35	U12
Argyle St.		
Cardonald Dr. G52	48	P14
Cardonald Gdns. G52	48	P14
Cardonald Pl. Rd. G52	48	P14
Cardow Rd. G21	23	Z10
Cardowan Dr. G33	25	CC9
Cardowan Rd. G32	38	AA13
Cardowan Rd. G33	25	DD9
Cardrona St. G33	24	BB10
Cardross Ct. G31	36	X12
Cardross St. G31	36	X12
Cardwell St. G41	51	V14
Cardyke St. G21	23	Y10
Careston Pl. G64	11	Z7
Carfin St. G42	51	V15
Carfrae St. G3	34	T12
Cargill Sq. G64	23	Y8
Cargill St. G31	54	AA14
Carham Cres. G52	33	Q13
Carham Dr. G52	33	Q13
Carillon Rd. G51	34	T13
Carisbrooke Cres. G64	11	Y6
Carlaverock Rd. G43	62	T17
Carleith Av., Clyde.	4	K5
Carleith Quad. G51	33	Q12
Carleith Ter., Clyde.	4	K5
Carleith Av.		
Carleston St. G21	22	X10
Atlas Rd.		
Carleton Dr. G46	62	T18
Carleton Gate G46	62	T18
Carlibar Av. G13	18	N9
Carlibar Dr. G78	59	M18
Carlibar Gdns. G78	59	M18
Commercial Rd.		
Carlibar Rd. G78	59	L18
Carlile La., Pais.	30	K13
New Sneddon St.		
Carlile Pl., Pais.	30	K13
Carlisle St. G21	22	W10
Carlowrie Av. G72	68	FF19
Carlton Ct. G5	35	V13
Carlton Pl. G5	35	V13
Carlton Ter. G20	21	U10
Wilton St.		
Carlyle Av. G52	32	N13
Carlyle Rd., Pais.	30	K13
Carlyle Ter. G73	53	Y15
Carmaben Rd. G33	39	DD12
Carment Dr. G41	50	T16
Carment La. G41	50	T16
Carmichael Pl. G42	51	U16
Carmichael St. G51	34	S13
Carmunnock La. G44	63	V17
Madison Av.		
Carmunnock Rd. G44	51	V16
Carmunnock Rd. G45	64	W17
Carmunnock Rd. G76	64	W19
Carmyle Av. G32	54	BB15
Carna Dr. G44	64	W17
Carnarvon St. G3	35	U11
Carnbooth Ct. G45	64	X19
Carnbroe St. G20	35	V11
Carnegie Rd. G52	32	P13
Carnock Cres. G78	59	L19
Carnock Rd. G53	49	Q16
Carnoustie Ct. G71	69	GG19
Carnoustie Cres. G64	11	Z7
Carnoustie St. G5	35	U13
Carntyne Gdns. G32	38	AA12
Abbeyhill St.		
Carntyne Pl. G32	37	Z12
Carntyne Rd. G31	37	Z13
Carntyne Rd. G32	38	AA12
Carntynehall Rd. G32	38	AA12
Carnwadric Rd. G46	61	R18
Carnwath Av. G43	63	U17
Caroline St. G31	38	AA13
Carolside Dr. G15	6	P6
Carradale Gdns. G64	11	Z7
Thrums Av.		
Carradale Pl., Pais.	28	E13
Carrbridge Dr. G20	20	T9
Glenfinnan Dr.		
Carriagehill Dr., Pais.	46	K15
Carrick Cres. G46	62	T19
Carrick Dr. G32	55	DD14
Carrick Dr. G73	65	Y17
Carrick Gro. G32	55	DD14
Carrick Rd. G64	11	Z7
Carrick Rd. G67	71	PP2
Carrick Rd. G73	64	X17
Carrick St. G2	35	V12
Carrickarden Rd. G61	7	R6
Carrickstone Rd. G68	70	NN1
Carrickstone Vw. G68	70	NN1
Carriden Pl. G33	39	DD12
Carrington St. G4	35	U11
Carroglen Gdns. G32	39	CC13
Carroglen Gro. G32	39	CC13
Carron Ct. G72	67	CC17
Carron Cres. G22	22	W9
Carron Cres. G61	7	Q6
Carron Cres. G64	11	Y7
Carron Cres. G66	13	DD6
Carron La., Pais.	31	L12
Kilearn Rd.		
Carron Pl. G22	22	X9

Street	Page	Grid
Claremont Pl. G3	35	U11
Claremont Ter.		
Claremont St. G3	35	U12
Claremont Ter. G3	35	U11
Claremont Ter. La. G3	35	U11
Clifton St.		
Claremount Av. G46	62	T19
Clarence Dr. G11	20	S10
Clarence Dr. G12	20	S10
Clarence Dr., Pais.	47	L14
Clarence Gdns. G11	20	S10
Clarence St., Clyde.	5	M6
Clarence St., Pais.	31	L13
Clarendon La. G20	35	V11
Clarendon St.		
Clarendon Pl. G20	35	V11
Clarendon St. G20	35	V11
Clarion Cres. G13	18	P8
Clarion Rd. G13	18	P8
Clark St. G41	35	U13
Tower St.		
Clark St., Clyde.	4	K6
Clark St., John.	43	D14
Clark St., Pais.	30	J13
Clark St., Renf.	17	L10
Clarkston Av. G44	63	U18
Clarkston Rd. G44	63	U18
Clarkston Rd. G76	63	U19
Clathic Av. G61	8	S6
Claud Rd., Pais.	31	L13
Claude Av. G72	67	DD18
Claudhall Av. G69	27	GG8
Clavens Rd. G52	32	N13
Claverhouse Pl., Pais.	47	L14
Claverhouse Rd. G52	32	N12
Clavering St. E., Pais.	30	J13
Well St.		
Clavering St. W., Pais.	30	J13
King St.		
Clayhouse Rd. G33	25	DD9
Claypotts Pl. G33	38	BB11
Claypotts Rd. G33	38	BB11
Clayslaps Rd. G3	34	T11
Argyle St.		
Claythorn Av. G40	36	X13
Claythorn Circ. G40	36	X13
Claythorn Av.		
Claythorn Ct. G40	36	X13
Claythorn Pk.		
Claythorn Pk. G40	36	X13
Claythorn St. G40	36	X13
Claythorn Ter. G40	36	X13
Claythorn Pk.		
Clayton Ter. G31	36	X12
Cleddans Cres., Clyde.	5	M5
Cleddans Rd., Clyde.	5	M5
Cleddens Ct. G64	11	Y7
Cleeves Pl. G53	60	P17
Cleeves Quad. G53	60	P17
Cleeves Rd. G53	60	P17
Cleghorn St. G22	21	V10
Cleland La. G5	36	W13
Cleland St.		
Cleland St. G5	36	W13
Clelland Av. G64	23	Y8
Clerwood St. G32	37	Z13
Cleveden Cres. G12	20	S9
Cleveden Cres. La. G12	20	S9
Cleveden Dr.		
Cleveden Dr. G12	20	S9
Cleveden Dr. G73	65	Z17
Cleveden Gdns. G12	20	S9
Cleveden Pl. G12	20	S9
Cleveden Rd. G12	20	S9
Cleveland St. G3	35	U12
Cliff Rd. G3	35	U11
Clifford Gdns. G51	34	S13
Clifford La. G51	34	T13
Gower St.		
Clifford Pl. G51	34	T13
Clifford St.		
Clifford St. G51	34	S13
Clifton Pl. G3	35	U11
Clifton St.		
Clifton Rd. G46	62	S18
Clifton St. G3	35	U11
Clifton Ter. G72	66	AA18
Clifton Ter., John.	44	E15
Clincart Rd. G42	51	V16
Clincarthill Rd. G73	53	Y16
Clinton Av. G71	69	GG17
Clippens Rd., Pais.	28	E13
Cloan Av. G15	6	P7
Cloan Cres. G64	11	Y6
Cloberhill Rd. G13	7	Q7
Cloch St. G33	38	BB12
Clochoderick Av., John.	42	B15
Mackenzie Dr.		
Clonbeith St. G33	39	DD11
Closeburn St. G22	22	W9
Cloth St. G78	59	M19
Clouden Rd. G67	71	PP3
Cloudhowe Ter. G72	68	FF19
Clouston Ct. G20	21	U10
Clouston La. G20	20	T10
Clouston St.		
Clouston St. G20	20	T10
Clova Pl. G71	69	GG17
Clova St. G46	61	R18
Clover Av. G64	10	X7
Cloverbank St. G21	37	Y11
Clovergate G64	10	X7
Clunie Rd. G52	49	R14
Cluny Av. G61	8	S7
Cluny Dr. G61	8	S7
Cluny Dr., Pais.	31	L13
Cluny Gdns. G14	19	R10
Cluny Gdns. G69	56	EE14
Cluny Vills. G14	19	Q10
Westland Dr.		
Clutha St. G51	35	U13
Paisley Rd. W.		
Clyde Av. G71	69	GG19
Clyde Av. G78	59	M19
Clyde Ct., Clyde.	4	K6
Little Holm		
Clyde Pl. G5	35	V13
Clyde Pl. G72	67	CC18
Clyde Pl., John.	43	C16
Clyde Rd., Pais.	31	L12
Clyde St. G1	35	V13
Clyde St., Clyde.	17	M8
Clyde St., Renf.	17	M9
Clyde Ter. G71	69	HH19
Clyde Tunnel G14	33	R11
Clyde Tunnel G51	33	R11
Clyde Tunnel Expressway G51	33	Q12
Clyde Vale G71	69	HH19
Clyde Vw., Pais.	47	L15
Clydebrae Dr. G71	69	HH19
Clydebrae St. G51	34	S12
Clydeford Dr. G32	54	AA14
Clydeford Dr. G71	56	FF16
Clydeford Rd. G72	54	BB16
Clydeholm Rd. G14	33	Q11
Clydeholm Ter., Clyde.	17	M8
Clydeneuk Dr. G71	56	FF16
Clydesdale Av., Pais.	31	L11
Clydeside Expressway G3	34	T11
Clydeside Expressway G14	19	Q10
Clydeside Rd. G73	52	X15
Clydesmill Dr. G32	54	BB16
Clydesmill Gro. G32	54	BB16
Clydesmill Pl. G32	54	BB16
Clydesmill Rd. G32	54	BB16
Clydeview G11	34	S11
Dumbarton Rd.		
Clydeview La. G11	33	R11
Broomhill Dr.		
Clydeview Ter. G32	55	CC16
Clydeview Ter. G40	52	X14
Newhall St.		
Clynder St. G51	34	S13
Clyth Dr. G46	62	T19
Coalhill St. G31	37	Y13
Coatbridge Rd. (Baillieston) G69	41	GG13
Coatbridge Rd. (Gartcosh) G69	27	GG10
Coates Cres. G53	49	Q16
Coats Cres. G69	40	EE13
Coats Dr., Pais.	45	H14
Coatshill Av. G72	68	FF19
Cobblerigg Way G71	69	GG17
Cobden Rd. G21	36	X11
Cobinshaw St. G32	38	BB13
Cobinton Pl. G33	38	BB11
Coburg St. G5	35	V13
Cochno St., Clyde.	17	M8
Cochran St., Pais.	46	K14
Cochrane St. G1	36	W12
Cochrane St. G78	59	L19
Cochranemill Rd., John.	43	C15
Cockels Ln., Renf.	31	L11
Cockenzie St. G32	38	BB13
Cockmuir St. G21	23	Y10
Cogan Rd. G43	62	T17
Cogan St. G43	50	T16
Cogan St. G78	59	L19
Colbert St. G40	52	X14
Colbreggan Ct., Clyde.	5	M5
St. Helena Cres.		
Colbreggan Gdns., Clyde.	5	M5
Colchester Dr. G12	20	S9
Coldingham Av. G14	18	N9
Coldstream Dr. G73	65	Z17
Coldstream Dr., Pais.	45	H15
Coldstream Pl. G21	22	W10
Keppochhill Rd.		
Coldstream Rd., Clyde.	5	L7
Colebrook St. G72	66	BB17
Colebrooke La. G12	21	U10
Colebrooke St.		
Colebrooke Pl. G12	21	U10
Belmont St.		
Colebrooke St. G12	21	U10
Colebrooke Ter. G12	21	U10
Colebrooke St.		
Coleridge G71	69	HH18
Colfin St. G34	40	FF11
Colgrain St. G20	21	V9
Colgrave Cres. G32	54	AA14
Colinbar Circle G78	59	L19
Colinslee Av. G53	46	K15
Colinslee Cres., Pais.	46	K15
Colinslee Dr., Pais.	46	K15
Colinslie Rd. G53	49	Q16
Colinton Pl. G32	38	BB12
Colintraive Av. G33	24	AA10
Coll Av., Renf.	31	M11
Coll Pl. G21	37	Y11
Coll St. G21	37	Y11
Colla Gdns. G64	11	Z7
College La. G1	36	W13
High St.		
College St. G1	36	W12
Collessie Dr. G33	39	CC11
Collier St., John.	43	D14
Collina St. G20	20	T9
Collins St. G4	36	X12
Collylin Rd. G61	7	R6
Colmonell Av. G13	18	N8
Colonsay Av., Renf.	31	M11
Colonsay Rd. G52	33	R13
Colonsay Rd., Pais.	46	J16
Colquhoun Av. G52	32	P12
Colquhoun Dr. G61	7	Q5
Colston Av. G64	22	X8
Colston Dr. G64	22	X8
Colston Gdns. G64	22	X8
Colston Path G64	22	X8
Colston Gdns.		
Colston Pl. G64	22	X8
Colston Rd. G64	22	X8
Coltmuir Av. G64	22	X8
Coltmuir Dr.		
Coltmuir Cres. G64	22	X8

Street	G	No.	Grid
Coltmuir Dr. G64	22	X8	
Coltmuir Gdns. G64	22	X8	
Coltmuir Dr.			
Coltmuir St. G22	21	V9	
Coltness La. G33	39	CC12	
Coltness St. G33	39	CC12	
Coltpark Av. G64	22	X8	
Coltpark La. G64	22	X8	
Coltsfoot Dr. G53	60	P18	
Columba Path, Clyde.	5	M7	
Onslow Rd.			
Columba St. G51	34	S12	
Colvend Dr. G73	65	Y18	
Colvend St. G40	52	X14	
Colville Dr. G73	65	Z17	
Colwood Av. G53	60	P18	
Colwood Gdns. G53	60	P18	
Colwood Av.			
Colwood Path G53	60	P18	
Parkhouse Rd.			
Colwood Pl. G53	60	P18	
Colwood Sq. G53	60	P18	
Colwood Av.			
Comedie Rd. G33	25	DD10	
Comely Pk. St. G31	37	Y13	
Comley Pl. G31	37	Y13	
Gallowgate			
Commerce St. G5	35	V13	
Commercial Ct. G5	36	W13	
Commercial Rd. G5	52	W14	
Commercial Rd. G78	59	M18	
Commonhead Rd. G34	40	FF12	
Commonhead Rd. G69	41	GG12	
Commore Av. G78	59	M19	
Commore Dr. G13	18	P8	
Comrie Rd. G33	25	CC9	
Comrie St. G32	54	BB14	
Cona St. G46	61	R18	
Conan St. G52	67	CC17	
Condorrat Ring Rd. G67	70	MM4	
Congleton St. G53	60	N17	
Nitshill Rd.			
Congress Rd. G3	35	U12	
Conifer Pl. G66	12	BB5	
Conisborough Path G34	39	DD11	
Balfluig St.			
Conisborough Rd. G34	39	DD11	
Conistone Cres. G69	55	DD14	
Connal St. G40	53	Y14	
Conniston St. G32	38	AA12	
Conon Av. G61	7	Q6	
Consett La. G33	39	CC12	
Consett St. G33	39	CC12	
Consett La.			
Contin Pl. G12	20	T9	
Convair Way, Renf.	31	M11	
Lismore Av.			
Conval Way, Pais.	30	J12	
Abbotsburn Way			
Cook St. G5	35	V13	
Coopers Well La. G11	34	T11	
Dumbarton Rd.			
Coopers Well St. G11	34	T11	
Dumbarton Rd.			
Copland Pl. G51	34	S13	
Copland Quad. G51	34	S13	
Copland Rd. G51	34	S13	
Coplaw St. G42	51	V14	
Copperfield La. G71	57	HH16	
Hamilton Vw.			
Corbett St. G32	54	BB14	
Corbiston Way G67	71	PP3	
Cordiner St. G44	51	V16	
Corkerhill Gdns. G52	49	R14	
Corkerhill Pl. G52	49	Q15	
Corkerhill Rd. G52	49	Q15	
Corlaich Av. G42	52	X16	
Corlaich Dr. G42	52	X16	
Corn St. G4	35	V11	
Cornaig Rd. G53	48	P16	
Cornalee Gdns. G53	48	P16	
Cornalee Pl. G53	48	P16	
Cornalee Rd. G53	48	P16	

Street	G	No.	Grid
Cornhill St. G21	23	Y9	
Cornoch St. G23	8	T7	
Torrin Rd.			
Cornock Cres., Clyde.	5	L6	
Cornock St., Clyde.	5	L6	
Cornwall Av. G73	65	Z17	
Cornwall St. G41	34	T13	
Coronation Pl. G69	27	GG8	
Coronation Way G61	8	S7	
Corpach Pl. G34	40	FF11	
Corran St. G33	38	AA12	
Corrie Dr., Pais.	48	N14	
Corrie Gro. G44	63	U18	
Corrie Pl. G66	13	DD6	
Corrour Rd. G43	50	T16	
Corse Rd. G52	32	N13	
Corsebar Av., Pais.	46	J15	
Corsebar Cres., Pais.	46	J15	
Corsebar Dr., Pais.	46	J15	
Corsebar La., Pais.	45	H15	
Balgonie Av.			
Corsebar Rd., Pais.	46	J15	
Corsebar Way, Pais.	46	J14	
Corseford Av., John.	43	C16	
Corsehill Pl. G34	40	FF12	
Corsehill St. G34	40	FF12	
Corselet Rd. G53	60	P18	
Corsewall Av. G32	55	DD14	
Corsford Dr. G53	61	Q17	
Corsock St. G31	37	Z12	
Corston St. G33	37	Z12	
Cortachy Pl. G64	11	Z7	
Coruisk Way, Pais.	45	G16	
Spencer Dr.			
Corunna St. G3	35	U12	
Coshneuk Rd. G33	24	BB9	
Cottar St. G20	21	U8	
Cotton Av., Pais.	28	E13	
Cotton St. G40	53	Y15	
Cotton St., Pais.	46	K14	
Coulters La. G40	36	X13	
Countess Wk. G69	41	HH13	
County Av. G72	53	Z16	
County Pl., Pais.	30	K13	
Moss St.			
County Sq., Pais.	30	K13	
Couper St. G4	36	W11	
Courthill G61	7	Q5	
Courthill Av. G44	63	V17	
Coustonhill St. G43	50	T16	
Pleasance St.			
Coustonholm Rd. G43	50	T16	
Coventry Dr. G31	37	Y12	
Cowal Dr., Pais.	28	E13	
Cowal Rd. G20	20	T8	
Cowal St. G20	20	T8	
Cowan Clo. G78	59	M18	
Cowan Cres. G78	59	M19	
Cowan La. G12	35	U11	
Cowan St.			
Cowan Rd. G68	70	MM3	
Cowan St. G12	35	U11	
Cowan Wilson Av. G72	68	FF19	
Cowan Wynd G71	57	HH16	
Cowcaddens Rd. G4	35	V11	
Cowden Dr. G64	11	Y6	
Cowden St. G51	33	Q12	
Cowdenhill Circ. G13	19	Q8	
Cowdenhill Pl. G13	19	Q8	
Cowdenhill Rd. G13	19	Q8	
Cowdie St., Pais.	30	J12	
Cowdray Cres., Renf.	17	M10	
Cowell St., Clyde.	5	L6	
Granville St.			
Cowglen Pl. G53	49	Q16	
Cowglen Rd.			
Cowglen Rd. G53	49	Q16	
Cowglen Ter. G53	49	Q16	
Cowie St. G41	35	U13	
Cowlairs Rd. G21	22	X10	
Coxhill St. G21	22	W10	
Coxton Pl. G33	39	CC11	
Coylton Rd. G43	63	U17	

Street	G	No.	Grid
Craggan Dr. G14	18	N9	
Crags Av., Pais.	46	K15	
Crags Cres., Pais.	46	K15	
Crags Rd., Pais.	46	K15	
Craig Rd. G44	63	V17	
Craigallian Av. G72	67	CC18	
Craiganour La. G43	62	T17	
Craiganour Pl. G43	62	T17	
Craigard Pl. G73	66	AA18	
Inverclyde Gdns.			
Craigbank Dr. G53	60	P17	
Craigbank St. G22	22	W10	
Craigbarnet Cres. G33	24	BB10	
Craigbo Av. G23	8	T7	
Craigbo Ct. G23	20	T8	
Craigbo Dr. G23	20	T8	
Craigbo Pl. G23	20	T8	
Craigbo Rd. G23	20	T8	
Craigbo St. G23	8	T7	
Craigbog Av., John.	43	C15	
Craigdonald Pl., John.	43	D14	
Craigellan Rd. G43	62	T17	
Craigenbay Cres. G66	13	CC5	
Craigenbay Rd. G66	13	CC6	
Craigenbay St. G21	23	Y10	
Craigencart Ct., Clyde.	4	K5	
Gentle Row			
Craigend Pl. G13	19	R9	
Craigend St. G13	19	R9	
Craigendmuir Rd. G33	25	DD10	
Craigendmuir St. G33	37	Z11	
Craigendon Oval, Pais.	58	J17	
Craigendon Rd., Pais.	58	J17	
Craigends Dr., John.	42	B14	
High Barholm			
Craigenfeoch Av.,	43	C15	
John.			
Craigfaulds Av., Pais.	45	H15	
Craigflower Gdns. G53	60	P18	
Craigflower Rd. G53	60	P18	
Craighalbert Rd. G68	70	MM2	
Craighalbert Way G68	70	MM2	
Craighall Rd. G4	35	V11	
Craighead Av. G33	23	Z10	
Craighead St. G78	59	L19	
Craighead Way G78	59	L19	
Craighouse St. G33	38	BB11	
Craigie Pk. G66	13	DD5	
Craigie St. G42	51	V15	
Craigiebar Dr., Pais.	46	J16	
Craigieburn Gdns. G20	20	S8	
Craigieburn Rd. G67	70	NN3	
Craigiehall Pl. G51	34	T13	
Craigiehall St. G51	35	U13	
Craigiehall Pl.			
Craigielea Dr., Pais.	29	H13	
Craigielea Pk., Renf.	17	L10	
Craigielea Rd., Renf.	17	M10	
Craigielea St. G31	37	Y12	
Craigielinn Av., Pais.	58	J17	
Craigievar St. G33	39	DD11	
Craigleith St. G32	38	AA13	
Craiglockhart St. G33	39	CC11	
Craigmaddie Ter. La. G3	35	U12	
Derby St.			
Craigmillar Rd. G42	51	V16	
Craigmont Dr. G20	21	U9	
Craigmont St. G20	21	U9	
Craigmore St. G31	37	Z13	
Craigmount Av., Pais.	58	J17	
Craigmuir Cres. G52	32	N13	
Craigmuir Pl. G52	32	N13	
Craigmuir Rd.			
Craigmuir Rd. G52	32	N13	
Craigneil St. G33	39	DD11	
Craignestock Pl. G40	36	X13	
London Rd.			
Craignestock St. G40	36	X13	
Craignethan Gdns. G11	34	S11	
Lawrie St.			
Craignure Rd. G73	65	Y13	
Craigpark G31	37	Y12	
Craigpark Dr. G31	37	Y12	

Name	Page	Grid
Craigpark Ter. G31	37	Y12
Craigpark		
Craigpark Way G71	57	HH16
Newton Dr.		
Craigs Av., Clyde.	5	M5
Craigston Pl., John.	43	D15
Craigston Rd., John.	43	D15
Craigton Av. G78	60	N19
Craigton Dr. G51	33	R13
Craigton Dr. G78	60	N19
Craigton Pl. G51	33	R13
Craigton Dr.		
Craigton Pl. G72	68	FF19
Craigton Rd. G51	33	R13
Craigvicar Gdns. G32	39	CC13
Hailes Av.		
Craigview Av., John.	43	C16
Craigwell Av. G73	65	Z17
Crail St. G31	37	Z13
Cramond Av., Renf.	32	N11
Cramond St. G5	52	W15
Cramond Ter. G32	38	BB13
Cranborne Rd. G12	20	S9
Cranbrooke Dr. G20	20	T8
Cranston St. G3	35	U12
Cranworth La. G12	20	T10
Great George St.		
Cranworth St. G12	20	T10
Crarae Av. G61	7	R7
Crathie Dr. G11	34	S11
Crathie La. G11	34	S11
Exeter Dr.		
Craw Rd., Pais.	46	J14
Crawford Av. G66	13	DD6
Crawford Ct. G46	62	S19
Milverton Rd.		
Crawford Cres. G71	57	GG16
Crawford Cres. G72	68	FF19
Crawford Dr. G15	6	N7
Crawford La. G11	34	S11
Crawford Path G11	34	S11
Crawford St.		
Crawford St. G11	34	S11
Crawfurd Dr., Pais.	29	H13
Crawfurd Gdns. G73	65	Y18
Crawfurd Rd. G73	65	Y18
Crawriggs Av. G66	13	CC5
Crebar Dr. G78	59	M19
Crebar St. G46	61	R18
Credon Gdns. G73	65	Z18
Cree Av. G64	11	Z7
Cree Gdns. G32	38	AA13
Kilmany Dr.		
Creran St. G40	36	X13
Tobago St.		
Crescent Ct., Clyde.	4	K6
Swindon St.		
Crescent Rd. G13	18	P9
Crescent Rd. G14	18	P9
Cresswell La. G12	20	T10
Great George St.		
Cresswell St. G12	20	T10
Cressy St. G51	33	R12
Crest Av. G13	18	P8
Crestlea Av., Pais.	46	K16
Creswell Ter. G71	57	GG16
Kylepark Dr.		
Crichton Ct. G45	64	X19
Crichton Pl. G21	22	X10
Crichton St.		
Crichton St. G21	22	X10
Crieff Ct. G3	35	U12
North St.		
Criffell Gdns. G32	55	CC14
Criffell Rd. G32	55	CC14
Crimea St. G2	35	V12
Crinan Gdns. G64	11	Y7
Crinan Rd. G64	11	Y7
Crinan St. G31	37	Y12
Cripps Av., Clyde.	5	M7
Croft Rd. G72	66	BB17
Croft Wynd G71	69	HH17
Croftbank Av. G71	69	HH19
Croftbank Cres. (Bothwell) G71	69	HH19
Croftbank Cres. (Uddingston) G71	69	GG17
Croftbank St. G21	22	X10
Croftbank St. G71	69	GG17
Croftburn Dr. G44	64	W18
Croftcroighn Rd. G33	38	BB11
Croftend Av. G44	64	X17
Croftfoot Cotts. G69	27	HH9
Croftfoot Cres. G45	65	Y18
Croftfoot Dr. G45	64	X18
Croftfoot Quad. G45	64	X18
Croftfoot Rd. G44	64	W18
Croftfoot Rd. G45	64	W18
Croftfoot St. G45	65	Y18
Croftfoot Ter. G45	64	X18
Crofthead St. G71	69	GG17
Crofthill Av. G71	69	GG17
Crofthill Rd. G44	64	W17
Crofthouse Dr. G44	64	X18
Croftmont Av. G44	64	X18
Croftmoraig Av. G69	15	HH6
Crofton Av. G44	64	W18
Croftpark Av. G44	64	W18
Croftside Av. G44	64	X18
Croftspar Av. G32	39	CC13
Croftspar Dr. G32	39	CC13
Croftspar Pl. G32	39	CC13
Croftwood G64	11	Y6
Croftwood Av. G44	64	W18
Cromart Pl. G69	14	FF7
Cromarty Av. G43	63	U17
Cromarty Av. G64	11	Z7
Cromarty Gdns. G76	63	V19
Crombie Gdns. G69	56	EE14
Cromdale St. G51	33	R13
Cromer La., Pais.	30	J12
Abbotsburn Way		
Cromer St. G20	21	U9
Cromer Way, Pais.	30	J12
Mosslands Rd.		
Crompton Av. G44	63	V17
Cromwell La. G20	35	V11
Cromwell St.		
Cromwell St. G20	35	V11
Cronberry Quad. G52	48	N14
Cronberry Ter. G52	48	N14
Crookedshields Rd. G72	66	BB19
Crookston Av. G52	48	P14
Crookston Ct. G52	48	P14
Crookston Dr. G52	48	N14
Crookston Dr., Pais.	48	N14
Crookston Gdns. G52	48	N14
Crookston Gro. G52	48	P14
Crookston Pl. G52	48	N14
Crookston Quad. G52	48	N14
Crookston Rd. G52	48	N15
Crookston Rd. G53	48	P15
Crookston Ter. G52	48	P14
Crookston Rd.		
Crosbie Dr., Pais.	45	G16
Crosbie St. G20	20	T8
Crosbie Wds., Pais.	45	H15
Cross, The G1	36	W13
Cross, The, Pais.	30	K13
Cross Arthurlie St. G78	59	L19
Cross Rd., Pais.	45	H15
Cross St. G32	55	CC15
Cross St., Pais.	46	J14
Crossbank Av. G42	52	X15
Crossbank Dr. G42	52	X15
Crossbank Rd. G42	52	W15
Crossbank Ter. G42	52	W15
Crossflat Cres., Pais.	31	L13
Crossford Dr. G23	9	U7
Crosshill Av. G42	51	V15
Crosshill Av. G66	13	CC5
Crosshill Dr. G73	65	Y17
Crosshill Rd. G64	11	Z5
Crosshill Rd. G66	12	BB6
Crosshill Sq. G69	56	FF14
Crosslee St. G52	33	R13
Crosslees Ct. G46	61	R18
Main St.		
Crosslees Dr. G46	61	R18
Crosslees Pk. G46	61	R18
Crosslees Rd. G46	61	R19
Crossloan Pl. G51	33	R12
Crossloan Rd. G51	33	R12
Crossloan Ter. G51	33	R12
Crossmill Av. G78	59	M18
Crossmyloof Gdns. G41	50	T15
Crosspoint Dr. G23	9	U7
Invershiel Rd.		
Crosstobs Rd. G53	48	P15
Crossview Av. G69	40	FF13
Swinton Av.		
Crossview Pl. G69	40	FF13
Crovie Rd. G53	48	P16
Crow Ct., The G64	10	X7
Kenmure Av.		
Crow La. G13	19	R9
Crow Rd. G11	19	R10
Crow Rd. G13	19	R10
Crow Wd. Rd. G69	26	EE8
Crow Wd. Ter. G69	26	EE8
Crowflats Rd. G71	69	GG17
Lady Isle Cres.		
Crowhill Rd. G64	22	X8
Crowhill St. G22	22	W9
Crowlin Cres. G33	38	BB12
Crown Av., Clyde.	5	L6
Crown Circ. G12	20	S10
Crown Rd. S.		
Crown Ct. G1	36	W12
Virginia St.		
Crown Gdns. G12	20	S10
Crown Rd. N.		
Crown Mans. G11	20	S10
North Gardner St.		
Crown Rd. N. G12	20	S10
Crown Rd. S. G12	20	S10
Crown St. G5	52	W14
Crown St. G69	55	DD14
Crown Ter. G12	20	S10
Crown Rd. S.		
Crownpoint Rd. G40	36	X13
Crowpoint Rd. G40	37	Y13
Alma St.		
Croy Pl. G21	23	Z9
Croy Rd.		
Croy Rd. G21	23	Z9
Cruachan Av., Renf.	31	M11
Cruachan Cres., Pais.	46	K16
Cruachan Dr. G78	59	M19
Cruachan Rd. G73	65	Z18
Cruachan St. G46	61	R18
Cruachan Way G78	59	M19
Cruden St. G51	33	R13
Crum Av. G46	62	S18
Crusader Av. G13	7	Q7
Cubie St. G40	36	X13
Cuilhill Rd. G69	41	GG12
Cuillin Way G78	59	M19
Cuillins, The G71	56	FF15
Cuillins Rd. G73	65	Z18
Culbin Dr. G13	18	N8
Cullen Pl. G71	57	HH16
Cullen St. G32	54	BB14
Cullins, The G69	15	HH6
Culloden St. G31	37	Y12
Coventry Dr.		
Culrain Gdns. G32	38	BB13
Culrain St. G32	38	BB13
Culross La. G32	55	CC14
Culross St. G32	55	CC14
Cult Rd. G66	13	DD6
Cults St. G51	33	R13
Culzean Cres. G69	56	EE14
Huntingtower Rd.		
Culzean Dr. G32	39	CC13
Cumberland Ct. G1	36	W13
Gallowgate		
Cumberland La. G5	51	V14
Cumberland St.		

Devonshire Gdns. G12	20	S10
Devonshire Gdns. La. G12	20	S10
Hyndland Rd.		
Devonshire Ter. G12	20	S10
Devonshire Ter. La. G12	20	S10
Hughenden Rd.		
Dewar Clo. G71	57	HH15
Diana Av. G13	18	P8
Dick St. G20	21	U10
Henderson St.		
Dickens Av., Clyde.	4	K6
Dilwara Av. G14	33	R11
Dimity St., John.	43	D15
Dinard Dr. G46	62	T18
Dinart St. G33	37	Z11
Dinduff St. G34	40	FF11
Dingwall St. G3	34	T12
Kelvinhaugh St.		
Dinmont Pl. G41	51	U15
Norham St.		
Dinmont Rd. G41	50	T15
Dinwiddie St. G21	37	Z11
Dipple Pl. G15	6	P7
Dirleton Av. G41	51	U16
Dirleton Dr., Pais.	45	H15
Dirleton Gate G61	7	Q7
Dixon Av. G42	51	V15
Dixon Rd. G42	52	W15
Dixon St. G1	35	V13
Dixon St., Pais.	46	K14
Dobbies Ln. G4	35	V11
Dobbies Ln. Pl. G4	36	W12
Dochart Av., Renf.	32	N11
Dochart St. G33	38	AA11
Dock St., Clyde.	17	M8
Dodhill Pl. G13	18	P9
Dodside Gdns. G32	55	CC14
Dodside Pl. G32	55	CC14
Dodside St. G32	55	CC14
Dolan St. G69	40	EE13
Dollar Ter. G20	20	T8
Crosbie St.		
Dolphin Rd. G41	50	T15
Don Av., Renf.	32	N11
Don Dr., Pais.	45	G15
Don Pl., John.	43	C16
Don St. G33	37	Z12
Donald Way G71	57	HH16
Donaldson Dr., Renf.	17	M10
Ferguson St.		
Donaldswood Rd., Pais.	46	J16
Doncaster St. G20	21	V10
Doon Cres. G61	7	Q6
Doon Side G67	71	PP3
Doon St., Clyde.	5	M6
Doonfoot Rd. G43	62	T17
Dora St. G40	53	Y14
Dorchester Av. G12	20	S9
Dorchester Ct. G12	20	S9
Dorchester Av.		
Dorchester Pl. G12	20	S9
Dorlin Rd. G33	25	DD9
Dormanside Rd. G53	48	P14
Dornal Av. G13	18	N8
Dornford Av. G32	55	CC15
Dornford Rd. G32	55	CC15
Dornie Dr. G32	55	CC16
Dornie Dr. G46	61	R18
Dornoch Av. G46	62	T19
Dornoch Pl. G64	11	Z7
Dornoch Pl. G69	14	FF7
Dornoch Rd. G61	7	Q7
Dornoch St. G40	36	X13
Dornoch Way G68	71	PP1
Dorset Sq. G3	35	U12
Dorset St.		
Dorset St. G3	35	U12
Dosk Av. G13	18	N8
Dosk Pl. G13	18	N8
Dougalston Rd. G23	9	U7
Douglas Av. G32	54	BB15
Douglas Av. G46	62	T19
Douglas Av. G66	13	CC5
Douglas Av. G73	65	Z17
Douglas Av., John.	44	E15
Douglas Ct. G66	13	CC5
Douglas Cres. G71	57	HH16
Douglas Dr. G15	6	N7
Douglas Dr. G69	39	DD13
Douglas Dr. G71	69	HH19
Douglas Dr. G72	66	AA17
Douglas Gdns. G46	62	T19
Douglas Gdns. G61	7	R6
Douglas Gdns. G66	13	CC5
Douglas Gdns. G71	69	GG17
Douglas La. G2	35	V12
West George St.		
Douglas Pk. Cres. G61	8	S5
Douglas Pl. G61	7	R5
Douglas Pl. G66	13	CC5
Douglas Rd., Pais.	31	L12
Douglas Rd., Renf.	31	L12
Douglas St. G2	35	V12
Douglas St. G71	57	HH16
Douglas St., Pais.	30	J13
Douglas Ter. G41	51	U14
Shields Rd.		
Douglas Ter., Pais.	30	K11
Dougray Pl. G78	59	M19
Dougrie Dr. G45	64	W18
Dougrie Pl. G45	64	X18
Dougrie Rd. G45	64	W19
Dougrie St. G45	64	X18
Dougrie Ter. G45	64	W18
Doune Cres. G64	11	Y6
Doune Gdns. G20	21	U10
Doune Quad. G20	21	U10
Dove St. G53	60	P17
Dovecot G43	50	T16
Shawhill Rd.		
Dovecothall St. G78	59	M18
Dover St. G3	35	U12
Downfield Rd. G67	70	NN3
Downhill Pl. G11	34	T11
Old Dumbarton Rd.		
Downhill St. G11	34	T11
Downhill St. G2	34	T11
Downside La. G12	20	T10
Byres Rd.		
Downside Rd. G12	20	T10
Downvale Ter. G11	34	S11
White St.		
Downcraig Dr. G45	64	W19
Downcraig Rd. G45	64	W19
Downcraig Ter. G45	64	W19
Downfield Gdns. G71	69	GG19
Downfield St. G32	54	AA14
Downiebrae Rd. G73	53	Y15
Downs St. G21	22	X10
Dowrie Cres. G53	48	P15
Dows Pl. G4	21	V10
Possil Rd.		
Drainie St. G34	40	EE12
Westerhouse Rd.		
Drake St. G40	36	X13
Drakemire Av. G45	64	W18
Drakemire Dr. G44	64	W18
Drakemire Dr. G45	64	W18
Dreghorn St. G31	37	Z12
Drem Pl. G11	34	S11
Merkland St.		
Drimnin Rd. G33	25	DD9
Drive Rd. G51	33	R12
Drochil St. G34	40	EE11
Drumbeg Dr. G53	60	P17
Drumbeg Pl. G53	60	P17
Drumbottie Rd. G21	23	Y9
Drumby Cres. G76	62	T19
Drumcavel Rd. G69	26	FF8
Drumchapel Gdns. G15	6	P7
Drumchapel Pl. G15	6	P7
Drumchapel Rd. G15	6	P7
Drumclog Gdns. G33	24	AA9
Drumclutha Dr. G71	69	HH19
Drumcross Rd. G53	49	Q15
Drumhead Pl. G32	54	AA15
Drumhead Rd. G32	54	AA15
Drumilaw Rd. G73	65	Y17
Drumilaw Way G73	65	Y17
Drumlaken Av. G23	8	T7
Drumlaken Ct. G23	8	T7
Drumlaken St. G23	8	T7
Drumlanrig Av. G34	40	FF11
Drumlanrig Pl. G34	40	FF11
Drumlanrig Quad. G34	40	FF11
Drumlochy Rd. G33	38	BB11
Drummond Av. G73	52	X16
Drummond Dr., Pais.	47	M14
Drummond Gdns. G13	19	R9
Crow Rd.		
Drummore Rd. G15	6	P5
Drumover Dr. G31	54	AA14
Drumoyne Av. G51	33	R12
Drumoyne Circ. G51	33	R13
Drumoyne Dr. G51	33	R12
Drumoyne Pl. G51	33	R13
Drumoyne Circ.		
Drumoyne Quad. G51	33	R13
Drumoyne Rd. G51	33	R13
Drumoyne Sq. G51	33	R12
Drumpark St. G46	61	R18
Drumpark St., Coat.	57	HH14
Dunnachie Dr.		
Drumpellier Av. G69	56	EE14
Drumpellier Pl. G69	56	EE14
Drumpellier Rd. G69	56	EE14
Drumpellier St. G33	37	Z11
Drumreoch Dr. G42	52	X16
Drumreoch Pl. G42	52	X16
Drumry Pl. G15	6	N7
Drumry Rd., Clyde.	5	L6
Drumry Rd. E. G15	5	M7
Drums Av., Pais.	30	J13
Drums Cres., Pais.	30	J13
Drums Rd. G53	48	P14
Drumsack Av. G69	26	FF8
Drumsargard Rd. G73	65	Z17
Drumshaw Dr. G32	55	CC16
Drumvale Dr. G69	15	GG7
Drury St. G2	35	V12
Dryad St. G46	61	R17
Dryborough Av., Pais.	45	H15
Dryburgh Av. G73	53	Y16
Dryburgh Gdns. G20	21	U10
Dryburgh Rd. G61	7	Q5
Dryburgh Wk. G69	15	HH6
Dryburn Av. G52	32	P13
Drygate G4	36	X12
Drygrange Rd. G33	39	CC11
Drymen Pl. G66	13	CC6
Drymen Rd. G61	7	Q5
Drymen St. G52	33	R13
Morven St.		
Drymen Wynd G61	7	R6
Drynoch Pl. G22	21	V8
Drysdale St. G14	18	N9
Duart Dr., John.	44	E15
Duart St. G20	20	T8
Dubs Rd. G78	60	N18
Dubton Path G34	40	EE11
Dubton St. G34	40	EE11
Duchall Pl. G14	18	P10
Duchess Pl. G73	53	Z16
Duchess Rd. G73	53	Z15
Duchray Dr., Pais.	48	N14
Duchray La. G33	37	Z11
Duchray St.		
Duchray St. G33	37	Z11
Ducraig St. G32	38	BB13
Dudhope St. G33	39	CC11
Dudley Dr. G12	20	S10
Duffus Pl. G32	55	CC16
Duffus St. G34	40	EE11
Duffus Ter. G32	55	CC16
Duich Gdns. G23	9	U7
Duisdale Rd. G32	55	CC16
Duke St. G4	36	X12
Duke St. G31	36	X12
Duke St., Pais.	46	K15

Name	No.	Grid
Duke St. (Linwood), Pais.	28	F13
Dukes Gate G71	69	GG18
Dukes Rd. G69	41	HH13
Dukes Rd. G72	65	Z17
Dukes Rd. G73	65	Z17
Dulnain St. G72	67	DD17
Dulsie Rd. G21	23	Z9
Dumbarton Rd. G11	34	S11
Dumbarton Rd. G14	18	N9
Dumbarton Rd. G60	4	J6
Dumbarton Rd., Clyde.	4	J6
Dumbarton Rd.	4	K5
(Duntocher), Clyde.		
Dumbreck Av. G41	50	S14
Dumbreck Ct. G41	50	S14
Dumbreck Pl. G66	13	DD6
Dumbreck Rd. G41	50	S14
Dumbreck Sq. G41	50	S14
Dumbreck Av.		
Dunagoil Rd. G45	64	W19
Dunagoil St. G45	64	X19
Dunagoil Ter. G45	64	X19
Dunalistair Dr. G33	24	BB9
Dunan Pl. G33	39	DD12
Dunard Rd. G73	53	Y16
Dunard St. G20	21	U10
Dunard Way, Pais.	30	J12
Mosslands Rd.		
Dunaskin St. G11	34	T11
Dunbar Av. G73	53	Z16
Dunbar Av., John.	43	D16
Dunbar Rd., Pais.	45	H15
Dunbeith Pl. G20	20	T9
Dunblane St. G4	35	V11
Dunbrach Rd. G68	70	MM2
Duncan Av. G14	19	Q10
Duncan La. G14	19	Q10
Duncan Av.		
Duncan La. N. G14	19	Q10
Ormiston Av.		
Duncan St., Clyde.	5	L6
Duncansby Rd. G33	39	CC13
Dunchattan Pl. G31	36	X12
Duke St.		
Dunchattan St. G31	36	X12
Dunchurch Rd., Pais.	31	M13
Dunclutha Dr. G71	69	HH19
Dunclutha St. G40	53	Y15
Duncombe St. G20	20	T8
Duncombe Vw., Clyde.	5	M6
Kirkoswald Dr.		
Duncraig Cres., John.	43	C16
Duncrub Dr. G64	10	X7
Duncruin St. G20	20	T8
Duncryne Av. G32	55	CC14
Duncryne Gdns. G32	55	DD14
Duncryne Pl. G64	22	X8
Dundas La. G1	36	W12
Dundas St. G1	36	W12
Dundasvale Ct. G4	35	V11
Maitland St.		
Dundasvale Rd. G4	35	V11
Maitland St.		
Dundee Dr. G52	48	P14
Dundee Path G52	49	Q14
Dundee Dr.		
Dundonald Av., John.	43	C15
Dundonald Rd. G12	20	T10
Dundonald Rd., Pais.	31	L12
Dundrennan Rd. G42	51	U16
Dunearn Pl., Pais.	47	L14
Dunearn St. G4	35	U11
Dunellan St. G52	33	R13
Dungeonhill Rd. G34	40	FF12
Dunglass Av. G14	19	Q10
Dunglass La. N. G14	19	Q10
Verona Av.		
Dungoil Av. G68	70	LL2
Dungoil Rd. G66	13	DD6
Dungoyne St. G20	20	T8
Dunira St. G32	54	AA14
Dunivaig St. G33	39	DD12
Dunkeld Av. G73	53	Y16
Dunkeld Dr. G61	8	S6
Dunkeld Gdns. G64	11	Y7
Dunkeld La. G69	15	HH7
Burnbrae Av.		
Dunkeld St. G31	53	Z14
Dunkenny Pl. G15	6	N6
Dunkenny Rd. G15	6	N6
Dunkenny Sq. G15	6	N6
Dunlop Cres. G71	69	HH19
Dunlop Cres., Renf.	17	M10
Hairst St.		
Dunlop Gro. G71	57	HH15
Dunlop St. G1	36	W13
Dunlop St. G72	67	DD17
Dunlop St., Pais.	28	F13
Dunlop St., Renf.	17	M10
Hairst St.		
Dunmore La. G5	35	V13
Norfolk St.		
Dunmore St. G5	35	V13
Dunmore St., Clyde.	17	M8
Dunn St. G40	53	Y14
Dunn St., Clyde.	4	K6
Dunn St.	4	K5
(Duntocher), Clyde.		
Dunn St., Pais.	47	L14
Dunnachie Dr., Coat.	57	HH14
Dunnichen Pl. G64	11	Z7
Dunning St. G31	53	Z14
Dunolly St. G21	37	Y11
Dunottar St. G33	38	BB11
Dunottar St. G64	11	Z7
Dunphail Dr. G34	40	FF12
Dunphail Rd. G34	40	FF12
Dunragit St. G31	37	Z12
Dunrobin Av., John.	44	E15
Dunrobin St. G31	37	Y13
Dunrod St. G32	54	BB14
Dunside Dr. G53	60	P17
Dunskaith Pl. G34	40	FF12
Dunskaith St. G34	40	FF12
Dunsmuir St. G51	34	S12
Dunster Gdns. G64	11	Y6
Dunswin Av., Clyde.	4	K6
Dunswin Ct., Clyde.	4	K6
Dunswin Av.		
Dunsyre Pl. G23	9	U7
Dunsyre St. G33	38	AA12
Duntarvie Cres. G34	40	FF12
Duntarvie Dr. G34	40	EE12
Duntarvie Pl. G34	40	EE12
Duntarvie Quad. G34	40	FF12
Duntarvie Rd. G34	40	EE12
Dunterle Ct. G78	59	M18
Dunterlie Av. G13	18	P9
Duntiglennan Rd., Clyde.	5	L5
Duntocher Rd. G61	6	P5
Duntocher Rd., Clyde.	4	K6
Duntocher Rd.	5	L5
(Duntocher), Clyde.		
Duntocher St. G21	22	X10
Northcroft Rd.		
Duntreath Av. G13	18	N8
Duntreath Av. G15	18	N8
Duntroon St. G31	37	Y12
Dunure Dr. G73	64	X17
Dunure St. G20	20	T8
Dunvegan Av., John.	44	F15
Dunvegan Ct. G13	18	P9
Kintillo Dr.		
Dunvegan Dr. G64	11	Y6
Dunvegan Quad., Renf.	17	L10
Kirklandneuk Rd.		
Dunwan Av. G13	18	N8
Dunwan Pl. G13	18	N8
Durban Av., Clyde.	4	J6
Durham St. G41	34	T13
Durness Av. G61	8	S5
Durno Path G33	39	DD12
Duror St. G32	38	BB13
Durris Gdns. G32	55	CC14
Durrockstock Cres., Pais.	45	G16
Durrockstock Rd., Pais.	45	G16
Durward Av. G41	50	T15
Durward Cres., Pais.	45	G15
Durwood Ct. G41	50	T15
Duthil St. G51	33	Q13
Dyce La. G11	34	S11
Dyers La. G1	36	W13
Turnbull St.		
Dyers Wynd, Pais.	30	K13
Gilmour St.		
Dyke Pl. G13	18	P8
Dyke Rd. G13	18	N9
Dyke Rd. G14	18	N9
Dyke St. G69	40	FF13
Dykebar Av. G13	18	P9
Dykebar Cres., Pais.	47	L15
Dykefoot Dr. G53	49	Q16
Dykehead La. G33	39	CC12
Dykehead Rd. G69	41	GG13
Dykehead St. G33	39	CC12
Dykemuir Pl. G21	23	Y10
Dykemuir Quad. G21	23	Y10
Dykemuir St.		
Dykemuir St. G21	23	Y10

E

Name	No.	Grid
Eagle Cres. G61	6	P5
Eagle St. G4	36	W11
Eaglesham Ct. G51	35	U13
Blackburn St.		
Eaglesham Pl. G51	35	U13
Earl Haig Rd. G52	32	N12
Earl Pl. G14	19	Q10
Earl St. G14	18	P10
Earlbank Av. G14	19	Q10
Earlbank La. N. G14	19	Q10
Dunglass Av.		
Earlbank La. S. G14	19	Q10
Earls Ct. G69	15	GG7
Longdale Rd.		
Earls Gate G71	69	GG18
Earls Hill G68	70	LL2
Earlsburn Rd. G66	13	DD6
Earlspark Av. G43	51	U16
Earn Av. G61	8	S6
Earn Av., Renf.	32	N11
Almond Av.		
Earn St. G33	38	AA11
Earnock St. G33	23	Z10
Earnside St. G32	38	BB13
Easdale Dr. G32	54	BB14
East Av., Renf.	17	M10
East Barns St., Clyde.	17	M8
East Bath La. G2	35	V12
Sauchiehall St.		
East Buchanan St., Pais.	30	K13
East Campbell St. G1	36	X13
East Fulton Holdings,	28	E12
Pais.		
East Greenlees Av. G72	67	CC18
East Greenlees Cres. G72	66	BB18
East Greenlees Dr. G72	66	BB18
East Greenlees Rd. G72	66	BB18
East Hallhill Rd. G69	40	EE13
East Kilbride Expressway G72	66	BB19
East Kilbride Rd. G73	65	Z17
East La., Pais.	47	L14
East Reid St. G73	53	Z16
East Rd., John.	42	B14
East Springfield Ter. G64	23	Y8
East Thomson St., Clyde.	5	L6
East Whitby St. G31	53	Z14
Eastburn Rd. G21	23	Y9
Eastcote Av. G14	19	R10
Eastcroft G73	53	Y16
Eastcroft Ter. G21	23	Y10
Easter Av. G71	69	GG17
Easter Garngaber Rd. G66	13	DD5
Easter Ms. G71	69	GG17
Church St.		
Easter Queenslie Rd. G33	39	DD12

Name	Map	Grid
Eastercraigs G31	37	Y12
Easterhill Pl. G32	54	AA14
Easterhill St. G32	54	AA14
Easterhouse Path G34	40	FF12
Easterhouse Pl. G34	40	FF12
Easterhouse Quad. G34	40	FF12
Easterhouse Rd. G34	40	FF12
Easterhouse Rd. G69	40	FF12
Eastfield Av. G72	66	AA17
Eastfield Rd. G21	22	X10
Eastgate G69	27	HH9
Eastmuir St. G32	38	BB13
Eastvale Pl. G3	34	T12
Eastwood Av. G41	50	T16
Eastwood Av. G46	62	T19
Eastwood Ct. G46	61	R18
Main St.		
Eastwood Cres. G46	61	R18
Eastwood Rd. G69	15	GG7
Eastwood Vw. G72	67	DD17
Eastwoodmains Rd. G46	62	S19
Eastwoodmains Rd. G76	62	S19
Easwald Bk., John.	42	B15
Eccles St. G22	22	X9
Eckford St. G32	54	BB14
Eday St. G22	22	W9
Edderton Pl. G34	40	EE12
Eddleston Pl. G72	67	DD17
Eddlewood Path G33	39	DD12
Eddlewood Rd. G33	39	DD12
Edelweiss Ter. G11	34	S11
Gardner St.		
Eden La. G33	37	Z11
Eden Pk. G71	69	GG19
Eden Pl. G72	67	CC17
Eden Pl., Renf.	32	N11
Eden St. G33	37	Z11
Edenwood St. G31	38	AA13
Edgam Dr. G52	33	Q13
Edgefauld Av. G21	22	X10
Edgefauld Dr. G21	22	X10
Edgefauld Pl. G21	22	X9
Balgrayhill Rd.		
Edgefauld Rd. G21	22	X10
Edgehill La. G11	20	S10
Marlborough Av.		
Edgehill Rd. G11	20	S10
Edgehill Rd. G61	7	R5
Edgemont St. G41	51	U16
Edinbeg Av. G42	52	X16
Edinbeg Pl. G42	52	X16
Edinburgh Rd. G33	37	Z12
Edinburgh Rd. G69	39	DD12
Edington Gdns. G69	15	GG6
Edington St. G4	35	V11
Edison St. G52	32	N12
Edmiston Dr. G51	33	R13
Edmiston Dr., Pais.	28	E13
Edmiston St. G31	53	Z14
Edmondstone Ct., Clyde.	17	M8
Yokerburn Ter.		
Edrom Path G32	38	AA13
Edrom St.		
Edrom St. G32	38	AA13
Edward Av., Renf.	18	N10
Edward St. G3	34	T12
Lumsden St.		
Edward St. G69	41	GG13
Edward St.,	17	M8
Clyde.		
Edwin St. G51	34	T13
Edzell Ct. G14	33	Q11
Edzell Dr., John.	44	F15
Edzell Gdns. G64	23	Z8
Edzell Pl. G14	33	Q11
Edzell St. G14	33	Q11
Egidia Av. G46	62	S19
Egilsay Cres. G22	22	W8
Egilsay Pl. G22	22	W8
Egilsay St. G22	22	W8
Egilsay Ter. G22	22	W8
Eglinton Ct. G5	35	V13
Eglinton Dr. G46	62	T19
Eglinton La. G5	51	V14
Eglinton St.		
Eglinton St. G5	51	V14
Eighth St. G71	57	GG15
Eildon Dr. G78	59	M19
Eileen Gdns. G64	11	Y7
Elba La. G31	37	Z13
Elcho St. G40	36	X13
Elder Gro. G71	57	HH16
Elder St. G51	33	R12
Elderbank G61	7	R6
Elderpark Gdns. G51	33	R12
Elderpark Gro. G51	33	R12
Elderpark St. G51	33	R12
Elderslie St. G3	35	U11
Eldon Gdns. G64	10	X7
Eldon Pl., John.	44	E15
Eldon St. G3	35	U11
Eldon Ter. G11	34	S11
Caird Dr.		
Elgin Dr., Pais.	28	E13
Elgin St. G40	37	Y13
Elibank St. G33	38	BB11
Elie St. G11	34	T11
Elizabeth Cres. G46	62	S18
Elizabeth St. G51	34	T13
Elizabethan Way, Renf.	31	M11
Cockels Ln.		
Ellangowan Rd. G41	50	T16
Ellergreen Rd. G61	7	R6
Ellerslie St., John.	44	E14
Ellesmere St. G22	21	V10
Ellinger Ct., Clyde.	4	K6
Scott St.		
Elliot Av. G46	62	T19
Elliot Av., Pais.	45	G16
Elliot Dr. G46	62	T18
Elliot La. G3	35	U12
Elliot St.		
Elliot Pl. G3	35	U12
Elliot St. G3	35	U12
Ellisland Av., Clyde.	5	M6
Ellisland Cres. G73	64	X17
Ellisland Rd. G43	62	T17
Ellisland Rd. G67	71	PP3
Ellismuir Fm. Rd. G69	56	FF14
Ellismuir Pl. G69	56	FF14
Ellismuir Rd. G69	56	FF14
Elliston Av. G53	61	Q17
Elliston Cres. G53	61	Q17
Elliston Dr. G53	61	Q17
Elliston Pl. G53	61	Q17
Ravenscraig Dr.		
Elm Av. G66	13	CC5
Elm Av., Renf.	17	M10
Elm Bk. G64	11	Y7
Elm Dr., John.	43	D16
Elm Gdns. G61	7	R5
Elm Rd. G73	65	Y18
Elm Rd., Clyde.	5	L5
Elm Rd., Pais.	47	L15
Elm St. G14	19	Q10
Elm Wk. G61	7	R5
Elmbank Av. G71	57	HH16
Elmbank Cres. G2	35	V12
Elmbank St.		
Elmbank La. G3	35	U12
North St.		
Elmbank St. G2	35	V12
Elmbank St. La. G3	35	U12
North St.		
Elmfoot St. G5	52	W15
Elmira Rd. G69	26	FF8
Elmore Av. G44	63	V17
Elmore La. G44	63	V17
Elmslie Ct. G69	56	EE14
Elmvale Row G21	22	X10
Elmvale Row E. G21	22	X10
Elmvale Row		
Elmvale Row W. G21	22	X10
Elmvale Row		
Elmvale St. G21	22	X9
Elmwood Av. G11	19	R10
Elmwood Ct. G71	69	HH19
Blantyre Mill Rd.		
Elmwood Gdns. G11	19	R10
Randolph Rd.		
Elmwood Gdns. G66	12	BB5
Elmwood La. G11	19	R10
Elmwood Av.		
Elmwood Ter. G11	19	R10
Crow Rd.		
Elphin St. G23	8	T7
Invershiel Rd.		
Elphinstone Pl. G51	34	T12
Elrig Rd. G44	63	V17
Elspeth Gdns. G64	11	Y7
Eltham St. G22	21	V10
Elvan Ct. G32	38	AA13
Edrom St.		
Elvan St. G32	38	AA13
Embo Dr. G13	18	P9
Emerson Rd. G64	11	Y7
Emerson St. G20	21	V9
Emily Pl. G31	36	X13
Endfield Av. G12	20	S9
Endrick Bk. G64	11	Y6
Endrick Dr. G61	7	R6
Endrick Dr., Pais.	31	L13
Endrick St. G21	22	W10
Endsleigh Gdns. G11	20	S10
Partickhill Rd.		
Ensay St. G22	22	W8
Enterkin St. G32	54	AA14
Ericht Rd. G43	62	T17
Eriska Av. G14	18	P9
Erradale St. G22	21	V8
Erriboll Pl. G22	21	V8
Erriboll St. G22	21	V8
Errogie St. G34	40	EE12
Erskine Av. G41	50	S14
Erskine Sq. G52	32	N12
Erskine Vw., Clyde.	5	L6
Singer St.		
Erskinefauld Rd., Pais.	28	E13
Ervie St. G34	40	FF12
Esk Av., Renf.	32	N11
Esk Dr., Pais.	45	G15
Esk St. G14	18	N9
Esk Way, Pais.	45	G15
Eskbank St. G32	38	BB13
Eskdale Dr. G73	53	Z16
Eskdale Rd. G61	7	Q7
Eskdale St. G42	51	V15
Esmond St. G3	34	T11
Espedair St., Pais.	46	K14
Essenside Av. G15	7	Q7
Essex Dr. G14	19	R10
Essex La. G14	19	R10
Esslemont Av. G14	18	P9
Estate Quad. G32	55	CC16
Estate Rd. G32	55	CC16
Etive Av. G61	8	S6
Etive Ct., Clyde.	5	M5
Etive Cres. G64	11	Y7
Etive Dr. G46	62	T19
Etive St. G32	38	BB13
Eton Gdns. G12	35	U11
Oakfield Av.		
Eton La. G12	35	U11
Great George St.		
Eton Pl. G12	35	U11
Oakfield Av.		
Eton Ter. G12	35	U11
Oakfield Av.		
Ettrick Av., Renf.	32	N11
Ettrick Ct. G72	67	DD18
Gateside Av.		
Ettrick Cres. G73	53	Z16
Ettrick Oval, Pais.	45	G16
Ettrick Pl. G43	50	T16
Ettrick Ter., John.	43	C16
Ettrick Way, Renf.	32	N11
Evan Cres. G46	62	T19
Evan Dr. G46	62	T19

Evanton Dr. G46	61	R18	Faskin Cres. G53	48	N16	Fifth Av. G66	13	CC7
Evanton Pl. G46	61	R18	Faskin Pl. G53	48	N16	Fifth Av., Renf.	31	M11
Evanton Dr.			Faskin Rd. G53	48	N16	Finart Dr., Pais.	47	L15
Everard Ct. G21	22	X8	Fasque Pl. G15	6	N6	Finch Pl., John.	43	C16
Everard Dr. G21	22	X8	Fastnet St. G33	38	BB12	Findhorn Av., Renf.	18	N10
Everard Pl. G21	22	X8	Fauldhouse St. G5	52	W14	Findhorn Cres., Pais.	45	G15
Everard Quad. G21	22	X8	Faulds G69	40	FF13	Findhorn St. G33	37	Z12
Everglades, The G69	26	EE8	Faulds Gdns. G69	40	FF13	Findochty St. G33	39	CC11
Eversley St. G32	54	BB14	Fauldshead Rd., Renf.	17	M10	Fingal La. G20	20	T8
Everton Rd. G53	49	Q15	Fauldspark Cres. G69	40	FF13	*Fingal St.*		
Ewart Pl. G3	34	T12	Fauldswood Cres., Pais.	45	H15	Fingal St. G20	20	T8
Kelvinhaugh St.			Fauldswood Dr., Pais.	45	H15	Fingask St. G32	55	CC14
Ewing Pl. G31	37	Z13	Fearnmore Rd. G20	20	T8	Finglas Av., Pais.	47	L15
Ewing St. G73	53	Y16	Fendoch St. G32	54	BB14	Fingleton Av. G78	59	M19
Ewing St., John.	42	B14	Fenella St. G32	38	BB13	Finhaven St. G32	54	AA14
Exchange Pl. G1	36	W12	Fennsbank Av. G73	65	Z18	Finlarig St. G34	40	FF12
Buchanan St.			Fenwick Dr. G78	59	M19	Finlas St. G22	22	W10
Exeter Dr. G11	34	S11	Fenwick Pl. G46	62	S19	Finlay Dr. G31	37	Y12
Exeter La. G11	34	S11	Fenwick Rd. G46	62	T18	Finnart Sq. G40	52	X14
Exeter Dr.			Fereneze Av. G78	59	L18	Finnart St. G40	52	X14
Exhibition Way G3	35	U12	Fereneze Av., Renf.	31	L12	Finnieston Pl. G3	35	U12
Eynort St. G22	21	V8	Fereneze Cres. G13	18	P8	*Finnieston St.*		
			Fereneze Dr., Pais.	46	J16	Finnieston St. G3	35	U12
F			Fereneze Rd. G78	58	J19	Finsbay St. G51	33	R13
			Fergus Ct. G20	21	U10	Fintry Av., Pais.	46	K16
Fagan Ct. G72	69	GG19	Fergus Dr. G20	21	U10	Fintry Cres. G64	11	Z7
Faifley Rd., Clyde.	5	L5	Ferguslie, Pais.	45	H14	Fintry Cres. G78	59	M19
Fairbairn Cres. G46	62	S19	Ferguslie Pk., Pais.	29	G13	Fintry Dr. G44	52	W16
Fairbairn Path G40	53	Y14	Ferguslie Pk. Av., Pais.	29	H13	Fir Pl. G69	56	EE14
Ruby St.			Ferguslie Wk., Pais.	45	H14	Fir Pl. G72	67	CC17
Fairbairn St. G40	53	Y14	Ferguson Av., Renf.	17	M10	*Caledonian Circuit*		
Dalmarnock Rd.			Ferguson St., John.	43	D14	Fir Pl., John.	44	E15
Fairburn St. G32	54	AA14	Ferguson St., Renf.	17	M10	Firbank Ter. G78	60	N19
Fairfax Av. G44	64	W17	Fergusson Rd. G67	70	NN3	Firdon Cres. G15	6	P7
Fairfield Gdns. G51	33	R12	Ferguston Rd. G61	7	R6	Firhill Rd. G20	21	V10
Fairfield Pl. G51	33	R12	Fern Av. G64	23	Y8	Firhill St. G20	21	V10
Fairfield Pl. G71	69	HH19	Fern Av. G66	13	CC5	Firpark Pl. G31	36	X12
Fairfield St. G51	33	R12	Fern Dr. G78	59	L18	*Firpark St.*		
Fairhaven Dr. G23	20	T8	Fernan St. G32	38	AA13	Firpark Rd. G64	23	Y8
Fairhill Av. G53	49	Q16	Fernbank Av. G72	67	CC18	Firpark St. G31	36	X12
Fairholm St. G32	54	AA14	Fernbank St. G21	22	X9	Firpark Ter. G31	36	X12
Fairley St. G51	34	S13	Fernbank St. G22	22	X9	*Ark La.*		
Fairlie Pk. Dr. G11	34	S11	Fernbrae Rd. G73	65	Z18	First Av. G33	24	BB10
Fairway Av., Pais.	46	J16	Fernbrae Way G73	65	Y18	First Av. G44	63	U19
Fairways G61	6	P5	Ferncroft Dr. G44	64	W17	First Av. G61	8	S6
Fairways Vw., Clyde.	5	M5	Ferndale Ct. G23	20	T8	First Av. G66	13	CC7
Fairyknowe Gdns. G71	69	HH19	*Rothes Dr.*			First Av. G71	57	GG16
Falcon Cres., Pais.	29	H13	Ferndale Dr. G23	20	T8	First Av., Renf.	31	M11
Falcon Rd., John.	43	C16	Ferndale Gdns. G23	20	T8	First Gdns. G41	50	S14
Falcon Ter. G20	20	T8	Ferndale Pl. G23	20	T8	First St. G71	57	GG16
Falfield St. G5	51	V14	*Rothes Dr.*			First Ter., Clyde.	5	L6
Falkland Cres. G64	23	Z8	Ferness Oval G21	23	Z8	Firwood Dr. G44	64	W17
Falkland Mans. G12	20	S10	Ferness Pl. G21	23	Z8	Fischer Gdns., Pais.	29	G13
Clarence Dr.			Ferness Rd. G21	23	Z9	Fisher Av., Pais.	45	G14
Falkland St. G12	20	S10	Ferngrove Av. G12	20	S9	Fisher Ct. G31	36	X12
Falloch Rd. G42	51	V16	Fernhill Gra. G71	69	HH19	Fisher Cres., Clyde.	5	L5
Falloch Rd. G73	7	Q7	Fernhill Rd. G73	65	Y18	Fisher Dr., Pais.	45	G14
Fallside Rd. G71	69	HH19	Fernlea G61	7	R6	Fisher Way, Pais.	45	G14
Falside Av., Pais.	46	K15	Fernleigh Pl. G69	15	GG7	*Fisher Dr.*		
Falside Rd. G32	54	BB14	Fernleigh Rd. G43	62	T17	Fishers Rd., Renf.	17	M9
Falside Rd., Pais.	46	J15	Ferry Rd. G3	34	S12	Fishescoates Av. G73	65	Z18
Fara St. G23	21	U8	Ferry Rd.	69	HH19	Fishescoates Gdns. G73	65	Z17
Farie St. G73	53	Y16	(Bothwell) G71			*Fishescoates Rd.*		
Farm Ct. G71	69	HH18	Ferry Rd.	68	FF17	Fishescoates Rd. G73	65	Z17
Farm La. G71	69	HH17	(Uddingston) G71			Fitzalan Dr., Pais.	31	L13
Myers Cres.			Ferry Rd., Renf.	17	M10	Fitzalan Rd., Renf.	31	L11
Farm Pk. G66	13	CC6	Ferry Vw. Cres. G14	18	N9	Fitzroy La. G3	35	U12
Farm Rd. G41	50	S14	Ferryden St. G14	33	R11	*North Claremont St.*		
Farm Rd. G72	68	FF19	Fersit St. G43	62	T17	Fitzroy Pl. G3	35	U12
Farm Rd.	4	J6	Fetlar Dr. G44	64	W17	*North Claremont St.*		
(Dalmuir), Clyde.			Fettercairn Av. G15	6	N6	Flax Rd. G71	69	HH17
Farm Rd.	5	L5	Fettercairn Gdns. G64	11	Z7	Fleet Av., Renf.	32	N11
(Duntocher), Clyde.			Fettes St. G33	38	AA12	Fleet St. G32	54	BB14
Farme Cross G73	53	Y15	Fidra St. G33	38	AA12	Fleming Av. G69	26	FF8
Farmeloan Rd. G73	53	Y16	Fielden Pl. G40	37	Y13	Fleming Av., Clyde.	17	M8
Farmington Av. G32	39	CC13	Fielden St. G40	37	Y13	Fleming Rd. G67	70	NN3
Farmington Gdns. G32	39	CC13	Fieldhead Dr. G43	62	S17	Fleming St. G31	37	Y13
Farmington Gate G32	39	CC13	Fieldhead Sq. G43	62	S17	Fleming St., Pais.	30	K12
Farmington Gro. G32	39	CC13	Fife Av. G52	48	P14	Flemington Rd. G72	67	DD19
Farne Dr. G44	63	V18	Fife Cres. G71	69	HH19	Flemington St. G21	22	X10
Farnell St. G4	35	V11	Fife Way G64	23	Z8	Fleurs Av. G41	50	S14
Farrier Ct., John.	43	D14	Fifth Av. G12	19	R9	Fleurs Rd. G41	50	S14
Faskally Av. G64	10	X6	Fifth Av. G33	24	BB9	Floors St., John.	43	D15

Street	No.	Grid
Floorsburn Cres., John.	43	D15
Flora Gdns. G64	11	Z7
Florence Dr. G46	62	T19
Florence Gdns. G73	65	Z18
Florence St. G5	36	W13
Florentine Pl. G12	35	U11
Gibson St.		
Florentine Ter. G12	35	U11
Southpark Av.		
Florida Av. G42	51	V16
Florida Cres. G42	51	V16
Florida Dr. G42	51	V16
Florida Gdns. G69	40	EE13
Florida Sq. G42	51	V16
Florida St. G42	51	V16
Flowerdale Pl. G53	60	P19
Waukglen Dr.		
Flures Av., Ersk.	16	K8
Flures Cres., Ersk.	16	K8
Flures Dr., Ersk.	16	K8
Flures Pl., Ersk.	16	K8
Fochabers Dr. G52	33	Q13
Fogo Pl. G20	20	T9
Forbes Dr. G40	36	X13
Forbes Pl., Pais.	46	K14
Forbes St. G40	36	X13
Ford Rd. G12	20	T10
Fordneuk St. G40	37	Y13
Fordoun St. G34	40	FF12
Fordyce St. G11	34	S11
Fore St. G14	19	Q10
Forehouse Rd., John.	42	A14
Forest Dr. G71	69	HH18
Forest Gdns. G66	12	BB6
Forest Pl. G66	12	BB6
Forest Pl., Pais.	46	K15
Brodie Pk. Av.		
Forest Rd. G67	71	QQ3
Forest Vw. G67	71	QQ2
Foresthall Cres. G21	23	Y10
Foresthall Dr. G21	23	Y10
Forfar Av. G52	48	P14
Forfar Cres. G64	23	Z8
Forgan Gdns. G64	23	Z8
Forge, The G46	62	T18
Braidpark Dr.		
Forge Pl. G21	37	Y11
Forge St. G21	37	Y11
Forglen St. G34	40	EE11
Formby Dr. G23	8	T7
Forres Av. G46	62	T18
Forres Gate G46	62	T19
Forres Av.		
Forres St. G23	9	U7
Tolsta St.		
Forrest St. G40	37	Y13
Forrestfield St. G21	37	Y11
Fortevoit Av. G69	40	FF13
Fortevoit Pl. G69	40	FF13
Forth Av., Pais.	45	G15
Forth Av., Renf.	31	M11
Third Av.		
Forth Pl., John.	43	C16
Forth Rd. G61	7	Q7
Forth St. G41	51	U14
Fortingall Av. G12	20	T9
Grandtully Dr.		
Fortingall Pl. G12	20	T9
Fortrose St. G11	34	S11
Foswell Pl. G15	6	N5
Fotheringay La. G41	51	U15
Beaton Rd.		
Fotheringay Rd. G41	50	T15
Foulis La. G13	19	R9
Foulis St. G13	19	R9
Foundary St. G21	22	X10
Foundry La. G78	59	L19
Main St.		
Foundry Open G31	37	Y13
Fountain St. G31	36	X13
Fountainwell Av. G21	36	W11
Fountainwell Dr. G21	36	W11
Fountainwell Pl. G21	36	W11
Fountainwell Rd. G21	36	W11
Fountainwell Sq. G21	36	X11
Fountainwell Ter. G21	36	X11
Fourth Av. G33	24	BB9
Fourth Av. G66	13	CC7
Fourth Av., Renf.	31	M11
Third Av.		
Fourth Gdns. G41	50	S14
Fourth St. G71	57	GG15
Fox La. G1	36	W13
Fox St. G1	35	V13
Foxbar Cres., Pais.	45	G16
Foxbar Dr. G13	18	P9
Foxbar Dr., Pais.	45	G16
Foxbar Rd., John.	45	G16
Foxbar Rd., Pais.	45	G16
Foxes Gro. G66	13	DD5
Foxglove Pl. G53	60	P18
Foxhills Pl. G23	9	U7
Foxley St. G32	55	CC15
Foyers Ct. G13	18	P9
Kirkton Av.		
Foyers Ter. G21	23	Y10
Francis St. G5	51	V14
Frankfield Rd. G33	25	DD9
Frankfield St. G33	37	Z11
Frankfort St. G41	51	U15
Franklin St. G40	52	X14
Fraser Av. G73	53	Z16
Fraser Av., John.	44	E15
Fraser St. G72	66	AA17
Fraserbank St. G21	22	W10
Keppochhill Rd.		
Frazer St. G40	37	Y13
Freeland Ct. G53	60	P17
Freeland Dr. G53	60	P17
Freeland Dr., Renf.	16	J9
Freelands Ct. G60	4	J5
Freelands Pl. G60	4	J6
Freelands Rd. G60	4	J5
French St. G40	52	X14
French St., Clyde.	4	K6
French St., Renf.	31	L11
Freuchie St. G34	40	EE12
Friar Av. G64	11	Y6
Friars Ct. Rd. G69	14	EE7
Friars Pl. G13	19	Q8
Friarscourt Av. G13	7	Q7
Friarscourt La. G13	19	Q8
Arrowsmith Av.		
Friarton Rd. G43	63	U17
Friendship Way, Renf.	31	M11
Fruin Pl. G22	22	W10
Fruin Rd. G15	6	N7
Fruin St. G22	22	W10
Fulbar Av., Renf.	17	M10
Fulbar Ct., Renf.	17	M10
Fulbar Av.		
Fulbar Cres., Pais.	45	G15
Fulbar Gdns., Pais.	45	G15
Peacock Dr.		
Fulbar La., Renf.	17	M10
Fulbar Rd. G51	33	Q12
Fulbar Rd., Pais.	45	G14
Fulbar St., Renf.	17	M10
Fullarton Av. G32	54	BB15
Fullarton Rd. G32	54	AA16
Fullarton Rd. G68	70	NN1
Fullerton St., Pais.	30	J12
Fullerton Ter., Pais.	30	K12
Fulmar Ct. G64	22	X8
Fulmar Pl., John.	43	C16
Fulton Cres., John.	42	B14
Fulton St. G13	19	Q8
Fulwood Av. G13	18	N8
Fulwood Av., Pais.	28	E13
Fulwood Pl. G13	18	N8
Fyvie Av. G43	62	S17

G

Street	No.	Grid
Gadie Av., Renf.	32	N11
Gadie St. G33	37	Z12
Gadloch Av. G66	13	CC7
Gadloch Gdns. G66	13	CC6
Gadloch St. G22	22	W9
Gadlock Vw. G66	13	CC7
Gadsburn Ct. G21	23	Z9
Wallacewell Quad.		
Gadshill St. G21	36	X11
Gailes Pk. G71	69	GG19
Gailes Rd. G68	70	NN1
Gailes St. G40	53	Y14
Gairbraid Av. G20	20	T9
Gairbraid Ct. G20	20	T9
Gairbraid Pl. G20	20	T9
Gairbraid Ter. G69	41	HH13
Gairn St. G11	34	S11
Castlebank St.		
Gala Av., Renf.	32	N11
Gala St. G33	38	AA11
Galbraith Av. G51	33	R12
Burghead Dr.		
Galbraith St. G51	33	Q12
Moss Rd.		
Galdenoch St. G33	38	BB11
Gallacher Av., Pais.	45	H15
Gallan Av. G23	9	U7
Galloway Dr. G73	65	Y18
Galloway St. G21	22	X9
Gallowflat St. G73	53	Y16
Reid St.		
Gallowgate G1	36	W13
Gallowgate G4	36	W13
Gallowgate G31	37	Y13
Gallowgate G40	37	Y13
Gallowhill Av. G66	13	CC5
Gallowhill Gro. G66	13	CC5
Gallowhill Rd. G66	13	CC5
Gallowhill Rd., Pais.	30	K13
Galston St. G53	60	N17
Gamrie Dr. G53	48	P16
Gamrie Gdns. G53	48	P16
Gamrie Rd. G53	48	P16
Gannochy Dr. G64	11	Z7
Gantock Cres. G33	38	BB12
Gardenside Av. G32	54	BB16
Gardenside Av. G71	69	GG17
Gardenside Cres. G32	54	BB16
Gardenside Pl. G32	54	BB16
Gardenside St. G71	69	GG17
Gardner Gro. G71	57	HH16
Gardner La. G69	56	FF14
Church St.		
Gardner St. G11	34	S11
Gardyne St. G34	40	EE11
Garfield St. G31	37	Y13
Garforth Rd. G69	55	DD14
Gargrave Av. G69	55	DD14
Garion Dr. G13	18	P9
Talbot Dr.		
Garlieston Rd. G33	39	DD13
Garmouth Ct. G51	33	R12
Garmouth St.		
Garmouth Gdns. G51	33	R12
Garmouth St. G51	33	R12
Garnet La. G3	35	V11
Garnet St.		
Garnet St. G3	35	V11
Garnethill St. G3	35	V11
Garngaber Av. G66	13	CC5
Garngaber Ct. G66	13	DD5
Woodilee Rd.		
Garnie Av., Ersk.	4	J7
Garnie Cres., Ersk.	4	J7
Garnie La., Ersk.	4	J7
Garnie Oval, Ersk.	4	J7
Garnie Pl., Ersk.	4	J7
Garnieland Rd., Ersk.	4	J7
Garnkirk La. G33	25	DD9
Garnkirk St. G21	36	X11
Garnock St. G21	36	X11
Garrell Way G67	70	NN3
Garrioch Cres. G20	20	T9
Garrioch Dr. G20	20	T9
Garrioch Gate G20	20	T9

Garrioch Quad. G20	20	T9	Generals Gate G71	69	GG17	Glasgow St. G12	21	U10
Garrioch Rd. G20	20	T10	*Cobblerigg Way*			Glassel Rd. G34	40	FF11
Garriochmill Rd. G20	21	U10	Gentle Row, Clyde.	4	K5	Glasserton Pl. G43	63	U17
Raeberry St.			George Av., Clyde.	5	M6	Glasserton Rd. G43	63	U17
Garriochmill Way G20	21	U10	*Robert Burns Av.*			Glassford St. G1	36	W12
Woodside Rd.			George Cres., Clyde.	5	M6	Glebe, The G71	69	HH19
Garrowhill Dr. G69	55	DD14	George Gray St. G73	53	Z16	Glebe Av. G71	69	HH19
Garry Av. G61	8	S7	George Mann Ter. G73	65	Y17	*Green St.*		
Garry Dr., Pais.	45	H15	George Pl., Pais.	46	K14	Glebe Ct. G4	36	W12
Garry St. G44	51	V16	George Reith Av. G12	19	R9	Glebe Hollow G71	69	HH19
Garscadden Rd. G15	6	P7	George Sq. G2	36	W12	*Glebe Wynd*		
Garscadden Rd. S. G13	18	P8	George St. G1	36	W12	Glebe Pl. G72	66	BB17
Garscadden Vw., Clyde.	5	M6	George St. G69	56	EE14	Glebe Pl. G73	52	X16
Kirkoswald Dr.			George St. G78	59	L18	Glebe St. G4	36	W11
Garscube Mill G61	8	S7	George St., John.	43	D14	Glebe St., Renf.	17	M10
Maryhill Rd.			George St., Pais.	46	J14	Glebe Wynd G71	69	HH19
Garscube Rd. G4	21	V10	Gertrude Pl. G78	59	L19	Gleddoch Rd. G52	32	N13
Garscube Rd. G20	21	V10	Gibb St. G21	36	X11	Glen Affric Av. G53	61	Q18
Gartartan Rd., Pais.	32	N13	*Royston Rd.*			Glen Affric Dr. G53	61	Q18
Gartcarron Hill G68	70	MM2	Gibson Cres., John.	43	D15	Glen Affric Pl. G53	61	Q18
Dunbrach Rd.			Gibson Rd., Renf.	31	L11	Glen Alby Pl. G53	61	Q18
Gartconnell Dr. G61	7	R5	Gibson St. G12	35	U11	Glen Av. G32	38	BB13
Gartconnell Gdns. G61	7	R5	Gibson St. G40	36	X13	Glen Av. G69	15	GG7
Gartconnell Rd. G61	7	R5	Giffnock Pk. Av. G46	62	T18	Glen Clunie Av. G53	61	Q18
Gartcosh Rd. G69	41	HH12	Gifford Dr. G52	32	P13	Glen Clunie Dr. G53	61	Q18
Gartcraig Path G33	38	AA11	Gilbert St. G3	34	T12	Glen Clunie Pl. G53	61	Q18
Gartcraig Pl.			Gilbertfield Pl. G33	38	BB11	Glen Cona Dr. G53	61	Q17
Gartcraig Pl. G33	38	AA11	Gilbertfield Rd. G72	67	CC18	Glen Cres. G13	18	N8
Gartcraig Rd. G33	38	AA12	Gilbertfield St. G33	38	BB11	Glen Douglas Dr. G68	70	MM2
Gartferry Av. G69	15	GG7	Gilfillan Way, Pais.	45	G16	Glen Esk Dr. G53	61	Q18
Gartferry Rd. G69	15	GG7	*Ashton Way*			Glen Etive Pl. G73	66	AA19
Gartferry St. G21	23	Y10	Gilhill St. G20	20	T8	Glen Fyne Rd. G68	70	LL2
Garth St. G1	36	W12	Gilia St. G72	66	AA17	Glen Gdns., John.	44	F14
Garthamlock Rd. G33	39	DD11	Gillies La. G69	56	FF14	Glen La., Pais.	30	K13
Garthland Dr. G31	37	Y12,	*Bredisholm Rd.*			Glen Lednock Dr. G68	70	MM2
Garthland La., Pais.	30	K13	Gills Ct. G31	37	Y13	Glen Livet Pl. G53	61	Q18
Gartliston Ter. G69	41	HH13	Gilmerton St. G32	54	BB14	Glen Loy Pl. G53	61	Q18
Gartloch Cotts.	26	EE9	Gilmour Av., Clyde.	5	L5	Glen Mallie Dr. G53	61	Q18
(Chryston) G69			Gilmour Cres. G73	52	X16	Glen Markie Dr. G53	61	Q18
Gartloch Cotts.	27	GG10	Gilmour Pl. G5	52	W14	Glen Moriston Rd. G53	61	Q18
(Gartcosh) G69			Gilmour St., Clyde.	5	M6	Glen Nevis Pl. G73	65	Z19
Gartloch Rd. G33	38	AA11	Gilmour St., Pais.	30	K13	Glen Ogle St. G32	55	CC14
Gartloch Rd. G34	39	CC11	Girthon St. G32	55	CC14	Glen Orchy Dr. G53	61	Q18
Gartloch Rd. G69	26	EE10	Girvan St. G33	37	Z11	Glen Orchy Pl. G53	61	Q18
Gartly St. G44	63	U18	Gladney Av. G13	18	N8	Glen Pk. Av. G46	61	R19
Clarkston Rd.			Gladsmuir Rd. G52	32	P13	Glen Rd. G32	38	BB12
Gartmore Gdns. G71	57	GG16	Gladstone Av. G78	59	L19	Glen Sax Dr., Renf.	32	N11
Gartmore La. G69	15	HH7	Gladstone St. G4	35	V11	Glen Sq. G33	24	BB10
Gartmore Rd., Pais.	47	M14	Gladstone St., Clyde.	4	K7	Glen St. G72	67	CC18
Gartmore Ter. G72	66	AA18	Glaive Rd. G13	7	Q7	Glen St. G78	59	M18
Gartness St. G31	37	Y12	Glamis Av., John.	44	E15	Glen St., Pais.	30	K13
Gartocher Rd. G32	39	CC13	Glamis Gdns. G64	11	Y6	Glen Vw. G67	71	QQ2
Gartochmill Rd. G20	21	U10	Glamis Pl. G31	53	Z14	Glenacre Cres. G71	57	GG16
Gartons Rd. G21	23	Z10	*Glamis Rd.*			Glenacre Dr. G45	64	W18
Gartshore Rd. G66	15	GG5	Glamis Rd. G31	53	Z14	Glenacre Quad. G45	64	W18
Gartshore Rd. G69	15	GG5	Glanderston Av. G78	60	N19	Glenacre Rd. G67	70	NN4
Garturk St. G42	51	V15	Glanderston Dr. G13	18	P8	Glenacre Ter. G45	64	W18
Garvald Ct. G40	53	Y14	Glaselune St. G34	40	FF12	Glenallan Way, Pais.	45	G16
Baltic St.			*Lochdochart Rd.*			Glenalmond Rd. G73	65	Z18
Garvald St. G40	53	Y14	Glasgow Airport, Pais.	30	J11	Glenalmond St. G32	54	BB14
Garve Av. G44	63	V18	Glasgow Bri. G1	35	V13	Glenapp Av., Pais.	47	L15
Garvel Cres. G33	39	DD13	Glasgow Bri. G5	35	V13	Glenapp Pl. G69	15	GG6
Garvel Rd. G33	39	DD13	Glasgow Grn. G1	36	W13	*Whithorn Cres.*		
Garvock Dr. G43	62	S17	Glasgow Grn. G40	36	W13	Glenapp Rd., Pais.	47	L15
Gas St., John.	44	E14	Glasgow Rd. G53	60	N18	Glenapp St. G41	51	U14
Gask Pl. G13	18	N8	Glasgow Rd. G67	71	PP2	Glenarklet Dr., Pais.	47	L15
Gatehouse St. G32	38	BB13	Glasgow Rd.	70	MM4	Glenartney Row G69	14	FF7
Gateside Av. G72	67	CC17	(Greenfaulds) G67			Glenashdale Way, Pais.	47	L15
Gateside Cres. G78	59	L19	Glasgow Rd. G69	55	DD14	*Glenbrittle Dr.*		
Gateside Pl., John.	42	B14	Glasgow Rd. G71	56	FF16	Glenavon Av. G73	65	Z18
Gateside Rd. G78	59	L19	Glasgow Rd.	68	FF19	Glenavon Rd. G20	20	T8
Gateside St. G31	37	Y13	(Blantyre) G72			*Thornton St.*		
Gauldry Av. G52	49	Q14	Glasgow Rd.	54	AA16	Glenavon Ter. G11	34	S11
Gauze St., Pais.	30	K13	(Cambuslang) G72			*Crow Rd.*		
Gavins Rd., Clyde.	5	L5	Glasgow Rd.	66	AA19	Glenbank Av. G66	13	CC6
Gavinton St. G44	63	U18	(Turnlaw) G72			Glenbank Dr. G46	61	R19
Gear Ter. G40	53	Y15	Glasgow Rd. G73	52	X15	Glenbank Rd. G66	13	CC6
Geary St. G23	8	T7	Glasgow Rd. G78	59	M18	Glenbarr St. G21	36	X11
Torrin Rd.			Glasgow Rd., Clyde.	17	L8	Glenbervie Cres. G68	70	NN2
Geddes Rd. G21	23	Z8	Glasgow Rd.	5	L5	Glenbervie Pl. G23	8	T7
Gelston St. G32	54	BB14	(Hardgate), Clyde.			Glenbrittle Dr., Pais.	47	L15
General Terminus Quay	35	U13	Glasgow Rd., Pais.	31	L13	Glenbrittle Way, Pais.	46	K15
G51			Glasgow Rd., Renf.	18	N10			

Street	No.	Grid
Glenbuck Av. G33	24	AA9
Glenbuck Dr. G33	24	AA9
Glenburn Av. (Baillieston) G69	40	FF13
Glenburn Av. (Chryston) G69	15	GG7
Glenburn Av. G72	65	Z17
Glenburn Cres., Pais.	46	J16
Glenburn Gdns. G64	10	X7
Glenburn Rd. G46	62	S19
Glenburn Rd. G61	7	Q5
Glenburn Rd., Pais.	45	H16
Glenburn St. G20	21	U8
Glenburnie Pl. G34	40	EE12
Glencairn Dr. G41	50	T15
Glencairn Dr. G69	15	GG7
Glencairn Dr. G73	52	X16
Glencairn Gdns. G41	51	U15
Glencairn Dr.		
Glencairn Rd. G67	71	QQ3
Glencairn Rd., Pais.	31	L12
Glencart Gro., John.	43	C15
Milliken Pk. Rd.		
Glenclora Dr., Pais.	47	L15
Glencloy St. G20	20	T8
Glencoats Cres., Pais.	29	H13
Glencoats Dr., Pais.	29	H13
Glencoe Pl. G13	19	R8
Glencoe Rd. G73	65	Z18
Glencoe St. G13	19	R8
Glencorse Rd., Pais.	46	J15
Glencorse St. G32	38	AA12
Glencroft Av. G71	57	GG16
Glencroft Rd. G44	64	W17
Glencryan Rd. G67	71	PP4
Glendale Cres. G64	23	Z8
Glendale Dr. G64	23	Z8
Glendale Pl. G31	37	Y13
Glendale St.		
Glendale Pl. G64	23	Z8
Glendale St. G31	37	Y13
Glendaruel Av. G61	8	S6
Glendaruel Rd. G73	66	AA19
Glendee Gdns., Renf.	31	M11
Glendee Rd., Renf.	31	M11
Glendenning Rd. G13	7	R7
Glendevon Pl., Clyde.	4	K6
Glendevon Sq. G33	38	BB11
Glendore St. G14	33	R11
Glendower Way, Pais.	45	G16
Spencer Dr.		
Glenduffhill Rd. G69	39	DD13
Gleneagles Av. G67	71	PP1
Gleneagles Cotts. G14	19	Q10
Dumbarton Rd.		
Gleneagles Dr. G64	11	Y6
Gleneagles Gdns. G64	11	Y6
Gleneagles La. N. G14	19	Q10
Dunglass Av.		
Gleneagles Pk. G71	69	GG19
Gleneagles Ter. G14	19	Q10
Dumbarton Rd.		
Glenelg Quad. G34	40	FF11
Glenfarg Cres. G61	8	S6
Glenfarg Rd. G73	65	Y18
Glenfarg St. G20	35	V11
Glenfield Cres., Pais.	58	J17
Glenfield Rd., Pais.	58	J17
Glenfinnan Dr. G20	20	T9
Glenfinnan Dr. G61	8	T6
Glenfinnan Pl. G20	20	T9
Glenfinnan Rd. G20	20	T9
Glenfruin Dr., Pais.	47	L15
Glengarry Dr. G52	33	Q13
Glengavel Cres. G33	24	AA9
Glengyre St. G34	40	FF11
Glenhead Cres. G22	22	W9
Glenhead Rd. G66	13	CC6
Glenhead Rd., Clyde.	5	L5
Glenhead St. G22	22	W9
Glenholme, Pais.	45	H15
Glenhove Rd. G67	71	PP3
Gleniffer Av. G13	18	P9
Gleniffer Cres., John.	44	F15
Gleniffer Dr. G78	59	L17
Gleniffer Rd., Pais.	45	H16
Gleniffer Rd., Renf.	31	L11
Gleniffer Vw., Clyde.	5	M6
Kirkoswald Dr.		
Glenisa Av. G69	15	HH6
Glenisla St. G31	53	Z14
Glenkirk Dr. G15	6	P7
Glenlee Cres. G52	48	N14
Glenlora Dr. G53	48	P16
Glenlora Ter. G53	48	P16
Glenluce Dr. G32	55	CC14
Glenluce Gdns. G69	15	HH6
Brady Cres.		
Glenlui Av. G73	65	Y17
Glenlyon Pl. G73	65	Z18
Glenmalloch Pl., John.	44	F14
Glenmanor Av. G69	15	GG7
Glenmore Av. G42	52	X16
Glenmuir Dr. G53	60	P17
Glenpark Rd. G31	37	Y13
Glenpark St. G31	37	Y13
Glenpark Ter. G72	54	AA16
Glenpatrick Bldgs., John.	44	F15
Glenpatrick Rd., John.	44	F15
Glenraith Rd. G33	24	BB10
Glenraith Sq. G33	24	BB10
Glenraith Wk. G33	25	CC10
Glenshee St. G31	53	Z14
Glenshiel Av., Pais.	47	L15
Glenside Av. G53	48	P15
Glenside Dr. G73	65	Z17
Glenspean Pl. G43	62	T17
Glenspean St.		
Glenspean St. G43	62	T17
Glentanar Pl. G22	21	V8
Glentanar Rd. G22	21	V8
Glentarbert Rd. G73	65	Z18
Glenturret St. G32	54	BB14
Glentyan Av., John.	42	B14
Glentyan Dr. G53	60	P17
Glentyan Ter. G53	48	P16
Glenview Cres. G69	15	HH6
Glenview Pl. G72	68	FF19
Glenville Av. G46	62	S18
Glenwood Ct. G66	12	BB5
Glenwood Dr. G46	61	R19
Glenwood Gdns. G66	12	BB5
Glenwood Pl. G66	12	BB5
Glenwood Rd. G66	12	BB5
Gloucester Av. G73	65	Z17
Gloucester St. G5	35	V13
Gockston Rd., Pais.	30	J12
Gogar Pl. G33	38	AA12
Gogar St. G33	38	AA12
Goldberry Av. G14	18	P9
Goldie Rd. G71	69	HH18
Golf Ct. G44	63	U19
Golf Dr. G15	6	N7
Golf Dr., Pais.	47	M14
Golf Rd. G73	65	Y18
Golf Vw. G61	6	P5
Golf Vw., Clyde.	4	K6
Golfhill Dr. G31	37	Y12
Golfhill La. G31	37	Y12
Whitehill St.		
Golfhill Ter. G31	36	X12
Firpark St.		
Golspie St. G51	34	S12
Goosedubbs G1	36	W13
Stockwell St.		
Gopher Av. G71	57	HH16
Gorbals Cross G5	36	W13
Gorbals La. G5	35	V13
Oxford St.		
Gorbals St. G5	35	V13
Gordon Av. G44	63	U19
Gordon Av. G69	39	DD13
Gordon Dr. G44	63	U18
Gordon La. G1	35	V12
Gordon St.		
Gordon Rd. G44	63	U19
Gordon St. G1	35	V12
Gordon St., Pais.	46	K14
Gordon Ter. G72	68	FF19
Gorebridge St. G32	38	AA12
Gorget Av. G13	7	Q7
Gorget Pl. G13	7	Q7
Gorget Quad. G13	6	P7
Gorget Av.		
Gorse Dr. G78	59	L18
Gorse Pl. G71	57	HH16
Gorsewood G64	10	X7
Gorstan Pl. G20	20	T9
Wyndford Rd.		
Gorstan St. G23	20	T8
Gosford La. G14	18	N9
Dumbarton Rd.		
Goudie St., Pais.	30	J12
Gough St. G33	37	Z12
Gourlay Path G21	22	W10
Endrick St.		
Gourlay St. G21	22	X10
Crichton St.		
Gourock St. G5	51	V14
Govan Cross G51	34	S12
Govan Rd. G51	33	R12
Govanhill St. G42	51	V15
Gowan Brae G66	13	CC5
Gallowhill Rd.		
Gowanbank Gdns., John.	43	D15
Floors St.		
Gowanlea Av. G15	6	P7
Gowanlea Dr. G46	62	T18
Gowanlea Ter. G71	57	HH16
Gower La. G51	34	T13
Gower St.		
Gower St. G51	50	T14
Gower Ter. G41	34	T13
Goyle Av. G15	7	Q6
Grace Av. G69	41	GG13
Grace St. G3	35	U12
Graffham Av. G46	62	T18
Grafton Pl. G1	36	W12
Graham Av. G72	67	CC17
Graham Av., Clyde.	5	L6
Graham Sq. G31	36	X13
Graham St. G78	59	L18
Graham St., John.	43	D15
Graham Ter. G64	23	Y8
Grahamston Ct., Pais.	47	M16
Grahamston Cres., Pais.	47	M16
Grahamston Pk. G78	59	L17
Grahamston Pl., Pais.	47	M16
Grahamston Rd.		
Grahamston Rd. G78	59	L17
Grahamston Rd., Pais.	59	L17
Grainger Rd. G64	11	Z7
Grampian Av., Pais.	46	J16
Grampian Cres. G32	54	BB14
Grampian Pl. G32	54	BB14
Grampian St. G32	54	BB14
Grampian Way G78	59	M19
Gran St., Clyde.	18	N8
Granby La. G12	20	T10
Great George St.		
Granby Pl. G12	20	T10
Great George St.		
Grandtully Dr. G12	20	T9
Grange Gdns. G71	69	HH19
Blairston Av.		
Grange Rd. G42	51	V16
Grange Rd. G61	7	R5
Grangeneuk Gdns. G68	70	MM3
Grant St. G3	35	U11
Grantlea Gro. G32	55	CC14
Grantlea Ter. G32	55	CC14
Grantley Gdns. G41	50	T16
Grantley St. G41	50	T16
Granton St. G5	52	X15
Granville St. G3	35	U12
Granville St., Clyde.	5	L6
Gray Dr. G61	7	R6
Gray St. G3	34	T11

Great Dovehill G1	36	W13
Great George La. G12	20	T10
Great George St.		
Great George St. G12	20	T10
Great Hamilton St., Pais.	46	K15
Great Kelvin La. G12	21	U10
Glasgow St.		
Great Western Rd. G4	20	S9
Great Western Rd. G12	20	T10
Great Western Rd. G13	6	P7
Great Western Rd. G15	6	P7
Great Western Rd., Clyde.	4	J5
Great Western Ter. G12	20	T10
Green, The G40	36	X13
Green Fm. Rd., Pais.	28	E13
Green Lo. Ter. G40	52	X14
Greenhead St.		
Green Pk. G71	69	HH19
Green St.		
Green Rd. G73	53	Y16
Green Rd., Pais.	45	H14
Green St. G40	36	X13
Green St. G71	69	HH19
Green St., Clyde.	5	L6
Greenan Av. G42	52	X16
Greenbank Dr., Pais.	46	J16
Greenbank Rd. G68	70	MM3
Greenbank St. G43	62	S17
Harriet St.		
Greenbank St. G73	53	Y16
Greendyke St. G1	36	W13
Greenend Av., John.	43	C15
Greenend Pl. G32	39	CC12
Greenfaulds Cres. G67	71	PP4
Greenfaulds Rd. G67	70	NN4
Greenfield Av. G32	38	BB12
Greenfield Pl. G32	38	BB13
Budhill Av.		
Greenfield Rd. G32	39	CC13
Greenfield St. G51	33	R12
Greengairs Av. G51	33	Q12
Greenhead Rd. G61	7	R6
Greenhead Rd., Renf.	16	J8
Greenhead St. G40	52	X14
Greenhill G64	11	Y7
Greenhill Av. G46	62	S19
Greenhill Av. G69	27	GG8
Greenhill Ct. G73	53	Y16
Greenhill Cres., John.	44	F15
Greenhill Cres., Pais.	28	F13
Greenhill Dr., Pais.	28	F13
Greenhill Rd. G73	53	Y16
Greenhill Rd., Pais.	30	J13
Greenhill St. G73	53	Y16
Greenholm Av. G71	57	GG16
Greenholme St. G44	63	V17
Holmlea Rd.		
Greenknowe Rd. G43	62	S17
Greenlaw Av., Pais.	31	L13
Greenlaw Cres., Pais.	31	L13
Greenlaw Dr.		
Greenlaw Dr., Pais.	31	L13
Greenlaw Rd. G14	17	M9
Greenlaw Ter., Pais.	31	L13
Greenlaw Av.		
Greenlea Rd. G69	26	EE8
Greenlea St. G13	19	R9
Greenlees Gdns. G72	66	AA18
Greenlees Pk. G72	66	BB18
Greenlees Rd. G72	66	BB17
Greenloan Av. G51	33	Q12
Greenmount G22	21	V8
Greenock Av. G44	63	V17
Greenock Rd., Pais.	30	J12
Greenock Rd., Renf.	16	J9
Greenrig G71	69	GG17
Greenrig St. G33	23	Z10
Greenrig St. G71	69	GG17
Greenrigg Rd. G67	71	PP3
Greenshields Rd. G69	40	EE13
Greenside Cres. G33	24	AA10
Greenside St. G33	24	AA10
Greentree Dr. G69	55	DD14
Greenview St. G43	50	T16
Greenways Av., Pais.	45	H15
Greenways Ct., Pais.	45	H15
Greenwell Pl. G51	34	S12
Greenwell St. G51	34	S12
Govan Rd.		
Greenwood Av. G69	15	GG7
Greenwood Av. G72	67	DD17
Greenwood Dr. G61	8	S6
Greenwood Quad.,	5	M7
Clyde.		
Greer Quad., Clyde.	5	L6
Grenville Dr. G72	66	AA18
Greran Dr., Renf.	17	L10
Gretna St. G40	53	Y14
Greyfriars St. G32	38	AA12
Greystone Av. G73	65	Z17
Greywood St. G13	19	R8
Grier Path G31	37	Z13
Grierson La. G33	37	Z12
Lomax St.		
Grierson St. G33	37	Z12
Grieve Rd. G67	71	PP2
Griqua Ter. G71	69	HH19
Grogary Rd. G15	6	P6
Springside Pl.		
Grosvenor Cres. G12	20	T10
Observatory Rd.		
Grosvenor Cres. La. G12	20	T10
Byres Rd.		
Grosvenor La. G12	20	T10
Byres Rd.		
Grosvenor Mans. G12	20	T10
Observatory Rd.		
Grosvenor Ter. G12	20	T10
Grove, The, John.	42	B14
Grove Pk. G66	13	CC6
Groveburn Av. G46	62	S18
Grovepark Gdns. G20	35	V11
Grovepark Pl. G20	21	V10
Grovepark St. G20	21	V10
Groves, The G64	23	Z8
Woodhill Rd.		
Grudie St. G34	40	EE12
Gryffe Av., Renf.	17	L9
Gryffe Cres., Pais.	45	G15
Gryffe St. G44	63	V17
Guildford St. G33	39	CC11
Gullane Cres. G68	70	NN1
Gullane St. G11	34	S11
Purdon St.		
Guthrie Dr. G71	57	HH15
Guthrie St. G20	20	T9

H

Haberlea Av. G53	61	Q18
Haberlea Gdns. G53	61	Q19
Hagg Cres., John.	43	D14
Hagg Pl., John.	43	D14
Hagg Rd., John.	43	D15
Haggs Rd. G41	50	T15
Haggs Wd. Av. G41	50	S15
Haghill Rd. G31	37	Z12
Haig Dr. G69	55	DD14
Haig St. G21	23	Y10
Hailes Av. G32	39	CC13
Haining, The, Renf.	31	M11
Haining Rd., Renf.	17	M10
Hairmyres St. G42	51	V15
Govanhill St.		
Hairst St., Renf.	17	M10
Halbeath Av. G15	6	N6
Halbert St. G41	51	U15
Haldane La. G14	19	Q10
Haldane St.		
Haldane St. G14	19	Q10
Halgreen Av. G15	5	M6
Halifax Way, Renf.	31	M11
Britannia Way		
Hall St., Clyde.	5	L7
Hallbrae St. G33	38	AA11
Halley Dr. G13	18	N8
Halley Pl. G13	18	N9
Halley Sq. G13	18	N8
Halley St. G13	18	N8
Hallhill Cres. G33	39	DD13
Hallhill Rd. G32	38	BB13
Hallhill Rd. G33	39	DD13
Hallhill Rd., John.	43	C16
Hallidale Cres., Renf.	32	N11
Hallrule Dr. G52	33	Q13
Hallside Av. G72	67	DD17
Hallside Cres. G72	67	DD17
Hallside Dr. G72	67	DD17
Hallside Rd. G72	67	DD18
Hallside St. G5	52	W14
Hallydown Dr. G13	19	Q9
Halton Gdns. G69	55	DD14
Hamilton Av. G41	50	S14
Hamilton Cres. G72	67	CC18
Hamilton Cres., Renf.	17	M9
Hamilton Dr. G12	21	U10
Hamilton Dr. G46	62	T19
Hamilton Dr. G71	69	HH19
Hamilton Dr. G72	66	BB17
Hamilton Pk. Av. G12	21	U10
Hamilton Rd. G32	55	DD15
Hamilton Rd. G71	69	HH19
Hamilton Rd. G72	66	BB17
Hamilton Rd. G73	53	Y16
Hamilton St. G42	52	W15
Hamilton St., Clyde.	17	M8
Hamilton St., Pais.	30	K13
Hamilton Ter., Clyde.	17	M8
Hamilton Vw. G71	57	HH16
Hamiltonhill Cres. G22	21	V10
Hamiltonhill Rd.		
Hamiltonhill Rd. G22	21	V10
Hampden Dr. G42	51	V16
Cathcart Rd.		
Hampden La. G42	51	V16
Cathcart Rd.		
Hampden Ter. G42	51	V16
Cathcart Rd.		
Hampden Way, Renf.	31	M11
Lewis Av.		
Hangingshaw Pl. G42	52	W16
Hanover St. G1	36	W12
Hanson St. G31	36	X12
Hapland Av. G53	49	Q15
Hapland Rd. G53	49	Q15
Harbour La., Pais.	30	K13
Harbour Rd., Pais.	30	K12
Harburn Pl. G23	9	U7
Harbury Pl. G14	18	N9
Harcourt Dr. G31	37	Y12
Hardgate Dr. G51	33	Q12
Hardgate Gdns. G51	33	Q12
Hardgate Pl. G51	33	Q12
Hardgate Rd. G51	33	Q12
Hardie Av. G73	53	Z16
Hardridge Av. G52	49	Q15
Hardridge Rd.		
Hardridge Pl. G52	49	R15
Hardridge Rd. G52	49	Q15
Harefield Dr. G14	18	P9
Harelaw Av. G44	63	U18
Harelaw Av. G78	59	M19
Harelaw Cres., Pais.	46	J16
Harhill St. G51	33	R12
Harland Cotts. G14	33	Q11
South St.		
Harland St. G14	19	Q10
Harlaw Gdns. G64	11	Z7
Harley St. G51	34	T13
Harmetray St. G22	22	W9
Harmony Pl. G51	34	S12
Harmony Row G51	34	S12
Harmony Sq. G51	34	S12
Harmsworth St. G11	33	R11
Harport St. G46	61	R18
Harriet St. G73	53	Y16
Harris Rd. G23	9	U7
Harris Rd. G60	4	J5
Harrison Dr. G51	34	S13

Hillside Ct. G46	61	R18	Holmhill Av. G72	66	BB18	Hughenden Rd. G12	20	S10
Hillside Dr. G61	8	S5	Holmhills Dr. G72	66	AA18	Hughenden Ter. G12	20	S10
Hillside Dr. G64	11	Y7	Holmhills Gdns. G72	66	AA18	*Hughenden Rd.*		
Hillside Dr. G78	59	L18	Holmhills Gro. G72	66	AA18	Hugo St. G20	21	U9
Hillside Gdns. G11	20	S10	Holmhills Pl. G72	66	AA18	Hume Dr.	69	HH18
Turnberry Rd.			Holmhills Rd. G72	66	AA18	(Bothwell) G71		
Hillside Gdns. La. G11	20	S10	Holmhills Ter. G72	66	AA18	Hume Dr.	57	GG16
North Gardner St.			Holmlea Rd. G44	51	V16	(Uddingston) G71		
Hillside Gro. G78	59	L18	Holms Pl. G69	27	GG8	Hume Rd. G67	71	PP2
Hillside Quad. G43	62	S17	Holmswood Av. G72	68	FF19	Hume St., Clyde.	5	L7
Hillside Rd. G43	62	S17	Holmwood Av. G71	57	GG16	Hunter Pl., John.	42	B15
Hillside Rd. G78	59	L18	Holmwood Gdns. G71	69	GG17	Hunter Rd. G73	53	Z15
Hillside Rd., Pais.	47	L15	Holyrood Cres. G20	35	U11	Hunter St. G4	36	X13
Hillswick Cres. G22	21	V8	Holyrood Quad. G20	35	U11	Hunter St., Pais.	30	K13
Hilltop Rd. G69	15	GG7	Holywell St. G31	37	Y13	Hunterfield Dr. G72	66	AA17
Eastwood Rd.			Homeston Av. G71	69	HH18	Hunterhill Av., Pais.	46	K14
Hillview Cres. G71	57	GG16	Honeybog Rd. G52	32	N13	*Hunterhill Rd.*		
Hillview Dr. G72	68	FF19	Hood St., Clyde.	5	M7	Hunterhill Rd., Pais.	46	K14
Hillview Rd., John.	44	F15	Hope St. G2	35	V12	Huntersfield Rd., John.	43	C15
Hillview St. G32	38	AA13	Hopefield Av. G12	20	T9	Huntershill Rd. G64	22	X8
Hilton Gdns. G13	19	R8	Hopehill Pl. G20	21	V10	Huntershill St. G22	22	X9
Hilton Gdns. La. G13	19	R8	*Hopehill Rd.*			Huntershill Way G64	22	X8
Fulton St.			Hopehill Rd. G20	21	V10	*Crowhill Rd.*		
Hilton Pk. G64	10	X6	Hopeman Av. G46	61	R18	Huntingdon Rd. G21	36	X11
Hilton Rd. G64	10	X6	Hopeman Dr. G46	61	R18	Huntingdon Sq. G21	36	X11
Hilton Ter. G13	19	R8	Hopeman Path G46	61	R18	*Huntingdon Rd.*		
Hilton Ter. G64	10	X6	*Kennishead Pl.*			Huntingtower Rd. G69	56	EE14
Hilton Ter. G72	66	AA18	Hopeman Rd. G46	61	R18	Huntley Rd. G52	32	N12
Hinshaw St. G20	21	V10	Hopeman St. G46	61	R18	Huntly Av. G46	62	T19
Hinshelwood Dr. G51	34	S13	Hopetoun Pl. G23	9	U7	Huntly Dr. G72	66	BB18
Hinshelwood Pl. G51	34	S13	Hopetoun Ter. G21	23	Y10	Huntly Gdns. G12	20	T10
Edmiston Dr.			*Foresthall Dr.*			Huntly Path G69	15	HH7
Hirsel Pl. G71	69	HH18	Hornal Rd. G71	69	HH18	*Burnbrae Av.*		
Lomond Dr.			Hornbeam Dr., Clyde.	5	L6	Huntly Rd. G12	20	T10
Hobart Cres., Clyde.	4	J5	Hornbeam Rd. G71	57	HH16	Huntly Ter., Pais.	47	L15
Hobart St. G22	21	V10	Horndean Ct. G64	11	Y6	Hurlet Rd. G53	48	N16
Hobden St. G21	23	Y10	Horndean Cres. G33	39	CC11	Hurlet Rd., Pais.	47	M15
Hoddam Av. G45	64	X18	Horne St. G22	22	X9	Hurley Hawkin G64	23	Z8
Hoddam Ter. G45	65	Y18	*Hawthorn St.*			Hurlford Av. G13	18	N8
Hoey St. G51	34	T12	Hornshill Rd. G33	25	DD8	Hutcheson Rd. G46	62	S19
Hogan Ct., Clyde.	4	K5	Hornshill St. G21	23	Y10	Hutcheson St. G1	36	W12
Dalgleish Av.			Horsburgh St. G33	39	CC11	Hutchinson Ct. G2	35	V12
Hogarth Av. G32	37	Z12	Horse Shoe La. G61	7	R6	*Hope St.*		
Hogarth Cres. G32	37	Z12	Horse Shoe Rd. G61	7	R5	Hutchinson Pl. G72	67	DD18
Hogarth Dr. G32	37	Z12	Horslethill Rd. G12	20	T10	Hutchison Ct. G46	62	S19
Hogarth Gdns. G32	37	Z12	Hospital St. G5	51	V14	*Berryhill Rd.*		
Hogg Av., John.	43	D15	Hotspur St. G20	21	U10	Hutchison Dr. G61	8	S7
Hogganfield St. G33	37	Z11	Houldsworth La. G3	35	U12	Hutton Dr. G51	33	R12
Holburn Av., Pais.	29	H13	*Finnieston St.*			Huxley St. G20	21	U9
Hole Brae G67	71	PP2	Houldsworth St. G3	35	U12	Hydepark Pl. G21	22	X9
Holeburn Rd. G43	62	T17	Househillmuir Cres. G53	49	Q16	*Springburn Rd.*		
Holehouse Dr. G13	18	P9	Househillmuir La. G53	49	Q16	Hydepark St. G3	35	U12
Holland St. G2	35	V12	Househillmuir Pl. G53	49	Q16	Hyndal Av. G53	49	Q15
Hollinwell Rd. G23	21	U8	Househillmuir Rd. G53	60	P17	Hyndford St. G51	34	S12
Hollowglen Rd. G32	38	BB13	Househillwood Cres. G53	48	P16	Hyndland Av. G11	34	S11
Hollows Av., Pais.	45	G16	Househillwood Rd. G53	60	P17	Hyndland Rd. G12	20	S10
Hollows Cres., Pais.	45	G16	Housel Av. G13	18	P8	Hyndland St. G11	34	T11
Holly Dr. G21	23	Y10	Houston Pl. G5	35	U13	Hyndlee Dr. G52	33	Q13
Holly Pl., John.	44	E16	Houston Pl., John.	44	F15	Hyslop Pl., Clyde.	5	L6
Holly St., Clyde.	5	L6	Houston Sq., John.	43	D14	*Albert Rd.*		
Hollybank Pl. G72	66	BB18	Houston St. G5	35	U13			
Hollybank St. G21	37	Y11	Houston St., Renf.	17	M10	**I**		
Hollybrook St. G42	51	V15	Howard St. G1	35	V13			
Hollybush Av., Pais.	45	H16	Howard St., Pais.	47	L14	Iain Dr. G61	7	Q5
Hollybush Rd. G52	32	N13	Howat St. G51	34	S12	Iain Rd. G61	7	Q5
Hollymount G61	7	R7	Howden Dr., Pais.	28	E13	Ibrox St. G51	34	T13
Holm Av. G71	57	GG16	Howe St., Pais.	45	G14	Ibrox Ter. G51	34	S13
Holm Av., Pais.	46	K15	Howford Rd. G52	48	P14	Ibrox Ter. La. G51	34	S13
Holm Pl., Pais.	28	E12	Howgate Av. G15	6	N6	Ibroxholm La. G51	34	T13
Holm St. G2	35	V12	Howieshill Av. G72	66	BB17	*Paisley Rd. W.*		
Holmbank Av. G41	50	T16	Howieshill Rd. G72	66	BB18	Ibroxholm Oval G51	34	S13
Holmbrae Av. G71	57	GG16	Howth Dr. G13	19	R8	Ibroxholm Pl. G51	34	S13
Holmbrae Rd. G71	57	GG16	Howth Ter. G13	19	R8	Ilay Av. G61	19	R8
Holmbyre Rd. G45	64	W19	Howwood St. G41	35	U13	Ilay Ct. G61	20	S8
Holmbyre Ter. G45	64	W19	Hoylake Pk. G71	69	GG19	Ilay Rd. G61	20	S8
Holmes Av., Renf.	31	M11	Hoylake Pl. G23	9	U7	Inchbrae Rd. G52	49	Q14
Holmfauld Rd. G51	33	R11	Hozier Cres. G71	57	GG16	Inchfad Dr. G15	6	N6
Holmfauldhead Dr. G51	33	R12	Hozier St. G40	52	X14	Inchholm St. G11	33	R11
Holmfauldhead Pl. G51	33	R12	Hubbard Dr. G11	33	R11	Inchinnan Rd., Pais.	30	K12
Govan Rd.			Hugh Murray Gro. G72	67	CC17	Inchinnan Rd., Renf.	17	L10
Holmhead Cres. G44	63	V17	Hughenden Dr. G12	20	S10	Inchkeith Pl. G32	38	BB12
Holmhead Pl. G44	63	V17	Hughenden Gdns. G12	20	S10	Inchlee St. G14	33	R11
Holmhead Rd. G44	63	V17	Hughenden La. G12	20	S10	Inchmurrin Dr. G73	65	Z19

118

Name	Page	Grid
Inchmurrin Gdns. G73	65	Z19
Inchmurrin Pl. G73	65	Z19
Inchoch St. G33	39	DD11
Inchrory Pl. G15	6	N6
Incle St., Pais.	30	K13
India Dr., Renf.	16	J9
India St. G2	35	V12
Inga St. G20	21	U8
Ingerbreck Av. G73	65	Z18
Ingleby Dr. G31	37	Y12
Inglefield St. G42	51	V15
Ingleneuk Av. G33	24	BB9
Inglestone Av. G46	62	S19
Inglis St. G31	37	Y13
Ingram St. G1	36	W12
Inishail Rd. G33	39	CC11
Inkerman Rd. G52	32	N13
Innerwick Dr. G52	32	P13
Inver Rd. G33	39	DD12
Inveraray Dr. G64	11	Y6
Invercanny Dr. G15	6	N6
Invercanny Pl. G15	6	P6
Inverclyde Gdns. G11	19	R10
Broomhill Dr.		
Inverclyde Gdns. G73	66	AA18
Inveresk Cres. G32	38	BB13
Inveresk St. G32	38	BB13
Inverewe Av. G46	61	Q18
Inverewe Dr. G46	61	Q19
Inverewe Gdns. G46	61	Q19
Inverewe Pl. G46	61	Q18
Invergarry Av. G46	61	Q19
Invergarry Ct. G46	61	Q19
Invergarry Dr. G46	61	Q19
Invergarry Gdns. G46	61	Q19
Invergarry Gro. G46	61	Q19
Invergarry Pl. G46	61	Q19
Invergarry Quad. G46	61	R19
Invergarry Vw. G46	61	R19
Inverglas Av., Renf.	32	N11
Morriston Cres.		
Invergordon Av. G43	51	U16
Invergyle Dr. G52	32	P13
Inverkar Dr., Pais.	45	H15
Inverkip St. G5	36	W13
Inverlair Av. G43	63	U17
Inverlair Av. G44	63	U17
Inverleith St. G32	37	Z13
Inverlochy St. G33	39	CC11
Inverness St. G51	33	Q13
Inveroran Dr. G61	8	S6
Invershiel Rd. G23	8	T7
Invershin Dr. G20	20	T9
Wyndford Rd.		
Inverurie St. G21	22	W10
Inzievar Ter. G32	54	BB15
Iona Ct. G51	34	S12
Iona Cres. G60	4	J5
Iona Dr. G60	4	J5
Iona Dr., Pais.	46	J16
Iona Gdns. G60	4	J5
Iona La. G69	15	HH7
Heathfield Av.		
Iona Pl. G60	4	J5
Iona Rd. G73	66	AA18
Iona Rd., Renf.	31	M11
Iona St. G51	34	S12
Iris Av. G45	65	Y18
Irongray St. G31	37	Z12
Irvine Dr., Pais.	28	E13
Irvine St. G40	53	Y14
Irving Av., Clyde.	5	L5
Stewart Dr.		
Irving Quad., Clyde.	5	L5
Stewart Dr.		
Iser La. G41	51	U16
Island Rd. G67	70	MM4
Islay Av. G73	66	AA18
Islay Cres. G60	4	J5
Islay Cres., Pais.	46	J16
Islay Dr. G60	4	J5
Ivanhoe Rd. G13	19	Q8
Ivanhoe Rd. G67	70	NN4
Ivanhoe Rd., Pais.	45	G15
Ivanhoe Way, Pais.	45	G15
Ivanhoe Rd.		
Ivybank Av. G72	67	CC18

J

Name	Page	Grid
Jacks Rd. G71	69	HH17
Jagger Gdns. G69	55	DD14
Jamaica St. G1	35	V13
James Dunlop Gdns. G64	23	Y8
Graham Ter.		
James Gray St. G41	51	U16
James Morrison St. G1	36	W13
St. Andrews Sq.		
James Nisbet St. G21	36	X11
James St. G40	52	X14
James Watt La. G2	35	V12
James Watt St.		
James Watt St. G2	35	V12
Jamieson Ct. G42	51	V15
Jamieson Path G42	51	V15
Jamieson St.		
Jamieson St. G42	51	V15
Janebank Av. G72	67	CC18
Janefield Av., John.	43	D15
Janefield St. G31	37	Y13
Janes Brae G67	70	NN4
Janetta St., Clyde.	5	L6
Jardine St. G20	21	U10
Jardine Ter. G69	27	GG9
Jasgray St. G42	51	U15
Jean Armour Dr.,	5	M6
Clyde.		
Jedburgh Av. G73	53	Y16
Jedburgh Dr., Pais.	45	H15
Jedburgh Gdns. G20	21	U10
Jedworth Av. G15	6	P6
Jellicoe St., Clyde.	4	K6
Jenny's Well Rd., Pais.	47	L15
Jerviston Rd. G33	39	CC11
Jessie St. G42	52	W15
Jessiman Sq., Renf.	31	L11
Jocelyn Sq. G1	36	W13
John Brown Pl. G69	26	FF8
John Knox La. G4	36	X12
Drygate		
John Knox St. G4	36	X12
John Knox St., Clyde.	17	M8
John Lang St., John.	44	E14
John St. G1	36	W12
John St. G78	59	L18
John St., Pais.	46	J14
Johnshaven St. G43	50	T16
Bengal St.		
Johnston Rd. G69	27	HH9
Johnston St., Pais.	46	K14
Gordon St.		
Johnstone Av. G52	32	P13
Johnstone Av., Clyde.	17	M8
Johnstone Dr. G72	66	BB17
Johnstone Dr. G73	53	Y16
Joppa St. G33	38	AA12
Jordan St. G14	33	Q11
Jordanhill Cres. G13	19	Q9
Jordanhill Dr. G13	19	Q9
Jordanhill La. G13	19	R9
Austen Rd.		
Jordanvale Av. G14	33	Q11
Jowitt Av., Clyde.	5	M7
Jubilee Bk. G66	13	CC6
Heriot Rd.		
Jubilee Path G61	7	R6
Jubilee Ter., John.	43	C15
Julian Av. G12	20	T10
Julian La. G12	20	T10
Julian Av.		
Juniper Ct. G66	12	BB5
Juniper Pl. G32	55	DD14
Juniper Pl., John.	44	E16
Juniper Ter. G32	55	DD14
Jura Av., Renf.	31	M11
Jura Ct. G52	33	R13
Jura Dr. G60	4	J5
Jura Rd.		
Jura Dr. G72	68	FF18
Jura Gdns. G60	4	J5
Jura Rd.		
Jura Pl. G60	4	J5
Jura Rd.		
Jura Rd. G60	4	J5
Jura Rd., Pais.	46	J16
Jura St. G52	33	R13

K

Name	Page	Grid
Kaim Dr. G53	61	Q17
Kames St. G5	51	V14
Karol Path G4	35	V11
St. Peters St.		
Katewell Av. G15	6	N6
Katrine Av. G64	11	Y7
Katrine Dr., Pais.	45	G15
Katrine Pl. G72	66	BB17
Kay St. G21	22	X10
Kaystone Rd. G15	6	P7
Keal Av. G15	18	P8
Keal Cres. G15	18	P8
Keal Dr. G15	18	P8
Keal Pl. G15	18	P8
Kearn Av. G15	6	P7
Kearn Pl. G15	6	P7
Keats Pk. G71	69	HH18
Keir Dr. G64	10	X7
Keir St. G41	51	U14
Keirhill Rd. G68	70	MM3
Woodburn Rd.		
Keirs Wk. G72	66	BB17
Keith Av. G46	62	T18
Keith Ct. G11	34	T11
Keith St.		
Keith St. G11	34	T11
Kelbourne St. G20	21	U10
Kelburn St. G78	59	L19
Kelburne Dr., Pais.	31	L13
Kelburne Gdns. G69	56	EE14
Kelburne Gdns., Pais.	31	L13
Kelburne Oval, Pais.	31	L13
Kelhead Av. G52	32	N13
Kelhead Dr. G52	32	N13
Kelhead Path G52	32	P13
Kelhead Pl. G52	32	N13
Kellas St. G51	34	S13
Kells Pl. G15	6	N6
Kelso Av. G73	53	Y16
Kelso Av., Pais.	45	H15
Kelso Gdns. G69	15	GG6
Whithorn Cres.		
Kelso Pl. G14	18	N9
Kelso St. G13	18	N9
Kelso St. G14	18	N9
Kelton St. G32	54	BB14
Kelty Pl. G5	35	V13
Bedford St.		
Kelty St. G5	51	V14
Eglinton St.		
Kelvin Av. G52	32	N11
Kelvin Ct. G12	19	R9
Kelvin Cres. G61	7	R7
Kelvin Dr. G20	20	T10
Kelvin Dr. G64	11	Y7
Kelvin Dr. G69	15	GG7
Kelvin Dr. G78	59	M19
Kelvin Rd. G67	71	PP4
Kelvin Rd. G71	57	GG16
Kelvin Way G3	34	T11
Kelvin Way G71	69	HH18
Bracken Ter.		
Kelvindale Bldgs. G12	20	T9
Kelvindale Rd.		
Kelvindale Cotts. G12	20	T9
Kelvindale Rd.		
Kelvindale Gdns. G20	20	T9
Kelvindale Glen G12	20	T9
Kelvindale Rd.		
Kelvindale Pl. G20	20	T9

Name	Page	Grid
Kelvindale Rd. G12	20	T9
Kelvindale Rd. G20	20	T9
Kelvingrove St. G3	35	U12
Kelvingrove Ter. G3	35	U12
Kelvingrove St.		
Kelvinhaugh Pl. G3	34	T12
Kelvinhaugh St.		
Kelvinhaugh St. G3	34	T12
Kelvinside Av. G20	21	U10
Queen Margaret Dr.		
Kelvinside Dr. G20	21	U10
Kelvinside Gdns. G20	21	U10
Kelvinside Gdns. E. G20	21	U10
Kelvinside Ter. S. G20	21	U10
Kelvinside Ter. W. G20	21	U10
Kemp Av., Pais.	31	L11
Kemp St. G21	22	X10
Kempock St. G31	53	Z14
Kempsthorn Cres. G53	48	P15
Kempsthorn Path G53	48	P15
Kempsthorn Rd. G53	48	P15
Kendal Av. G12	20	S9
Kendal Av. G46	62	T18
Kendal Dr. G12	20	S9
Kendal Ter. G12	20	S9
Kendoon Av. G15	6	N6
Kenilworth Av. G41	50	T16
Kenilworth Cres. G61	7	Q5
Kenilworth Way, Pais.	45	G16
Kenmar Gdns. G71	56	FF16
Kenmore Gdns. G61	8	S5
Kenmore Rd. G67	71	PP3
Kenmore St. G32	38	BB13
Kenmuir Av. G32	55	DD14
Kenmuir Rd. G32	55	CC16
Kenmuirhill Rd. G32	55	CC15
Kenmure Av. G64	10	X7
Kenmure Cres. G64	10	X7
Kenmure Dr. G64	10	X7
Kenmure Gdns. G64	10	X7
Kenmure Row G22	9	V7
Kenmure St. G41	51	U14
Kenmure Way G73	65	Y18
Kennedar Dr. G51	33	R12
Kennedy Ct. G46	62	T18
Braidholm Cres.		
Kennedy St. G4	36	W12
Kennet St. G21	37	Y11
Kennishead Av. G46	61	R17
Kennishead Path G46	61	R17
Kennishead Pl.		
Kennishead Pl. G46	61	R17
Kennishead Rd. G43	61	R17
Kennishead Rd. G46	61	R17
Kennishead Rd. G53	61	Q18
Kennisholm Av. G46	61	R17
Kennisholm Path G46	61	R18
Kennisholm Av.		
Kennisholm Pl. G46	61	R17
Kennoway Dr. G11	33	R11
Kennoway La. G11	33	R11
Thornwood Dr.		
Kennyhill Sq. G31	37	Y12
Kensington Dr. G46	62	T19
Kensington Gate G12	20	T10
Kensington Rd.		
Kensington Rd. G12	20	T10
Kent Dr. G73	65	Z17
Kent Rd. G3	35	U12
Kent St. G40	36	X13
Kentallen Rd. G33	39	DD13
Kentigern Ter. G64	23	Y8
Keppel Dr. G44	52	X16
Keppoch St. G21	22	W10
Keppochhill Rd. G21	22	X10
Keppochhill Rd. G22	22	W10
Kerfield La. G15	6	N6
Kerfield Pl. G15	6	N6
Kerr St. G40	36	X13
Kerr St. G78	59	L19
Kerr St., Pais.	30	J13
Kerrera Pl. G33	39	CC13
Kerrera Rd. G33	39	CC13
Kerry Pl. G15	6	N6
Kerrycroy Av. G42	52	W16
Kerrycroy Pl. G42	52	W16
Kerrycroy Av.		
Kerrycroy St. G42	52	W16
Kerrydale St. G40	53	Y14
Kerrylamont Av. G42	52	X16
Kersland La. G12	20	T10
Kersland St.		
Kersland St. G12	20	T10
Kessington Dr. G61	8	S6
Kessington Rd. G61	8	S6
Kestral Ct., Clyde.	5	L5
Kestrel Pl., John.	43	C16
Kestrel Rd. G13	19	Q9
Kew Gdns. G12	20	T10
Ruthven St.		
Kew Gdns. G71	57	HH16
Kew La. G12	20	T10
Saltoun St.		
Kew Ter. G12	20	T10
Keyden St. G41	35	U13
Kibbleston Rd., John.	42	B14
Kidston St. G5	52	W14
Kierhill Rd. G68	70	MM3
Kilbarchan Rd., John.	43	C15
Kilbarchan St. G5	35	V13
Bedford St.		
Kilbeg Ter. G46	61	Q18
Kilberry St. G21	37	Y11
Kilbirnie St. G5	51	V14
Kilbowie Ct., Clyde.	5	L6
Crown Av.		
Kilbowie Rd. G67	71	PP3
Kilbowie Rd., Clyde.	5	L5
Kilbrennan Rd., Pais.	28	E13
Kilbride St. G5	52	W15
Kilbride Vw. G71	57	HH16
Hamilton Vw.		
Kilburn Gro. G72	68	FF19
Kilburn Pl. G13	18	P9
Kilchattan Dr. G44	52	W16
Kilchoan Rd. G33	39	CC11
Kilcloy Av. G15	6	P6
Kildale St. G73	52	X16
Kildale Way G73	52	X16
Kildary Av. G44	63	V17
Kildary Rd. G44	63	V17
Kildermorie Rd. G34	40	EE12
Kildonan Dr. G11	34	S11
Kildonan Ter. G51	34	S13
Copland Rd.		
Kildrostan St. G41	51	U15
Terregles Av.		
Kildrum Rd. G67	71	PP2
Kilearn Rd., Pais.	31	L12
Kilearn Way, Pais.	31	L12
Kilearn Dr., Pais.	48	N14
Kilearn St. G22	21	V10
Killermont Av. G61	8	S7
Killermont Ct. G61	8	S6
Killermont Meadows G71	69	GG19
Killermont Rd. G61	8	S6
Killermont St. G2	36	W12
Killermont Vw. G20	8	S7
Killiegrew Rd. G41	50	T15
Killin St. G32	54	BB14
Killoch Av., Pais.	29	H13
Killoch Dr. G13	18	P8
Killoch Dr. G78	59	M19
Killoch Rd., Pais.	29	H13
Kilmailing Rd. G44	63	V17
Kilmair Pl. G20	20	T9
Wyndford Rd.		
Kilmaluag Ter. G46	61	Q18
Kilmany Dr. G32	38	AA13
Kilmany Gdns. G32	38	AA13
St. Mark St.		
Kilmardinny Av. G61	7	R5
Kilmardinny Cres. G61	7	R5
Kilmardinny Dr. G61	7	R5
Kilmardinny Gate G61	7	R5
Kilmardinny Av.		
Kilmardinny Gro. G61	7	R5
Kilmarnock Rd. G41	62	T17
Kilmarnock Rd. G43	62	T17
Kilmartin Pl. G46	61	R18
Kilmaurs Dr. G46	63	U18
Kilmaurs St. G51	33	R13
Kilmorie Dr. G73	52	X16
Kilmory Av. G71	57	HH16
Spindlehowe Rd.		
Kilmuir Cres. G46	61	Q18
Kilmuir Dr. G46	61	R18
Kilmuir Rd. G46	61	R18
Kilmuir Rd. G71	57	GG15
Kilmun La. G20	20	T8
Kilmun St.		
Kilmun Pl. G20	20	T8
Kilmun St.		
Kilmun St. G20	20	T8
Kilnside Rd., Pais.	30	K13
Kiloran St. G46	61	R18
Kilpatrick Av., Pais.	45	H15
Kilpatrick Cres., Pais.	46	J15
Kilpatrick Dr., Renf.	31	L12
Campsie Dr.		
Kilpatrick Way G71	57	HH16
Kiltearn Rd. G33	39	DD12
Kilvaxter Dr. G46	61	R18
Kilwynet Way, Pais.	31	L12
Kimberley St., Clyde.	4	J5
Kinalty Rd. G44	63	V17
Kinarvie Cres. G53	48	N16
Kinarvie Gdns. G53	48	N16
Kinarvie Rd.		
Kinarvie Pl. G53	48	N16
Kinarvie Rd. G53	48	N16
Kinarvie Ter. G53	48	N16
Kinbuck St. G22	22	W10
Kincaid Gdns. G72	66	BB17
Kincardine Cres. G64	23	Y8
Graham Ter.		
Kincardine Dr. G64	23	Y8
Kincardine Pl. G64	23	Z8
Kincardine Sq. G33	39	CC11
Kincath Av. G73	65	Z18
Kinclaven Av. G15	6	P6
Kincraig St. G51	33	Q13
Kinellan Rd. G61	7	R7
Kinellar Dr. G14	18	P9
Kinfauns Dr. G15	6	N6
Kinfauns Ter. G51	34	S13
Copland Rd.		
King Edward Rd. G13	19	R9
King George V Bri. G1	35	V13
King George V Bri. G5	35	V13
King George V Dock G51	32	P11
King St. G1	36	W13
King St. G73	53	Y16
King St., Clyde.	17	M8
King St., Pais.	30	J13
Kingarth St. G42	51	V15
Kinghorn Dr. G44	52	W16
Kinglas Rd. G61	7	Q7
King's Bri. G5	52	W14
King's Bri. G40	52	W14
Kings Cres. G72	66	BB17
Kings Cres., John.	44	F14
Kings Cross G31	36	X12
King's Dr. G40	52	X14
Kings Dr. G68	70	NN1
Kings Inch Rd., Renf.	17	M9
Kings La. W., Renf.	17	M10
Bell St.		
King's Pk. Av. G44	63	V17
King's Pk. Av. G73	63	V17
Kings Pk. Rd. G44	51	V16
Kings Pl. G22	21	V8
Kings Rd., John.	44	E15
Kingsacre Rd. G44	52	W16
Kingsbarns Dr. G44	51	V16
Kingsborough Gdns. G12	20	S10

Kingsborough Gate G12	20	S10
Prince Albert Rd.		
Kingsborough Ter. G12	20	S10
Hyndland Rd.		
Kingsbrae Av. G44	52	W16
Kingsbridge Cres. G44	64	W17
Kingsbridge Dr. G44	64	W17
Kingsbridge Dr. G73	64	W17
Kingsburgh Dr., Pais.	31	L13
Kingsburn Dr. G73	65	Y17
Kingsburn Gro. G73	65	Y17
Kingscliffe Av. G44	64	W17
Kingscourt Av. G44	64	W17
Kingsdale Av. G44	52	W16
Kingsdyke Av. G44	52	W16
Kingsford Av. G44	63	U18
Kingsheath Av. G73	64	X17
Kingshill Dr. G44	64	W17
Kingshouse Av. G44	64	W17
Kingshurst Av. G44	52	W16
Kingsknowe Dr. G73	64	X17
Kingsland Cres. G52	32	P13
Kingsland Dr. G52	32	P13
Kingsley Av. G42	51	V15
Kingsley Ct. G71	57	HH16
Kingslynn Dr. G44	64	W17
Kingslynn La. G44	64	W17
Kingslynn Dr.		
Kingsmuir Dr. G73	64	X17
Kingston Av. G71	57	HH16
Kingston Bri. G3	35	U13
Kingston Bri. G5	35	U13
Kingston Pl., Clyde.	4	J6
Kingston St. G5	35	V13
Kingsway G14	18	P9
Kingsway Ct. G14	18	P9
Kingswood Dr. G44	64	W17
Kingussie Dr. G44	64	W17
Kiniver Dr. G15	6	P7
Kinloch Av. G72	66	BB18
Kinloch Av., Pais.	28	E13
Pentland Dr.		
Kinloch Rd., Renf.	31	L11
Kinloch St. G40	53	Z14
Kinmount Av. G44	51	V16
Kinmount La. G44	51	V16
Kinmount Av.		
Kinnaird Cres. G61	8	S6
Kinnaird Dr., Pais.	28	E13
Kinnaird Pl. G64	23	Y8
Kinnear Rd. G40	53	Y14
Kinnell Av. G52	49	Q14
Kinnell Cres. G52	49	Q14
Kinnell Path G52	49	Q14
Kinnell Cres.		
Kinnell Pl. G52	49	R15
Mosspark Dr.		
Kinnell Sq. G52	49	Q14
Kinning St. G5	35	U13
Kinnoul La. G12	20	T10
Dowanhill St.		
Kinpurnie Rd., Pais.	31	M13
Kinross Av. G52	48	P14
Kinsail Dr. G52	32	N13
Kinstone Av. G14	18	P9
Kintessack Pl. G64	11	Z7
Kintillo Dr. G13	18	P9
Kintore Rd. G43	63	U17
Kintra St. G51	34	S13
Kintyre Av., Pais.	28	E13
Kintyre St. G21	37	Y11
Kippen St. G22	22	W9
Kippford St. G32	55	CC14
Kirk La. G43	50	T16
Riverbank St.		
Kirk Pl. G71	69	GG17
Kirk Rd. G61	7	R5
Kirkaig Av., Renf.	32	N11
Kirkbean Av. G73	65	Y18
Kirkburn Av. G72	66	BB18
Kirkcaldy Rd. G41	50	T15
Kirkconnel Av. G13	18	N9
Kirkconnel Dr. G73	64	X17
Kirkdale Dr. G52	49	R14
Kirkfield Rd. G71	69	HH18
Kirkford Rd. G69	15	GG7
Bridgeburn Dr.		
Kirkhill Av. G72	66	BB18
Kirkhill Dr. G20	20	T9
Kirkhill Gdns. G72	66	BB18
Kirkhill Gro. G72	66	BB18
Kirkhill Pl. G20	20	T9
Kirkhill Rd. G69	27	GG9
Kirkhill Rd. G71	57	GG16
Kirkhill Ter. G72	66	BB18
Kirkhope Dr. G15	6	P7
Kirkinner Rd. G32	55	CC14
Kirkintilloch Rd. G64	22	X8
Kirkintilloch Rd. G66	13	CC5
Kirkland St. G20	21	U10
Kirklandneuk Cres., Renf.	17	L10
Kirklandneuk Rd.		
Kirklandneuk Rd., Renf.	17	L10
Kirklands Cres. G71	69	HH18
Kirklea Av., Pais.	29	H13
Kirklee Circ. G12	20	T10
Kirklee Gdns. G12	20	T9
Bellshaugh Rd.		
Kirklee Gdns. La. G12	20	T9
Bellshaugh Rd.		
Kirklee Pl. G12	20	T10
Kirklee Quad. G12	20	T10
Kirklee Quad. La. G12	20	T10
Kirklee Quad.		
Kirklee Rd. G12	20	T10
Kirklee Ter. G12	20	T10
Kirklee Ter. La. G12	20	T10
Kirklee Ter.		
Kirkliston St. G32	38	AA13
Kirkmuir Av., Renf.	31	L11
Kirkmuir Dr. G73	65	Y18
Kirknewton St. G32	38	BB13
Kirkoswald Dr., Clyde.	5	M6
Kirkoswald Rd. G43	62	T17
Kirkpatrick St. G40	37	Y13
Kirkriggs Av. G73	65	Y17
Kirkriggs Gdns. G73	65	Y17
Kirkriggs Way G73	65	Y17
Kirkstall Gdns. G64	11	Y6
Kirkton Av. G13	18	P9
Kirkton Cres. G13	18	P9
Kirkton Rd. G72	66	BB17
Kirktonside G78	59	L19
Kirkview Gdns. G71	57	GG16
Glencroft Av.		
Kirkville Pl. G15	6	P7
Kirkwall G67	71	PP1
Kirkwall Av. G72	68	FF18
Kirkwell Rd. G44	63	V17
Kirkwood Av., Clyde.	5	M7
Kirkwood Quad., Clyde.	5	M7
Kirkwood Av.		
Kirkwood Rd. G71	57	GG15
Newlands Rd.		
Kirkwood St. G51	34	T13
Kirkwood St. G73	53	Y16
Kirn St. G20	20	T8
Kilmun St.		
Kirriemuir Av. G52	49	Q14
Kirriemuir Gdns. G64	11	Z7
Kirriemuir Pl. G52	49	Q14
Kirriemuir Av.		
Kirriemuir Rd. G64	11	Z7
Kirtle Dr., Renf.	32	N11
Kirton Av. G78	59	L19
Kishorn Pl. G33	39	CC11
Knapdale St. G22	21	V8
Knights Gate G71	69	GG17
Knightsbridge Rd. G13	19	Q9
Knightsbridge St. G13	19	Q9
Knightscliffe Av. G13	19	Q8
Knightswood Cross G13	19	Q8
Knightswood Rd. G13	7	Q7
Knightswood Ter. G72	69	GG19
Knock Way, Pais.	31	L12
Knockburnie Rd. G71	69	HH18
Knockhall St. G33	39	CC11
Knockhill Dr. G44	51	V16
Knockhill La. G44	51	V16
Mount Annan Dr.		
Knockhill Rd., Renf.	31	L11
Knockside Av., Pais.	46	J16
Knowe Rd. G69	26	FF8
Knowe Rd., Pais.	31	L12
Knowe Ter. G22	21	V8
Hillend Rd.		
Knowehead Dr. G71	69	GG17
Knowehead Ter.		
Knowehead Gdns. G41	51	U14
Knowehead Gdns. G71	69	GG17
Knowehead Ter. G41	51	U14
Knowetap St. G20	21	U8
Knox St., Pais.	45	H14
Kyle Dr. G46	62	T18
Kyle Rd. G67	71	PP2
Kyle Sq. G73	65	Y17
Kyle St. G4	36	W11
Kyleakin Gdns. G72	68	EE19
Kyleakin Rd. G46	61	Q18
Kyleakin Ter. G46	61	Q18
Kylepark Av. G71	68	FF17
Kylepark Cres. G71	56	FF16
Kylepark Dr. G71	56	FF16
Kylerhea Rd. G46	61	Q18

L

La Belle Pl. G3	35	U11
La Crosse Ter. G12	21	U10
Laburnum Gdns. G66	12	BB5
Laburnum Gro.		
Laburnum Gro. G66	12	BB5
Laburnum Pl., John.	44	E16
Laburnum Rd. G41	50	T14
Laburnum Rd. G67	71	QQ3
Lacy St., Pais.	31	L13
Lade Ter. G52	48	P14
Ladeside Dr., John.	43	C15
Ladhope Pl. G13	18	N8
Lady Anne St. G14	18	N9
Lady Isle Cres. G71	69	GG17
Lady Jane Gate G71	69	GG18
Lady La., Pais.	46	J14
Ladybank Dr. G52	49	R14
Ladyburn St., Pais.	47	L14
Ladyhill Dr. G69	56	EE14
Ladykirk Cres. G52	32	P13
Ladykirk Cres., Pais.	46	K14
Ladykirk Dr. G52	32	P13
Ladyloan Av. G15	6	N6
Ladyloan Pl. G15	6	N6
Ladymuir Cres. G53	49	Q15
Ladysmith Av., John.	43	C15
Ladywell St. G4	36	X12
Laggan Rd. G43	63	U17
Laggan Rd. G64	11	Y7
Laggan Ter., Renf.	17	L10
Laidlaw Gdns. G71	57	GG15
Laidlaw St. G5	35	V13
Laigh Kirk La., Pais.	46	K14
Causeyside St.		
Laigh Possil Rd. G23	21	V8
Balmore Rd.		
Laighcartside St., John.	44	E14
Laighlands Rd. G71	69	HH19
Laighmuir St. G71	69	GG17
Laighpark Harbour, Pais.	30	K12
Lainshaw Dr. G45	63	V19
Laird Pl. G40	52	X14
Lairds Gate G71	69	GG17
Lairds Hill G67	70	NN3
Lairg Dr. G72	68	FF19
Lamb St. G22	21	V9
Lambhill St. G41	34	T13
Lamerton Dr. G52	32	P13
Lamerton Rd. G67	71	QQ3
Lamington Rd. G52	48	P14
Lamlash Cres. G33	38	BB12
Lammermoor Av. G52	49	Q14

Name	No.	Grid
Leven St. G41	51	U14
Leven Vw., Clyde.	5	L6
Radnor St.		
Leven Way, Pais.	45	G15
Levern Cres. G78	59	L19
Levern Gdns. G78	59	L18
Levernside Av. G78	59	L19
Levernside Cres. G53	48	P15
Levernside Rd. G53	48	P15
Lewis Av., Renf.	31	M11
Lewis Ct., John.	42	B15
Lewis Cres. G60	4	J5
Lewis Gdns. G60	4	J5
Lewis Cres.		
Lewis Gdns. G61	6	P5
Lewis Gro. G60	4	J5
Lewiston Dr. G23	8	T7
Lewiston Rd.		
Lewiston Pl. G23	8	T7
Lewiston Rd.		
Lewiston Rd. G23	8	T7
Lexwell Av., John.	44	F14
Lexwell Rd., Pais.	45	G15
Leyden Ct. G20	21	U9
Leyden St.		
Leyden Gdns. G20	21	U9
Leyden St.		
Leyden St. G20	21	U9
Leys, The G64	11	Y7
Liberton St. G33	37	Z12
Liberty Av. G69	41	HH13
Libo Av. G53	49	Q15
Liddale Way G73	52	X16
Liddel Rd. G67	70	NN3
Liddell St. G32	55	CC15
Liddesdale Av., Pais.	44	F16
Liddesdale Pl. G22	22	W8
Liddesdale Sq.		
Liddesdale Rd. G22	22	W8
Liddesdale Sq. G22	22	W8
Liddesdale Ter. G22	22	X8
Liff Gdns. G64	23	Z8
Liff Pl. G34	40	FF11
Lightburn Pl. G32	38	BB12
Lightburn Rd. G72	67	CC18
Lilac Av., Clyde.	4	K6
Lilac Gdns. G64	23	Y8
Lilac Pl., John.	44	E15
Lillyburn Pl. G15	6	N5
Lily St. G40	53	Y14
Lilybank Av. G69	26	FF8
Lilybank Av. G72	67	CC18
Lilybank Gdns. G12	34	T11
Lilybank Gdns. La. G12	20	T10
Great George St.		
Lilybank Ter. G12	20	T10
Great George St.		
Lilybank Ter. La. G12	20	T10
Great George St.		
Lime Gro. G66	13	CC5
Lime Gro. G72	68	FF19
Lime St. G14	19	Q10
Limecraigs Cres., Pais.	46	J16
Limecraigs Rd., Pais.	46	J16
Limeside Av. G73	53	Y16
Limeside Gdns. G73	53	Z16
Calderwood Rd.		
Limetree Av. G71	57	HH16
Limetree Dr., Clyde.	5	L6
Limeview Av., Pais.	45	H16
Limeview Cres., Pais.	45	H16
Limeview Rd., Pais.	45	H16
Limeview Av.		
Limeview Way, Pais.	45	H16
Limeview Av.		
Linacre Dr. G32	39	CC13
Linacre Gdns. G32	39	CC13
Linbank Av. G53	49	Q16
Linburn Pl. G52	32	P13
Linburn Rd. G52	32	N12
Linclive Link Rd., Pais.	28	F13
Linclive Ter., Pais.	28	F13
Lincoln Av. G13	18	P9
Lincoln Av. G71	57	GG15
Lindams G71	69	GG17
Linden Dr., Clyde.	5	L5
Linden Pl. G13	19	R8
Linden St. G13	19	R8
Lindores Av. G73	53	Y16
Lindores St. G42	51	V16
Somerville Dr.		
Lindrick Dr. G23	9	U7
Lindsay Dr. G12	20	S9
Lindsay Pl. G12	20	S9
Lindsay Pl. G66	13	CC6
Lindsaybeg Rd. G66	13	DD6
Lindsaybeg Rd. G69	14	EE7
Linfern Rd. G12	20	T10
Links Rd. G32	55	CC14
Links Rd. G44	64	W18
Linkwood Av. G15	6	N6
Kinfauns Dr.		
Linkwood Cres. G15	6	N6
Linkwood Dr. G15	6	N6
Linkwood Pl. G15	6	N6
Kinfauns Dr.		
Linlithgow Gdns. G32	39	CC13
Linn Cres., Pais.	46	J16
Linn Dr. G44	63	U18
Linn Pk. G44	63	V18
Linnet Av., John.	43	C16
Linnhe Av. G44	63	V18
Linnhe Av. G64	11	Y7
Linnhe Dr. G78	59	L17
Linnhe Pl. G72	68	FF19
Linnhead Dr. G53	60	P17
Linnhead Pl. G14	18	P10
Linnpark Av. G44	63	U19
Linnpark Ct. G44	63	U19
Linnpark Gdns., John.	44	E15
Lunn Brae		
Linnwood Ct. G44	63	V17
Bowling Grn. Rd.		
Linside Av., Pais.	47	L14
Lintfield Ln. G71	69	HH17
Myers Cres.		
Linthaugh Rd. G53	48	P15
Linthaugh Ter. G53	49	Q15
Linthaugh Rd.		
Linthouse Bldgs. G51	33	R12
Holmfauld Rd.		
Linthouse Rd. G51	33	R11
Lintlaw G72	68	FF19
Lintlaw Dr. G52	33	Q13
Linton St. G33	38	AA12
Linwell Cres., Pais.	46	J16
Linwood Moss Rd., Pais.	28	F13
Linwood Rd., Pais.	28	F13
Linwood Ter. G12	21	U10
Glasgow St.		
Lismore Av., Renf.	31	M11
Lismore Dr., Pais.	46	J16
Lismore Gdns., John.	43	C15
Lismore Pl. G69	15	HH6
Altnacreag Gdns.		
Lismore Rd. G12	20	S10
Lister Rd. G52	32	P12
Lister St. G4	36	W11
Lithgow Cres., Pais.	47	L15
Little Dovehill G1	36	W13
Little Holm, Clyde.	4	K6
Little St. G3	35	U12
Littlehill St. G21	22	X10
Edgefauld Rd.		
Littleton Dr. G23	8	T7
Rothes Dr.		
Littleton St. G23	8	T7
Rothes Dr.		
Livingstone Av. G52	32	P12
Livingstone Cres. G72	68	FF19
Livingstone St. G21	22	W10
Keppochhill Rd.		
Livingstone St., Clyde.	5	M7
Lloyd Av. G32	54	BB15
Lloyd St. G31	37	Y12
Lloyd St. G73	53	Y15
Loanbank Quad. G51	34	S12
Loancroft Av. G69	56	FF14
Loancroft Gdns. G71	69	GG17
Loancroft Pl. G69	56	EE14
Loanend Cotts. G72	67	DD19
Loanfoot Av. G13	18	P8
Loanhead Av., Pais.	28	E13
Loanhead Av., Renf.	17	M10
Loanhead La., Pais.	28	E13
Loanhead Rd.		
Loanhead Rd., Pais.	28	E13
Loanhead St. G32	38	AA12
Lobnitz Av., Renf.	17	M10
Loch Achray St. G32	55	CC14
Loch Katrine St. G32	55	CC14
Loch Laidon St. G32	55	CC14
Loch Voil St. G32	55	CC14
Lochaber Dr. G73	65	Z18
Lochaber Rd. G61	8	S7
Lochaline Av., Pais.	45	H15
Lochaline Dr. G44	63	V18
Lochalsh Dr., Pais.	45	H15
Lochalsh Pl. G72	68	EE19
Lochar Cres. G53	49	Q15
Lochard Dr., Pais.	45	H15
Lochay St. G32	55	CC14
Lochbrae Dr. G73	65	Z18
Lochbridge Rd. G34	40	EE12
Lochbroom Dr., Pais.	45	H15
Lochburn Cres. G20	21	U8
Lochburn Gro. G20	21	U8
Cadder Rd.		
Lochburn Pas. G20	21	U8
Lochburn Rd. G20	20	T9
Lochdochart Path G34	40	FF12
Lochdochart Rd.		
Lochdochart Rd. G34	40	FF12
Lochearn Cres., Pais.	45	H15
Lochearnhead Rd. G33	25	CC9
Lochend Av. G69	27	GG8
Lochend Cres. G61	7	Q6
Lochend Dr. G61	7	Q6
Lochend Rd. G34	40	EE11
Lochend Rd. G61	7	R6
Lochend Rd. G69	27	GG8
Locher Rd., John.	42	A14
Lochfauld Rd. G23	9	V7
Lochfield Cres., Pais.	46	K15
Lochfield Dr., Pais.	47	L15
Lochfield Rd., Pais.	46	K15
Lochgilp St. G20	20	T8
Lochgoin Av. G15	6	N6
Lochgreen St. G33	24	AA10
Lochhead Av., Pais.	28	E13
Lochiel La. G73	65	Z18
Lochiel Rd. G46	61	R18
Lochinver Cres., Pais.	45	H15
Lochinver Dr. G44	63	V18
Lochinver Gro. G72	67	CC17
Andrew Sillars Av.		
Lochlea Av., Clyde.	5	M6
Lochlea Rd. G43	62	T17
Lochlea Rd. G67	71	QQ2
Lochlea Rd. G73	64	X17
Lochleven La. G42	51	V16
Battlefield Rd.		
Lochleven Rd. G42	51	V16
Lochlibo Av. G13	18	N9
Lochlibo Cres. G78	59	L19
Lochlibo Rd. G78	59	L19
Lochlibo Ter. G78	59	L19
Lochmaben Rd. G52	48	N14
Lochmaddy Av. G44	63	V18
Lochside G61	7	R6
Drymen Rd.		
Lochside G69	27	GG9
Lochside St. G41	51	U15
Minard Rd.		
Lochview Cotts. G69	27	GG10
Lochview Cres. G33	24	AA10
Lochview Dr. G33	24	AA10
Lochview Gdns. G33	24	AA10
Lochview Pl. G33	24	AA10

Lochview Rd. G61	7	R6
Lochview Ter. G69	27	GG9
Lochwood St. G33	38	AA11
Lochy Av., Renf.	32	N11
Lochy Gdns. G64	11	Y7
Lockerbie Av. G43	63	U17
Lockhart Av. G72	67	CC17
Lockhart Dr. G72	67	CC17
Lockhart St. G21	37	Y11
Locksley Av. G13	19	Q8
Locksley Rd., Pais.	45	G15
Logan Dr. G68	70	MM2
Logan Dr., Pais.	30	J13
Logan St. G5	52	W15
Logan Twr. G72	67	DD18
Claude Av.		
Loganswell Dr. G46	61	Q19
Loganswell Gdns. G46	61	R19
Loganswell Pl. G46	61	R19
Loganswell Rd. G46	61	R19
Logie St. G51	34	S12
Lomax St. G33	37	Z12
Lomond Av., Renf.	31	L11
Lomond Ct. G78	59	M19
Lomond Cres., Pais.	46	J16
Lomond Dr. G71	69	HH18
Lomond Dr. G78	59	L18
Lomond Gdns., John.	44	F15
Lomond Pl. G33	25	CC10
Lomond Rd. G61	7	R7
Lomond Rd. G64	10	X6
Lomond Rd. G66	13	CC5
Lomond Rd. G71	57	GG15
Lomond St. G22	21	V9
Lomond Vw., Clyde.	5	L6
Granville St.		
London Arc. G1	36	W13
London Rd.		
London La. G1	36	W13
London Rd.		
London Rd. G1	36	W13
London Rd. G31	53	Z14
London Rd. G32	54	BB15
London Rd. G40	52	X14
London St., Renf.	17	M9
Long Row G69	40	FF13
Longay Pl. G22	22	W8
Longay St. G22	22	W8
Longcroft Dr., Renf.	17	M10
Longdale Rd. G69	15	GG7
Longden St.,	17	M8
Clyde.		
Longford St. G33	37	Z12
Longlee G69	56	EE14
Longmeadow, John.	43	C15
Longstone Rd. G33	38	BB12
Longwill Ter. G67	71	PP2
Lonmay Rd. G33	39	CC12
Lonsdale Av. G46	62	T18
Loom St. G40	36	X13
Stevenson St.		
Loom Wk., John.	42	B14
Shuttle St.		
Lora Dr. G52	49	R14
Loretto Pl. G33	38	AA12
Loretto St. G33	38	AA12
Lorne Av. G69	26	FF8
Lorne Cres. G64	11	Z7
Lorne Dr., Pais.	28	E13
Lorne Rd. G52	32	N12
Lorne St. G51	34	T13
Lorne Ter. G72	66	AA18
Lorraine Gdns. G12	20	T10
Kensington Rd.		
Lorraine Rd. G12	20	T10
Loskin Dr. G22	21	V8
Lossie Cres., Renf.	32	N11
Lossie St. G33	37	Z11
Lothian Cres., Pais.	46	J15
Lothian Gdns. G20	21	U10
Lothian St. G52	32	N12
Loudon Gdns.,	44	E14
John.		
Loudon Rd. G33	24	BB9
Loudon Ter. G12	20	T10
Observatory Rd.		
Lounsdale Cres., Pais.	45	H15
Lounsdale Dr., Pais.	45	H15
Lounsdale Pl. G14	18	P10
Lounsdale Rd., Pais.	45	H15
Lourdes Av. G52	49	Q14
Lovat Pl. G73	65	Z18
Lovat St. G4	36	W11
Love St., Pais.	30	K13
Low Barholm, John.	42	B15
Low Cres., Clyde.	18	N8
Low Parksail, Ersk.	16	J8
Low Rd., Pais.	46	J14
Lower Bourtree Dr.	65	Z18
G73		
Lower English Bldgs.	51	V14
G42		
Lower Millgate G71	57	GG16
Lowndes La., Pais.	30	K13
New Sneddon St.		
Lowndes St. G78	59	M19
Lowther Ter. G12	20	T10
Loyne Dr., Renf.	32	N11
Morrison Cres.		
Luath St. G51	34	S12
Lubas Av. G42	52	W16
Lubas Pl. G42	52	W16
Lubnaig Rd. G43	63	U17
Luckingsford Av., Renf.	16	J8
Luckingsford Dr., Renf.	16	J8
Luckingsford Rd.,	16	J8
Renf.		
Lucy Brae G71	57	GG16
Ludovic Sq., John.	43	D14
Luffness Gdns. G32	54	BB15
Lugar Dr. G52	49	R14
Lugar Pl. G44	64	X17
Luggiebank Pl. G69	57	HH14
Luing Rd. G52	33	R13
Lumloch St. G21	23	Y10
Lumsden La. G3	34	T12
Lumsden St.		
Lumsden St. G3	34	T12
Lunan Dr. G64	23	Z8
Lunan Pl. G51	33	R12
Luncarty Pl. G32	54	BB14
Luncarty St. G32	54	BB14
Lunderston Dr. G53	48	P16
Lundie Gdns. G64	23	Z8
Lundie St. G32	54	AA14
Lunn Brae, John.	43	D15
Luss Rd. G51	33	R12
Lusset Vw., Clyde.	5	L6
Radnor St.		
Lusshill Ter. G71	56	EE15
Lyall Pl. G21	22	W10
Keppochhill Rd.		
Lyall St. G21	22	W10
Lybster Cres. G73	65	Z18
Lye Brae G67	71	PP3
Lyle Ter., Pais.	46	K15
Lymburn St. G3	34	T12
Lyndale Pl. G20	20	T8
Lyndale Rd. G20	20	T8
Lyndhurst Gdns. G20	21	U10
Lyne Cft. G64	11	Y6
Lyne Dr. G23	9	U7
Lynedoch Cres. G3	35	U11
Lynedoch Pl. G3	35	U11
Lynedoch St. G3	35	U11
Lynedoch Ter. G3	35	U11
Lynn Gdns. G12	20	T10
Great George St.		
Lynn Wk. G71	69	HH17
Flax Rd.		
Lynnhurst G71	57	GG16
Lynton Av. G46	62	S19
Lyon Rd., Pais.	45	G15
Lyoncross Av. G78	59	M19
Lyoncross Cres. G78	59	M18
Lyoncross Rd. G53	48	P15
Lytham Dr. G23	9	U7
Lytham Meadows G71	69	GG19

M

Macbeth Pl. G31	53	Z14
Macbeth St.		
Macbeth St. G31	53	Z14
Macdonald St. G73	53	Y16
Greenhill Rd.		
Macdougal St. G43	50	T16
Macdowall St., John.	43	D14
Macdowall St., Pais.	30	J13
Macduff Pl. G31	53	Z14
Macduff St. G31	53	Z14
Mace Rd. G13	7	Q7
Macfarlane Rd. G61	7	R7
Machrie Dr. G45	64	X18
Machrie Rd. G45	64	X18
Machrie St. G45	64	X18
Mackean St., Pais.	30	J13
Mackechnie St. G51	34	S12
Mackeith St. G40	52	X14
Mackenzie Dr., John.	42	B15
Mackie St. G4	22	W10
Borron St.		
Mackiesmill Rd., John.	44	F16
Mackinlay St. G5	51	V14
Maclay Av., John.	42	B15
Maclean St. G41	35	U13
Maclean St. G51	34	T13
Maclehose Rd. G67	71	QQ2
Maclellan St. G41	34	T13
Macmillan Gdns. G71	57	HH15
Madison Av. G44	63	V17
Madison La. G44	63	V17
Carmunnock Rd.		
Madras Pl. G40	52	X14
Madras St.		
Madras St. G40	52	X14
Mafeking St. G51	34	S13
Magdalen Way, Pais.	44	F16
Magnus Cres. G44	63	V18
Mahon Ct. G69	15	GG7
Maida St. G43	50	S16
Maidland Rd. G53	49	Q16
Mailerbeg Gdns. G69	15	GG6
Mailing Av. G64	11	Y7
Main Rd., John.	44	F14
Main Rd., Pais.	46	J14
Main St. G40	52	X14
Main St. G46	61	R18
Main St. G67	71	PP1
Main St. (Baillieston) G69	56	EE14
Main St. (Chryston) G69	26	FF8
Main St. (Bothwell) G71	69	HH19
Main St.	69	GG17
(Uddingston) G71		
Main St. G72	66	BB17
Main St. G73	53	Y16
Main St. G78	59	L19
Mainhead Ter. G67	71	PP1
Roadside		
Mainhill Av. G69	40	FF13
Mainhill Dr. G69	40	FF13
Mainhill Pl. G69	40	FF13
Mainhill Rd. G69	41	GG13
Mains Av. G46	62	S19
Mains Dr., Ersk.	4	J7
Mains Hill, Ersk.	4	J7
Mains Holm, Ersk.	4	J7
Mains River, Ersk.	4	J7
Mains Wd., Ersk.	4	J7
Mainscroft, Ersk.	4	J7
Mair St. G51	35	U13
Maitland Pl., Renf.	31	L11
Maitland St. G4	35	V11
Malcolm St. G31	37	Z13
Malin Pl. G33	38	AA12
Mallaig Path G51	33	Q12
Mallaig Pl. G51	33	Q12
Mallaig Rd. G51	33	Q12
Mallard Rd., Clyde.	5	L5

Malloch Cres., John.	44	E15
Malloch St. G20	21	U9
Malta St., Clyde.	17	M8
Maltbarns St. G20	21	V10
Malvern Ct. G31	37	Y13
Malvern Way, Pais.	30	J12
Mambeg Dr. G51	33	R12
Mamore Pl. G43	62	T17
Mamore St. G43	62	T17
Manchester Dr. G12	20	S9
Manitoba Pl. G31	37	Y13
Janefield St.		
Mannering Ct. G41	50	T16
Pollokshaws Rd.		
Mannering Rd. G41	50	T16
Mannering Rd., Pais.	45	G16
Mannofield G61	7	Q6
Chesters Rd.		
Manor Rd. G14	19	R10
Manor Rd. G15	6	N7
Manor Rd. G69	27	GG9
Manor Rd., Pais.	45	G15
Manor Way G73	65	Y18
Manse Av. G61	7	R5
Manse Av. G71	69	HH19
Manse Brae G44	63	V17
Manse Ct. G78	59	M18
Manse Rd. G32	55	CC14
Manse Rd. G61	7	R5
Manse Rd. G69	41	GG13
Manse St., Renf.	17	M10
Mansefield Av. G72	66	BB18
Mansefield Dr. G71	69	GG17
Mansel St. G21	22	X9
Mansewood Rd. G43	62	S17
Mansfield Rd. G52	32	N12
Mansfield St. G11	34	T11
Mansion Ct. G72	66	BB17
Mansion St. G22	22	W9
Mansion St. G72	66	BB17
Mansionhouse Av. G32	55	CC16
Mansionhouse Dr. G32	39	CC13
Mansionhouse Gdns. G41	51	U16
Mansionhouse Rd.		
Mansionhouse Gro. G32	55	DD14
Mansionhouse Rd. G32	55	DD14
Mansionhouse Rd. G41	51	U16
Mansionhouse Rd. G42	51	U16
Mansionhouse Rd., Pais.	31	L13
Maple Dr. G66	12	BB5
Maple Dr., Clyde.	4	K5
Maple Dr., John.	44	E16
Maple Rd. G41	50	S14
Mar Gdns. G73	65	Z18
March La. G41	51	U15
Nithsdale Dr.		
March St. G41	51	U15
Marchfield G64	10	X6
Marchfield Av., Pais.	30	J12
Marchglen Pl. G51	33	Q12
Mallaig Rd.		
Marchmont Gdns. G64	10	X6
Marchmont Ter. G12	20	T10
Observatory Rd.		
Maree Dr. G52	49	R14
Maree Gdns. G64	11	Y7
Maree Rd., Pais.	45	H15
Marfield St. G32	38	AA13
Margaret St. G1	36	W12
Martha St.		
Margaretta Bldgs. G44	63	V17
Clarkston Rd.		
Marguerite Av. G66	13	CC5
Marguerite Dr. G66	13	CC5
Marguerite Gdns. G66	13	CC5
Marguerite Gdns. G71	69	HH18
Marguerite Gro. G66	13	CC5
Marine Cres. G51	35	U13
Marine Gdns. G51	35	U13
Mariscat Rd. G41	51	U15
Marjory Dr., Pais.	31	L12
Marjory Rd., Renf.	31	L11
Market St. G40	36	X13
Markinch St. G5	35	V13
West St.		
Marlborough Av. G11	19	R10
Marlinford Rd., Renf.	32	P11
Marlow St. G41	51	U14
Marlow Ter. G41	35	U13
Seaward St.		
Marmion Pl. G67	70	NN4
Marmion Rd. G67	70	NN4
Marmion Rd., Pais.	45	G16
Marmion St. G20	21	U10
Marne St. G31	37	Y12
Marnock Ter., Pais.	47	L15
Marnock Way G69	15	GG7
Braeside Av.		
Marshall's La., Pais.	46	K14
Mart St. G1	36	W13
Martha St. G1	36	W12
Martin Cres. G69	40	FF13
Martin St. G40	52	X14
Martlet Dr., John.	43	C16
Martyr St. G4	36	X12
Martyrs Pl. G64	23	Y8
Marwick St. G31	37	Y12
Marwood Av. G66	14	EE5
Mary St. G4	35	V11
Mary St., John.	44	E14
Mary St., Pais.	46	K15
Maryhill Rd. G20	20	S8
Maryhill Rd. G61	8	S7
Maryland Dr. G52	33	R13
Maryland Gdns. G52	33	R13
Marys La., Renf.	17	M10
Maryston Pl. G33	37	Z11
Maryston St. G33	37	Z11
Maryview Gdns. G71	56	FF15
Edinburgh Rd.		
Maryville Av. G46	62	T19
Maryville Vw. G71	56	FF15
Marywood Sq. G41	51	U15
Masonfield Av. G68	70	MM3
Masterton St. G21	22	W10
Mathieson La. G5	52	W14
Mathieson St.		
Mathieson Rd. G73	53	Z15
Mathieson St. G5	52	W14
Mathieson St., Pais.	31	L13
Matilda Rd. G41	51	U14
Mauchline St. G5	51	V14
Maukinfauld Ct. G32	54	AA14
Maukinfauld Rd. G32	54	AA14
Mauldslie St. G40	53	Y14
Maule Dr. G11	34	S11
Mavis Bk. G64	22	X8
Mavisbank Gdns. G51	35	U13
Mavisbank Rd. G51	34	S12
Govan Rd.		
Mavisbank Ter., Pais.	46	K14
Maxton Av. G78	59	L18
Maxton Gro. G78	59	L18
Maxton Ter. G72	66	AA18
Maxwell Av. G41	51	U14
Maxwell Av. G69	56	EE15
Maxwell Dr. G41	50	T14
Maxwell Dr. G69	40	EE13
Maxwell Gdns. G41	50	T14
Maxwell Gro. G41	50	T14
Maxwell Oval G41	51	U14
Maxwell Pl. G41	51	V14
Maxwell Rd. G41	51	U14
Maxwell Sq. G41	51	U14
Maxwell St. G1	36	W13
Maxwell St. G69	56	EE14
Maxwell St., Clyde.	4	K6
Maxwell St., Pais.	30	K13
Maxwellton Rd., Pais.	45	H14
Maxwellton St., Pais.	46	J14
Maxwelton Rd. G33	37	Z11
May Rd., Pais.	46	K16
May Ter. G42	51	V16
Prospecthill Rd.		
May Ter. G46	62	T18
Maybank La. G42	51	V15
Victoria Rd.		
Maybank St. G42	51	V15
Mayberry Cres. G32	39	CC13
Mayberry Gdns. G32	39	CC13
Mayberry Gro. G32	39	CC13
Maybole St. G53	60	N17
Mayfield St. G20	21	U9
McAlpine St. G2	35	V13
McArthur St. G43	50	T16
Pleasance St.		
McArthur St., Clyde.	17	M8
McAslin Ct. G4	36	W12
McAslin St. G4	36	X12
McCallum Av. G73	53	Y16
McClue Av., Renf.	17	L10
McClue Rd., Renf.	17	L10
McCracken Av., Renf.	31	L11
McCreery St., Clyde.	17	M8
McCulloch St. G41	51	U14
McDonald Av., John.	43	D15
McDonald Cres., Clyde.	17	M8
McEwan St. G31	37	Z13
McFarlane St. G4	36	X13
McFarlane St., Pais.	30	J12
McGhee St., Clyde.	5	L6
McGown St., Pais.	30	J13
McGregor Av., Renf.	31	L11
Porterfield Rd.		
McGregor Rd. G67	70	NN3
McGregor St. G51	33	R13
McGregor St., Clyde.	17	M8
McIntosh Ct. G31	36	X12
McIntosh St.		
McIntosh St. G31	36	X12
McIntyre Pl., Pais.	46	J15
McIntyre St. G3	35	U12
McIntyre Ter. G72	66	BB17
McIver St. G72	67	CC17
McKay Cres., John.	44	E15
McKenzie Av., Clyde.	5	L6
McKenzie St., Pais.	30	J13
McKerrel St., Pais.	31	L13
McLaren Av., Renf.	31	M11
Newmains Rd.		
McLaurin Cres., John.	43	C15
McLean Pl., Pais.	30	J12
McLean Sq. G51	34	T13
McLean St., Clyde.	18	N8
Wood Quad.		
McLennan St. G42	51	V16
McLeod St. G4	36	X12
McNair St. G32	38	BB13
McNeil St. G5	52	W14
McNeill Av., Clyde.	6	N7
McPhail St. G40	52	X14
McPhater St. G4	35	V11
Dunblane St.		
McPherson Dr. G71	69	HH18
Wordsworth Way		
McPherson St. G1	36	W13
High St.		
McTaggart Rd. G67	70	NN4
Meadow La., Renf.	17	M9
Meadow Rd. G11	34	S11
Meadow Vw. G67	71	QQ2
Meadowbank La. G71	69	GG17
Meadowburn G64	11	Y6
Meadowburn Av. G66	13	DD5
Meadowhead Av. G69	15	GG7
Meadowpark St. G31	37	Y12
Meadowside Av., John.	44	F15
Meadowside Quay G11	33	R11
Meadowside St. G11	34	S11
Meadowside St., Renf.	17	M9
Meadowwell St. G32	38	BB13
Meadside Av., John.	42	B14
Meadside Rd., John.	42	B14
Mears Way G64	11	Z7
Medlar Rd. G67	71	QQ3
Medwin St. G72	67	DD17
Mill Rd.		
Medwyn St. G14	19	Q10

Meek Pl. G72	66	BB17	Merrylee Pk. La. G46	62	T18	Millcroft Rd. G67	71	PP3
Meetinghouse La., Pais.	30	K13	Merrylee Pk. Ms. G46	62	T18	Millcroft Rd. G73	52	X15
Moss St.			Merrylee Rd. G43	62	T17	Miller St. G1	36	W12
Megan Gate G40	52	X14	Merrylee Rd. G44	62	T17	Miller St. G69	56	EE14
Megan St.			Merryton Av. G15	6	P6	Miller St., Clyde.	5	L7
Megan St. G40	52	X14	Merryton Av. G46	62	T18	Miller St., John.	44	E14
Meikle Av., Renf.	31	M11	Merryton Pl. G15	6	P6	Millerfield Pl. G40	53	Y14
Meikle Rd. G53	49	Q16	Merryvale Av. G46	62	T18	Millerfield Rd. G40	53	Y14
Meiklerig Cres. G53	49	Q15	Merryvale Pl. G46	62	T17	Millers Pl. G66	13	CC6
Meikleriggs Dr., Pais.	45	H15	Merton Dr. G52	32	P13	Millersneuk Av. G66	13	CC6
Meiklewood Rd. G51	33	Q13	Meryon Gdns. G32	55	CC15	Millersneuk Cres. G33	24	BB9
Melbourne Av., Clyde.	4	J5	Meryon Rd. G32	55	CC15	Millersneuk Dr. G66	13	CC6
Melbourne Ct. G46	62	T18	Methil St. G14	19	Q10	Millerston St. G31	37	Y13
Melbourne St. G31	36	X13	Methuen Rd., Pais.	31	L11	Millford Dr., Pais.	28	E13
Meldon Pl. G51	33	R12	Methven Av. G61	8	S5	Millgate G71	57	GG16
Meldrum Gdns. G41	50	T15	Methven St. G31	53	Z14	Millgate Av. G71	57	GG16
Meldrum St., Clyde.	18	N8	Methven St., Clyde.	4	K6	Millholm Rd. G44	63	V18
Melford Av. G46	62	T19	Metropole La. G1	35	V13	Millhouse Cres. G20	20	T8
Melford Way, Pais.	31	L12	*Howard St.*			Millhouse Dr. G20	20	T8
Knock Way			Micklehouse Oval G69	40	EE13	Millichen Rd. G23	8	T5
Melfort Av. G41	50	S14	*Micklehouse Rd.*			Milliken Dr., John.	43	C15
Melfort Av., Clyde.	5	L6	Micklehouse Pl. G69	40	EE13	Milliken Pk. Rd., John.	43	C15
Melfort Gdns., John.	43	C15	*Micklehouse Rd.*			Milliken Rd., John.	43	C15
Milliken Pk. Rd.			Micklehouse Rd. G69	40	EE13	Millpond Dr. G40	36	X13
Mellerstain Dr. G14	18	N9	Micklehouse Wynd G69	40	EE13	Millport Av. G44	52	W16
Melness Pl. G51	33	Q12	*Micklehouse Rd.*			Millroad Dr. G40	36	X13
Mallaig Rd.			Mid Cotts. G69	26	FF10	Millroad Gdns. G40	36	X13
Melrose Av. G69	41	GG13	Midcroft G64	10	X6	Millroad St. G40	36	X13
Melrose Av. G73	53	Y16	Midcroft Av. G44	64	W17	Millview G78	59	M18
Melrose Av., Pais.	45	H15	Middle Pk., Pais.	46	J15	Millview Pl. G53	60	P18
Melrose Av.	28	E13	Middlemuir Av. G66	13	CC5	Millwood St. G41	51	U16
(Linwood), Pais.			Middlemuir Rd. G66	13	CC5	Milnbank St. G31	37	Y12
Melrose Ct. G73	53	Y16	Middlerigg Rd. G68	70	MM3	Milncroft Rd. G33	38	BB11
Dunard Rd.			Middlesex St. G41	35	U13	Milner Rd. G13	19	R9
Melrose Gdns. G20	21	U10	Middleton Cres., Pais.	30	J13	Milngavie Rd. G61	7	R6
Melrose Gdns. G71	57	GG15	Middleton Rd., Pais.	28	F12	Milnpark Gdns. G41	35	U13
Lincoln Av.			Middleton St. G51	34	T13	Milnpark St. G41	35	U13
Melrose Pl. G72	68	FF19	Midland St. G1	35	V13	Milovaig St. G23	8	T7
Melrose St. G4	35	V11	Midlem Dr. G52	33	Q13	Milrig Rd. G73	52	X16
Queens Cres.			Midlem Oval G52	33	Q13	Milton Av. G72	66	AA17
Melvaig Pl. G20	20	T9	Midlock St. G51	34	T13	Milton Douglas Rd.,	5	L5
Melvick Pl. G51	33	Q12	Midlothian Dr. G41	50	T15	Clyde.		
Mallaig Rd.			Midton Cotts. G69	15	HH7	Milton Dr. G64	22	X8
Melville Ct. G1	36	W12	Midton St. G21	22	X10	Milton Gdns. G71	57	GG16
Brunswick St.			Midwharf St. G4	36	W11	Milton Mains Rd., Clyde.	5	L5
Melville Gdns. G64	11	Y7	Migvie Pl. G20	20	T9	Milton St. G4	35	V11
Melville St. G41	51	U14	*Wyndford Rd.*			Milverton Av. G61	7	Q5
Memel St. G21	22	X9	Milan St. G41	51	V14	Milverton Rd. G46	62	S19
Memus Av. G52	49	Q14	Milford St. G33	38	BB12	Minard Rd. G41	51	U15
Mennock Dr. G64	11	Y6	Mill Ct. G73	53	Y16	Minard Way G71	57	HH16
Menock Rd. G44	63	V17	Mill Cres. G40	52	X14	*Newton Dr.*		
Menteith Av. G64	11	Y7	Mill Pl., Pais.	28	E13	Minerva St. G3	35	U12
Menteith Dr. G73	65	Z19	Mill Ri. G66	13	CC6	Minerva Way G3	35	U12
Menteith Pl. G73	65	Z19	Mill Rd. G71	69	HH19	Mingarry La. G20	20	T10
Menzies Dr. G21	23	Y9	Mill Rd. G72	67	CC18	*Clouston St.*		
Menzies Pl. G21	23	Y9	Mill Rd. G78	59	L18	Mingarry St. G20	21	U10
Menzies Rd. G21	23	Y9	Mill Rd., Clyde.	17	M8	Mingulay Cres. G22	22	W8
Merchant La. G1	36	W13	Mill St. G40	52	X14	Mingulay Pl. G22	22	X8
Clyde St.			Mill St. G73	53	Y16	Mingulay St. G22	22	W8
Merchants Clo., John.	42	B14	Mill St., Pais.	46	K14	Minmoir Rd. G53	48	N16
Church St.			Mill Vennel, Renf.	18	N10	Minstrel Rd. G13	7	Q7
Merchiston St. G32	38	AA12	*High St.*			Minto Av. G73	65	Z18
Merkland Ct. G11	34	S11	Millands Av. G72	68	FF19	Minto Cres. G52	33	R13
Vine St.			Millar St., Pais.	30	K13	Minto St. G52	33	R13
Merkland St. G11	34	S11	Millar Ter. G73	53	Y15	Mireton St. G22	21	V9
Merksworth Way, Pais.	30	J12	Millarbank St. G21	22	X10	Mirrlees Dr. G12	20	T10
Mosslands Rd.			Millarston Av., Pais.	45	H14	Mirrlees La. G12	20	T10
Merlewood Av. G71	69	HH18	Millarston Dr., Pais.	45	H14	*Redlands Rd.*		
Merlin Way, Pais.	31	L12	Millbeg Cres. G33	39	DD13	Mitchell Av. G72	67	DD17
Merlinford Av., Renf.	18	N10	Millbeg Pl. G33	39	DD13	Mitchell Av., Renf.	31	L11
Merlinford Cres., Renf.	18	N10	Millbrae Ct. G42	51	U16	Mitchell Dr. G73	65	Y17
Merlinford Dr., Renf.	18	N10	*Millbrae Rd.*			Mitchell La. G1	35	V12
Merlinford Way, Renf.	18	N10	Millbrae Cres. G42	51	U16	*Buchanan St.*		
Merrick Gdns. G51	34	S13	Millbrae Cres., Clyde.	17	M8	Mitchell Rd. G67	71	PP3
Merrick Ter. G71	57	HH16	Millbrae Rd. G42	51	U16	Mitchell St. G1	35	V12
Merrick Way G73	65	Y18	Millbrix Av. G14	18	P9	Mitchell St., Coat.	57	HH14
Merryburn Av. G46	62	T17	Millburn Av. G73	65	Y17	Mitchellhill Rd. G45	64	X19
Merrycrest Av. G46	62	T18	Millburn Av., Clyde.	18	N8	Mitchison Rd. G67	71	PP2
Merrycroft Av. G46	62	T18	Millburn Av., Renf.	18	N10	Mitre Ct. G11	19	R10
Merryland Pl. G51	34	T12	Millburn Dr., Renf.	17	M10	*Mitre Rd.*		
Merryland St. G51	34	S12	Millburn Rd., Renf.	17	M10	Mitre La. G14	19	R10
Merrylee Cres. G46	62	T18	Millburn St. G21	37	Y11	Mitre La. W. G14	19	R10
Merrylee Pk. Av. G46	62	T18	Millburn Way, Renf.	18	N10	*Mitre La.*		

126

Street	No.	Grid
Mitre Rd. G11	19	R10
Mitre Rd. G14	19	R10
Moat Av. G13	19	Q8
Mochrum Rd. G43	63	U17
Moffat Pl. G72	68	FF19
Moffat St. G5	52	W14
Mogarth Av., Pais.	45	H16
Amochrie Rd.		
Moidart Av., Renf.	17	L10
Moidart Ct. G78	59	M17
Moidart Cres. G52	33	R13
Moidart Rd.		
Moidart Pl. G52	33	R13
Moidart Rd.		
Moidart Rd. G52	33	R13
Moir La. G1	36	W13
Moir St.		
Moir St. G1	36	W13
Molendinar St. G1	36	W13
Mollinsburn St. G21	22	X10
Monach Rd. G33	39	CC12
Monachie Gdns. G64	11	Z7
Muirhead Way		
Monart Pl. G20	21	U10
Caithness St.		
Moncrieff Av. G66	13	CC5
Moncrieff Gdns. G66	13	CC5
Moncrieff Pl. G4	35	V11
North Woodside Rd.		
Moncrieff St. G4	35	V11
Braid Sq.		
Moncur St. G40	36	X13
Moness Dr. G52	49	R14
Monica Gdns. G53	61	Q19
Monifieth Av. G52	49	Q14
Monikie Gdns. G64	11	Z7
Muirhead Way		
Monkcastle Dr. G72	66	BB17
Monkland Av. G66	13	CC5
Monkland Vw. G71	57	HH15
Lincoln Av.		
Monkland Vw. Cres. G69	41	HH13
Monksbridge Av. G13	7	Q7
Monkscroft Av. G11	20	S10
Monkscroft Ct. G11	34	S11
Monkscroft Gdns. G11	20	S10
Monkscroft Av.		
Monkton Dr. G15	6	P7
Monmouth Av. G12	20	S9
Monreith Av. G61	7	Q7
Monreith Rd. G43	62	T17
Monreith Rd. E. G44	63	V17
Monroe Dr. G71	57	GG15
Monroe Pl. G71	57	GG15
Montague La. G12	20	S10
Montague St. G4	35	U11
Montague Ter. G12	20	S10
Hyndland Rd.		
Montclair Pl., Pais.	28	E13
Monteith Dr. G76	63	V19
Monteith Pl. G40	36	X13
Monteith Row G40	36	X13
Monteith Row La. G40	36	X13
Monteith Pl.		
Montford Av. G44	52	W16
Montford Av. G73	52	W16
Montgomerie Gdns. G14	19	Q10
Lennox Av.		
Montgomery Av., Pais.	31	L12
Montgomery Dr. G46	62	T19
Montgomery Dr., John.	42	B14
Meadside Av.		
Montgomery La. G42	51	V16
Somerville Dr.		
Montgomery Rd., Pais.	31	L12
Montgomery St. G40	52	X14
London Rd.		
Montgomery St. G72	67	DD17
Mill Rd.		
Montrave St. G52	49	Q14
Montrave St. G73	53	Z15
Montreal Ho., Clyde.	4	J5
Perth Cres.		
Montron Dr. G15	6	• P7
Moraine Av.		
Montrose Av. G32	54	BB15
Montrose Av. G52	32	N12
Montrose Gdns. G72	68	FF19
Montrose Pl., Pais.	28	E13
Montrose Rd., Pais.	45	G16
Montrose St. G1	36	W12
Montrose St. G4	36	W12
Montrose St., Clyde.	5	L7
Montrose Ter. G64	23	Z8
Monymusk Gdns. G64	11	Z7
Monymusk Pl. G15	6	N5
Moodies Ct. G1	36	W13
Osborne St.		
Moodiesburn St. G33	37	Z11
Moorburn Av. G46	62	S18
Moore Dr. G61	7	R6
Moore St. G31	37	Y13
Gallowgate		
Moorehouse Av., Pais.	45	H15
Moorfoot G64	11	Z7
Moorfoot Av. G46	62	S18
Moorfoot Av., Pais.	46	J15
Moorfoot St. G32	38	AA13
Moorhouse Av. G13	18	N9
Moorhouse St. G78	59	M19
Moorpark Av. G52	32	N13
Moorpark Av. G69	26	FF8
Moorpark Dr. G52	32	P13
Moorpark Pl. G52	32	N13
Moorpark Sq., Renf.	31	L11
Morag Av. G72	68	FF19
Moraine Av. G15	6	P7
Moraine Circ. G15	6	P7
Moraine Dr. G15	6	P7
Moraine Pl. G15	6	P7
Moraine Dr.		
Morar Av., Clyde.	5	L6
Morar Ct. G67	70	LL4
Morar Ct., Clyde.	5	L6
Morar Cres. G64	10	X7
Morar Cres., Clyde.	5	L6
Morar Dr. G61	8	S6
Morar Dr. G67	70	LL4
Morar Dr. G73	65	Y18
Morar Dr., Clyde.	5	L6
Morar Dr., Pais.	45	H15
Morar Dr.	28	E13
(Linwood), Pais.		
Morar Pl., Clyde.	5	L6
Morar Pl., Renf.	17	L10
Morar Rd. G52	33	R13
Morar Rd., Clyde.	5	L6
Morar Ter. G71	57	HH16
Morar Ter. G73	65	Z18
Moravia Av. G71	69	HH18
Moray Gdns. G68	71	PP1
Moray Gdns. G71	57	GG16
Moray Gate G71	69	GG18
Moray Pl. G41	51	U15
Moray Pl. G64	11	Z7
Moray Pl., Pais.	28	E13
Mordaunt St. G40	53	Y14
Moredun Cres. G32	39	CC12
Moredun Dr., Pais.	45	H15
Moredun Rd., Pais.	45	H15
Moredun St. G32	39	CC12
Morefield Rd. G51	33	Q12
Morgan Ms. G42	51	V14
Morion Rd. G13	19	Q8
Morley St. G42	51	V16
Morna Pl. G14	33	R11
Victoria Pk. Dr. S.		
Morningside St. G33	37	Z12
Morrin Path G21	22	X10
Crichton St.		
Morrin Sq. G4	36	X12
Collins St.		
Morrin St. G21	22	X10
Morris Pl. G40	36	X13
Morrison Quad., Clyde.	6	N7
Morrison St. G5	35	V13
Morrison St., Clyde.	4	K5
Morrisons Ct. G2	35	V12
Argyle St.		
Morriston Cres., Renf.	32	N11
Morriston Pk. Dr. G72	54	BB16
Morriston St. G72	66	BB17
Mortimer St. G20	21	U10
Hotspur St.		
Morton Gdns. G41	50	T15
Morven Av. G64	11	Z7
Morven Av. G72	68	FF19
Morven Av., Pais.	46	J16
Morven Dr., Pais.	28	E13
Morven Gdns. G71	57	GG16
Morven Rd. G61	7	R5
Morven Rd. G72	66	AA18
Morven St. G52	33	R13
Mosesfield St. G21	22	X9
Mosesfield Ter. G21	22	X9
Balgrayhill Rd.		
Moss Av., Pais.	28	E13
Moss Dr. G78	59	L17
Moss Heights Av. G52	33	Q13
Moss Knowe G67	71	QQ3
Moss Path G69	55	DD14
Castle St.		
Moss Rd. G51	33	Q12
Moss Rd. G66	13	CC5
Moss Rd. G67	71	QQ2
Moss Rd. G69	26	FF8
Moss Sq. G33	38	BB11
Moss St., Pais.	30	K13
Moss-side Rd. G41	50	T15
Mossbank Dr. G33	24	AA10
Mosscastle Rd. G33	39	CC11
Mossend La. G33	39	CC12
Mossend Rd., Pais.	30	J12
Mosslands Rd.		
Mossend St. G33	39	CC12
Mossgiel Av. G73	65	Y17
Mossgiel Dr., Clyde.	5	M6
Mossgiel Gdns. G71	57	GG16
Mossgiel Pl. G73	65	Y17
Mossgiel Rd. G43	62	T17
Mossgiel Rd. G67	71	PP3
Mossgiel Ter. G72	68	FF19
Mossland Rd. G52	32	N12
Mosslands Rd., Pais.	30	J12
Mossneuk Dr., Pais.	46	J16
Mosspark Av. G52	49	R14
Mosspark Boul. G52	49	R14
Mosspark Dr. G52	49	Q14
Mosspark La. G52	49	R15
Mosspark Dr.		
Mosspark Oval G52	49	R14
Mosspark Sq. G52	49	R14
Mossvale Cres. G33	39	CC11
Mossvale La., Pais.	30	J13
Mossvale Path G33	25	CC10
Mossvale Rd. G33	24	BB10
Mossvale Sq. G33	39	CC11
Mossvale St., Pais.	30	J12
Mossvale Ter. G69	15	HH6
Mossvale Wk. G33	39	CC11
Mossvale Way G33	39	CC11
Mossview Cotts. G69	26	FF9
Mossview Quad. G52	33	Q13
Mossview Rd. G33	25	DD9
Mote Hill Rd., Pais.	31	L13
Moulin Circ. G52	48	P14
Moulin Pl. G52	48	P14
Moulin Rd. G52	48	P14
Moulin Ter. G52	48	P14
Mount Annan Dr. G44	51	V16
Mount Harriet Av. G33	25	DD9
Mount Harriet Dr. G33	25	CC9
Mount St. G20	21	U10
Mount Stuart St. G41	51	U16
Mount Vernon Av. G32	55	DD14
Mountainblue St. G31	37	Y13
Mountblow Ho., Clyde.	4	J5
Melbourne Av.		
Mountblow Rd., Clyde.	4	K5

128

Newfield Sq. G53	60	P17
Newhall St. G40	52	X14
Newhaven Rd. G33	38	BB12
Newhaven St. G32	38	BB12
Newhills Rd. G33	39	DD12
Newington St. G32	38	AA13
Newlands Gdns., John.	44	F15
Renshaw Rd.		
Newlands Rd. G43	63	U17
Newlands Rd. G44	63	V17
Newlands Rd. G71	57	GG16
Newlandsfield Rd. G43	50	T16
Newluce Dr. G32	55	CC14
Newmains Rd., Renf.	31	L11
Newmill Rd. G21	23	Z9
Newnham Rd., Pais.	48	N14
Newpark Cres. G72	54	BB16
Newshot Ct., Clyde.	17	M8
Clydeholm Ter.		
Newshot Dr., Ersk.	4	J7
Newstead Gdns. G23	9	U7
Newton Av. G72	67	CC17
Newton Av. G78	59	M19
Newton Av., John.	45	G14
Newton Av., Pais.	31	L12
Newton Brae G72	67	DD17
Newton Dr. G71	57	HH16
Newton Dr., John.	45	G14
Newton Fm. Rd. G72	55	DD16
Newton Pl. G3	35	U11
Newton Rd. G66	13	DD6
Newton Sta. Rd. G72	67	DD17
Newton St., Pais.	46	J14
Newton Ter. G3	35	U12
Sauchiehall St.		
Newton Ter. La. G3	35	U11
Elderslie St.		
Newtongrange Av. G32	54	BB15
Newtongrange Gdns. G32	54	BB15
Newtyle Pl. G64	11	Z7
Newtyle Rd., Pais.	47	M14
Nicholas St. G1	36	W12
Nicholson Ct. G33	25	CC9
Nicholson La. G5	35	V13
Nicholson St.		
Nicholson St. G5	35	V13
Niddrie Rd. G42	51	U15
Niddrie Sq. G42	51	U15
Niddry St., Pais.	30	K13
Nigel Gdns. G41	50	T15
Nigg Pl. G34	40	EE12
Nightingale Pl., John.	43	C16
Nimmo Dr. G51	33	R12
Nisbet St. G31	37	Z13
Nith Av., Pais.	45	G15
Nith Dr., Renf.	32	N11
Nith Pl., John.	43	C16
Nith St. G33	37	Z11
Nithsdale Cres. G61	7	Q5
Nithsdale Dr. G41	51	U15
Nithsdale Pl. G41	51	U14
Shields Rd.		
Nithsdale Rd. G41	50	S14
Nithsdale St. G41	51	U15
Nitshill Rd. G46	61	Q18
Nitshill Rd. G53	60	N17
Niven St. G20	20	T9
Noldrum Av. G32	55	CC16
Noldrum Gdns. G32	55	CC16
Norbreck Dr. G46	62	T18
Norby Rd. G11	19	R10
Norfield Dr. G44	51	V16
Norfolk Ct. G5	35	V13
Norfolk Cres. G64	10	X6
Norfolk La. G5	35	V13
Norfolk St.		
Norfolk St. G5	35	V13
Norham St. G41	51	U15
Norman St. G40	52	X14
Norse La. N. G14	19	Q10
Ormiston Av.		
Norse La. S. G14	19	Q10
Verona Av.		

Norse Rd. G14	19	Q10
North Av. G72	66	AA17
North Av., Clyde.	5	L7
North Bk. Pl., Clyde.	17	M8
North Bk. St.		
North Bk. St., Clyde.	17	M8
North Berwick Av. G68	70	NN1
North Berwick Gdns. G68	70	NN1
North Berwick Av.		
North Brae Pl. G13	18	P8
North British Rd. G71	69	GG17
North Canalbank St. G4	36	W11
North Carbrain Rd. G67	70	NN4
North Claremont St. G3	35	U11
North Corsebar Av., Pais.	46	J15
North Ct. La. G1	36	W12
Buchanan St.		
North Cft. St., Pais.	30	K13
North Deanpark Av. G71	69	HH18
North Douglas St., Clyde.	17	M8
North Dr. G1	36	W13
North Dr., Pais.	28	E13
North Elgin St., Clyde.	17	M8
North Erskine Pk. G61	7	Q5
North Frederick St. G1	36	W12
North Gardner St. G11	20	S10
North Gower St. G51	34	T13
North Gra. Rd. G61	7	R5
North Greenhill Rd., Pais.	30	J12
North Hanover Pl. G4	36	W11
North Hanover St. G1	36	W12
North Iverton Pk. Rd.,	44	E14
John.		
North Lo. Rd., Renf.	17	M10
North Moraine La. G15	7	Q7
Moraine Av.		
North Pk. Av. G46	61	R18
North Pl. G3	35	U12
North St.		
North Portland St. G1	36	W12
North Queen St. G2	36	W12
George Sq.		
North Rd., John.	43	D15
North Spiers Wf. G4	35	V11
North St. G3	35	U12
North St., Clyde.	5	L7
Dumbarton Rd.		
North St., Pais.	30	K13
North Vw. G61	7	Q7
North Wallace St. G4	36	W11
North Way G72	68	FF19
North Woodside Rd. G20	21	U10
Northampton Dr. G12	20	S9
Northampton La. G12	20	S9
Northampton Dr.		
Northbank Av. G72	67	CC17
Northbank St. G72	67	CC17
Northcroft Rd. G21	22	X10
Northcroft Rd. G69	15	GG7
Northgate Quad. G21	23	Z8
Northgate Rd. G21	23	Z8
Northinch St. G14	33	Q11
Northland Dr. G14	19	Q9
Northland La. G14	19	Q10
Northland Dr.		
Northmuir Rd. G15	6	P6
Northpark St. G20	21	U10
Northpark Ter. G12	21	U10
Hamilton Dr.		
Northumberland St. G20	21	U10
Norval St. G11	34	S11
Norwich Dr. G12	20	S9
Norwood G61	7	R6
Norwood Dr. G46	62	S19
Norwood Ter. G12	35	U11
Southpark Av.		
Norwood Ter. G71	57	HH16
Nottingham Av. G12	20	S9
Nottingham La. G12	20	S9
Northampton Dr.		
Novar Dr. G12	20	S10
Novar Gdns. G64	10	X7
Numrow Ct., Clyde.	4	K5

Nuneaton St. G40	53	Y14
Nurseries Rd. G69	39	DD13
Nursery La. G41	51	U15
Nursery St. G41	51	U15
Pollokshaws Rd.		
Nursery St. La. G41	51	U15
Nithsdale Dr.		
Nutberry Ct. G42	51	V15

O

Oak Cres. G69	56	EE14
Oak Dr. G66	12	BB5
Oak Dr. G72	67	CC18
Oak Pk. G64	11	Y7
Oak Rd., Clyde.	4	K5
Oak Rd., Pais.	47	L15
Oak St. G2	35	V12
Cadogan St.		
Oakbank Dr. G78	60	N19
Oakbank La. G20	21	V10
Oakbank Ter. G20	21	V10
Oakdene Av. G71	57	HH16
Oakfield Av. G12	35	U11
Oakfield Ter. G12	35	U11
Oakfield Av.		
Oakhill Av. G69	55	DD14
Oakley Dr. G44	63	U18
Oakley Ter. G31	36	X12
Oaks, The, John.	43	C15
Oakshaw Sch. Brae, Pais.	30	J13
Oakshaw St., Pais.	30	J13
Oakshawhead, Pais.	30	J13
Oakwood Av., Pais.	45	H15
Oatfield St. G21	23	Y10
Oban Ct. G20	21	U10
Oban Dr. G20	21	U10
Observatory La. G12	20	T10
Observatory Rd.		
Observatory Rd. G12	20	T10
Ochil Dr. G78	59	M19
Ochil Dr., Pais.	46	K16
Ochil Pl. G32	54	BB14
Ochil Rd. G64	11	Z7
Ochil Rd., Renf.	31	L11
Ochil St. G32	54	BB14
Ochil Vw. G71	57	HH16
Ochiltree Av. G13	19	R8
Ogilvie Pl. G31	54	AA14
Ogilvie St. G31	53	Z14
Old Bothwell Rd. G71	69	HH19
Old Castle Rd. G44	63	V17
Old Dalmarnock Rd. G40	52	X14
Old Dalnottar Rd. G60	4	J5
Old Dumbarton Rd. G3	34	T11
Old Edinburgh Rd. G71	57	GG15
Old Gartcosh Rd. G69	27	GG9
Old Glasgow Rd. G71	56	FF16
Old Govan Rd., Renf.	18	N10
Old Greenock Rd., Renf.	16	J8
Old Manse Rd. G32	39	CC13
Old Mill Rd.	69	HH19
(Bothwell) G71		
Old Mill Rd.	69	GG17
(Uddingston) G71		
Old Mill Rd. G72	67	CC17
Old Mill Rd., Clyde.	5	L5
Old Renfrew Rd., Renf.	32	P11
Old Rd., John.	44	F14
Old Roundknowe Rd. G71	56	FF15
Old Rutherglen Rd. G5	52	W14
Old Shettleston Rd. G32	38	AA13
Old Sneddon St., Pais.	30	K13
Old St., Clyde.	4	K5
Old Wd. Rd. G69	56	EE14
Old Wynd G1	36	W13
Oldhall Rd., Pais.	31	M13
Olifard Av. G71	69	HH18
Oliphant Cres., Pais.	45	G16
Olive St. G33	23	Z10
Olrig Ter. G41	51	U14
Shields Rd.		
Olympia St. G40	36	X13

O'Neil Av. G64	23	Y8
Onslow Dr. G31	37	Y12
Onslow Rd., Clyde.	5	M7
Onslow Sq. G31	37	Y12
Onslow Dr.		
Oran Gdns. G20	21	U9
Oran Gate G20	21	U10
Oran Pl. G20	21	U9
Oran St. G20	21	U9
Orbiston Gdns. G32	38	BB13
Balintore St.		
Orcades Dr. G44	63	V18
Orchard Av. G71	69	HH19
Orchard Ct. G32	54	BB16
Orchard Ct. G46	62	S18
Orchard Dr. G46	62	S18
Orchard Dr. G73	52	X16
Orchard Gro. G46	62	S18
Orchard Pk. G46	62	T18
Orchard Pk. Av. G46	62	S18
Orchard Sq., Pais.	46	K14
Orchard St. G69	55	DD14
Orchard St., Pais.	46	K14
Orchard St., Renf.	17	M10
Orchardfield G66	13	DD6
Orchy Ct., Clyde.	5	M5
Orchy Cres. G61	7	Q7
Orchy Cres., Pais.	45	G15
Orchy Dr. G76	63	U19
Orchy Gdns. G76	63	U19
Orchy St. G44	63	V17
Oregon Pl. G5	52	W14
Orion Way G72	66	BB17
Orkney Pl. G51	34	S12
Orkney St.		
Orkney St. G51	34	S12
Orleans Av. G14	19	R10
Orleans La. G14	19	R10
Ormiston Av. G14	19	Q10
Ormiston La. G14	19	Q10
Ormiston Av.		
Ormiston La. S. G14	19	Q10
Ormiston Av.		
Ormonde Av. G44	63	U18
Ormonde Ct. G44	63	U18
Ormonde Cres. G44	63	U18
Ormonde Dr. G44	63	U18
Ornsay St. G22	22	W8
Oronsay Cres. G61	8	S6
Orr Pl. G40	36	X13
Orr Sq., Pais.	30	K13
Orr St. G40	36	X13
Orr St., Pais.	30	K13
Orton St. G51	34	S13
Orwell St. G21	22	X10
Osborn Ter. G51	34	S13
Copland Rd.		
Osborne St. G1	36	W13
Osborne St., Clyde.	5	L6
Osborne Vill. G44	63	V17
Holmhead Rd.		
Osprey Dr. G71	57	HH16
Ossian Av., Pais.	32	N13
Auchmannoch Av.		
Ossian Rd. G43	63	U17
Oswald La. G1	35	V13
Oswald St.		
Oswald St. G1	35	V13
Otago La. G12	35	U11
Otago St.		
Otago La. N. G12	35	U11
Otago St.		
Otago St. G12	35	U11
Ottawa Cres., Clyde.	4	J6
Otter La. G11	34	S11
Castlebank St.		
Otterburn Dr. G46	62	T19
Otterswick Pl. G33	39	CC11
Oval, The G76	63	U19
Overbrae Pl. G15	6	N5
Overdale Av. G42	51	U16
Overdale Gdns. G42	51	U16
Overdale St. G42	51	U16

Overdale Vills. G42	51	U16
Overdale St.		
Overlea Av. G73	65	Z17
Overnewton Pl. G3	34	T12
Kelvinhaugh St.		
Overnewton Sq. G3	34	T12
Overnewton St. G3	34	T11
Overton Cres., John.	44	E14
Overton Rd. G72	67	CC18
Overton Rd., John.	44	E15
Overton St. G72	67	CC18
Overtoun Ct., Clyde.	4	K6
Dunswin Av.		
Overtoun Dr. G73	53	Y16
Overtoun Dr., Clyde.	4	K6
Overtoun Rd., Clyde.	4	K6
Overtown Av. G53	60	P17
Overtown St. G31	37	Y13
Overwood Dr. G44	64	W17
Oxford Dr., Pais.	28	E13
Oxford La. G5	35	V13
Oxford Rd., Renf.	17	M10
Oxford St. G5	35	V13
Oxton Dr. G52	32	P13
P		
Paisley Ct. G78	59	L18
Paisley Rd.		
Paisley Rd. G5	35	U13
Paisley Rd. G78	59	L18
Paisley Rd., Renf.	31	L11
Paisley Rd. W. G51	34	S13
Paisley Rd. W. G52	48	P14
Palace St. G31	53	Z14
Paladin Av. G13	19	Q8
Palermo St. G21	22	X10
Palladium Pl. G14	19	Q10
Palmer Av. G13	7	Q7
Palmerston Pl. G3	34	T12
Kelvinhaugh St.		
Palmerston Pl., John.	43	C16
Pandora Way G71	57	HH16
Hillcrest Rd.		
Panmure St. G20	21	V10
Park Av. G3	35	U11
Park Av. G64	11	Y6
Park Av. G78	59	L19
Park Av., John.	44	F15
Park Av., Pais.	46	J15
Park Brae, Ersk.	16	J8
Park Dr.		
Park Circ. G3	35	U11
Park Circ. La. G3	35	U11
Lynedoch Pl.		
Park Circ. Pl. G3	35	U11
Park Ct. G46	62	S19
Park Ct. G64	11	Y6
Park Ct., Clyde.	4	K6
Little Holm		
Park Cres. G61	6	P5
Park Cres. G64	11	Y6
Park Cres., Renf.	16	J8
Park Dr. G3	35	U11
Park Dr. G73	53	Y16
Park Dr., Ersk.	16	J8
Park Gdns. G3	35	U11
Park Gdns., John.	42	B14
Park Gdns. La. G3	35	U11
Clifton St.		
Park Gate G3	35	U11
Park Gro., Ersk.	16	J8
Park Holdings, Ersk.	16	J8
Park Inch, Ersk.	16	J8
Park La. G40	36	X13
Park La., Pais.	30	K13
Netherhill Rd.		
Park Pl. G20	20	T8
Fingal St.		
Park Quad. G3	35	U11
Park Ridge, Ersk.	16	J8
Park Dr.		
Park Rd. G4	35	U11

Park Rd. G46	62	T19
Park Rd. G64	11	Y7
Park Rd. (Baillieston) G69	41	GG13
Park Rd. (Chryston) G69	26	FF8
Park Rd., Clyde.	4	K6
Park Rd., John.	43	D15
Park Rd., Pais.	46	J15
Park Rd., Renf.	16	J8
Park St. S. G3	35	U11
Park Ter. G3	35	U11
Park Ter. G42	51	U15
Queens Dr.		
Park Ter. G46	62	T19
Park Top, Ersk.	16	J8
Park Vw., John.	42	B14
Park Vw., Pais.	46	J15
Park Way G67	71	PP2
Park Winding, Ersk.	16	J8
Parkburn Av. G66	13	CC5
Parker St. G14	33	R11
Parkgrove Av. G46	62	T18
Parkgrove Ct. G46	62	T18
Parkgrove Ter. G3	35	U11
Parkgrove Ter. La. G3	35	U12
Derby St.		
Parkhall Rd., Clyde.	4	K6
Parkhall Ter., Clyde.	4	K5
Parkhead Cross G31	37	Z13
Parkhill Dr. G73	53	Y16
Parkhill Rd. G43	50	T16
Parkholm La. G5	35	U13
Paisley Rd.		
Parkhouse Path G53	60	P18
Parkhouse Rd. G53	60	N18
Parkhouse Rd. G78	60	N18
Parklands Rd. G44	63	U18
Parklea G64	10	X6
Midcroft		
Parkneuk Rd. G43	62	T18
Parksail, Ersk.	16	J8
Parksail Dr., Ersk.	16	J8
Parkvale Av., Ersk.	16	J8
Parkvale Cres., Ersk.	16	J8
Parkvale Av.		
Parkvale Dr., Ersk.	16	J8
Parkvale Av.		
Parkvale Gdns., Ersk.	16	J8
Parkvale Av.		
Parkvale Pl., Ersk.	16	J8
Parkvale Av.		
Parkvale Way, Ersk.	16	J8
Parkvale Av.		
Parkview Av. G66	13	CC5
Parkview Ct. G66	13	CC5
Parkview Dr. G33	25	DD9
Parliament Rd. G21	36	X12
Parnie St. G1	36	W13
Parson St. G4	36	X12
Parsonage Row G1	36	W12
Parsonage Sq. G4	36	W12
Partick Bri. St. G11	34	T11
Partickhill Av. G11	20	S10
Partickhill Ct. G11	20	S10
Partickhill Av.		
Partickhill Rd. G11	20	S10
Paterson St. G5	35	V13
Pathead Gdns. G33	24	AA9
Patna St. G40	53	Y14
Paton St. G31	37	Y12
Patrick St., Pais.	46	K14
Patterton Dr. G78	59	M19
Pattison St., Clyde.	4	K6
Payne St. G4	36	W11
Peacock Av., Pais.	45	G15
Peacock Dr.		
Peacock Dr., Pais.	45	G14
Pearce St. G51	34	S12
Pearson Dr., Renf.	31	M11
Pearson Pl., Pais.	28	E13
Peat Pl. G53	60	P17
Peat Rd. G53	60	P17
Peathill Av. G69	26	EE8
Peathill St. G21	22	W10

Quay Rd. G73	53	Y15	
Quay Rd. N. G73	53	Y15	
Quebec Ho., Clyde.	4	J5	
Perth Cres.			
Queen Arc. G2	35	V12	
Renfrew St.			
Queen Elizabeth Av. G52	32	N12	
Queen Elizabeth Sq. G5	52	W14	
Queen Margaret Ct. G20	21	U10	
Queen Margaret Cres. G12	21	U10	
Hamilton Dr.			
Queen Margaret Dr. G12	20	T10	
Queen Margaret Dr. G20	21	U10	
Queen Margaret Rd. G20	21	U10	
Queen Mary Av. G42	51	V15	
Queen Mary Av., Clyde.	5	M7	
Queen Mary St. G40	52	X14	
Queen Sq. G41	51	U15	
Queen St. G1	36	W12	
Queen St. G73	53	Y16	
Queen St., Pais.	46	J14	
Queen St., Renf.	17	M10	
Queen Victoria Dr. G13	19	Q10	
Queen Victoria Dr. G14	19	Q10	
Queen Victoria Gate G13	19	Q9	
Queenbank Av. G69	27	GG8	
Queens Av. G72	66	BB17	
Queens Cres. G4	35	V11	
Queens Cres. G69	41	GG13	
Queens Cross G20	21	U10	
Queens Dr. G42	51	U15	
Queens Dr. G68	70	NN1	
Queens Dr. La. G42	51	V15	
Queens Gdns. G12	20	T10	
Victoria Cres. Rd.			
Queens Pk. Av. G42	51	V15	
Queens Pl. G12	20	T10	
Queens Rd., John.	44	F15	
Queensborough Gdns.	20	S10	
G12			
Queensby Av. G69	40	EE13	
Queensby Rd.			
Queensby Dr. G69	40	EE13	
Queensby Rd.			
Queensby Pl. G69	40	EE13	
Queensby Rd.			
Queensby Rd. G69	40	EE13	
Queensferry St. G5	52	X15	
Rosebery St.			
Queenshill St. G21	22	X10	
Queensland Ct. G52	33	Q13	
Queensland Dr. G52	33	Q13	
Queensland Gdns. G52	33	Q13	
Queensland La. E. G52	32	P13	
Kingsland Dr.			
Queensland La. W. G52	33	Q13	
Queensland Dr.			
Queenslie Ind. Est. G33	39	CC12	
Queenslie St. G33	37	Z11	
Quendale Dr. G32	54	AA14	
Quentin St. G41	51	U15	
Quinton Gdns. G69	40	EE13	

R

Raasay Dr., Pais.	46	J16	
Raasay Pl. G22	22	W8	
Raasay St. G22	22	W8	
Rachan St. G34	40	FF11	
Radnor St. G3	35	U12	
Argyle St.			
Radnor St., Clyde.	5	L6	
Raeberry St. G20	21	U10	
Raeswood Dr. G53	48	N16	
Raeswood Gdns. G53	48	N16	
Raeswood Pl. G53	48	N16	
Raeswood Rd. G53	48	N16	
Raglan St. G4	35	V11	
Raith Av. G44	64	W18	
Raithburn Av. G45	64	W18	
Raithburn Rd. G45	64	W18	
Ralston Av. G52	48	N14	
Ralston Av., Pais.	48	N14	

Ralston Ct. G52	48	N14	
Ralston Dr. G52	48	N14	
Ralston Path G52	48	N14	
Ralston Dr.			
Ralston Pl. G52	48	N14	
Ralston Rd. G61	7	R5	
Ralston Rd. G78	59	M19	
Ralston St., Pais.	47	L14	
Seedhill Rd.			
Ram St. G32	38	AA13	
Rampart Av. G13	18	P8	
Ramsay Av., John.	43	D15	
Ramsay Cres., John.	42	B15	
Ramsay Pl., John.	43	D15	
Ramsay St., Clyde.	4	K6	
Ranald Gdns. G73	65	Z18	
Randolph Av. G76	63	U19	
Randolph Dr. G76	63	U19	
Randolph Gdns. G76	63	U19	
Randolph Rd. G11	19	R10	
Randolph Ter. G72	66	BB17	
Hamilton Rd.			
Ranfurley Rd. G52	32	N13	
Rankine Pl., John.	43	D14	
Rankine St.			
Rankine St., John.	43	D14	
Rankines La., Renf.	17	M10	
Manse St.			
Rannoch Av. G64	11	Y7	
Rannoch Dr. G61	8	S7	
Rannoch Dr., Renf.	17	M10	
Rannoch Gdns. G64	11	Y7	
Rannoch Pl., Pais.	47	L14	
Rannoch Rd. G71	57	GG15	
Rannoch Rd., John.	43	D15	
Rannoch St. G44	63	V17	
Ranza Pl. G33	23	Z10	
Raploch Av. G14	18	P10	
Ratford St. G51	34	S12	
Rathlin St. G51	34	S12	
Ratho Dr. G21	22	X9	
Rattray St. G32	54	AA14	
Ravel Row G31	37	Z13	
Ravel Wynd G71	57	HH15	
Ravelston Rd. G61	7	R7	
Ravelston St. G32	37	Z13	
Ravens Ct. G64	22	X8	
Lennox Cres.			
Ravenscliffe Dr. G46	62	S18	
Ravenscraig Av., Pais.	46	J15	
Ravenscraig Dr. G53	60	P17	
Ravenscraig Ter. G53	61	Q17	
Ravenshall Rd. G41	50	T16	
Ravenstone Rd. G46	62	T18	
Ravenswood Av., Pais.	45	G16	
Ravenswood Dr. G41	50	T15	
Ravenswood Rd. G69	40	FF13	
Rayne Pl. G15	6	P6	
Red Rd. G21	23	Y10	
Red Rd. Ct. G21	23	Y10	
Redan St. G40	36	X13	
Redcastle Sq. G33	39	CC11	
Redford St. G33	37	Z12	
Redgate Pl. G14	18	P10	
Redhill Rd. G68	70	MM2	
Redhurst Cres., Pais.	45	H16	
Redhurst Way, Pais.	45	H16	
Redlands La. G12	20	T10	
Kirklee Rd.			
Redlands Rd. G12	20	T10	
Redlands Ter. G12	20	T10	
Redlands Ter. La. G12	20	T10	
Julian Av.			
Redlawood Pl. G72	68	EE17	
Redlawood Rd.			
Redlawood Rd. G72	68	EE17	
Redmoss St. G22	21	V9	
Rednock St. G22	22	W10	
Redpath Dr. G52	32	P13	
Redwood Dr. G21	23	Y10	
Foresthall Dr.			
Redwood Pl. G66	12	BB5	
Redwood Rd. G67	71	QQ3	

Reelick Av. G13	18	N8	
Reelick Quad. G13	18	N8	
Reen Pl. G71	69	HH18	
Regent Moray St. G3	34	T11	
Regent Pk. Sq. G41	51	U15	
Regent Pk. Ter. G41	51	U15	
Pollokshaws Rd.			
Regent Pl., Clyde.	4	K6	
Regent Sq. G66	13	CC6	
Regent St., Clyde.	4	K6	
Regent St., Pais.	31	L13	
Regents Gate G71	69	GG18	
Regwood St. G41	50	T16	
Reid Av. G61	8	S5	
Reid Av., Pais.	28	E13	
Reid Pl. G40	52	X14	
Muslin St.			
Reid St. G40	52	X14	
Reid St. G73	53	Y16	
Reidhouse St. G21	22	X10	
Muir St.			
Reids Row G69	56	FF14	
Reidvale St. G31	36	X13	
Renfield St. G2	35	V12	
Renfield St., Renf.	17	M10	
Renfrew Ct. G2	35	V12	
Renfrew St.			
Renfrew La. G2	35	V12	
Renfield St.			
Renfrew Rd. G51	32	P11	
Renfrew Rd., Pais.	30	K13	
Renfrew Rd., Renf.	32	P11	
Renfrew St. G2	35	V11	
Renfrew St. G3	35	V11	
Rennies Rd., Renf.	16	J8	
Renshaw Dr. G52	32	P13	
Renshaw Rd., John.	44	F15	
Renton St. G4	36	W11	
Renwick St. G41	35	U13	
Scotland St.			
Residdl Rd. G33	25	DD9	
Reston Dr. G52	32	P13	
Reuther Av. G73	53	Y16	
Revoch Dr. G13	18	P8	
Rhannan Rd. G44	63	V17	
Rhannan Ter. G44	63	V17	
Rhindhouse Pl. G69	40	FF13	
Rhindhouse Rd. G69	40	FF13	
Swinton Av.			
Rhindmuir Av. G69	40	FF13	
Rhindmuir Dr. G69	40	FF13	
Rhindmuir Gro. G69	40	FF13	
Rhindmuir Rd. G69	40	FF13	
Rhindmuir Vw. G69	40	FF13	
Rhinds St., Coat.	57	HH14	
Rhinsdale Cres. G69	40	FF13	
Rhumhor Gdns., John.	43	C15	
Rhymer St. G21	36	X11	
Rhymie Rd. G32	55	CC14	
Rhynie Dr. G51	34	S13	
Riccarton St. G42	52	W15	
Riccartsbar Av., Pais.	46	J14	
Richard St. G2	35	V12	
Cadogan St.			
Richard St., Renf.	17	M10	
Richmond Ct. G73	53	Z16	
Richmond Dr. G64	11	Y6	
Richmond Dr. G72	66	AA17	
Richmond Dr. G73	53	Z16	
Richmond Dr., Pais.	28	E12	
Richmond Gdns. G69	14	EE7	
Richmond Gro. G73	53	Z16	
Richmond Pl. G73	53	Z16	
Richmond St. G1	36	W12	
Richmond St., Clyde.	5	M7	
Riddell St., Clyde.	5	M6	
Riddon Av. G13	18	N8	
Riddon Av., Clyde.	18	N8	
Riddon Pl. G13	18	N8	
Riddrie Cres. G33	38	AA12	
Riddrie Knowes G33	38	AA12	
Riddrie Ter. G33	23	Z10	
Provanmill Rd.			

Name	Page	Grid
Riddrievale Ct. G33	38	AA11
Riddrievale St. G33	38	AA11
Rigby St. G32	37	Z13
Rigg Pl. G33	39	DD12
Rigghead Av. G67	71	PP1
Riggside Rd. G33	39	CC11
Riggside St. G33	39	CC11
Riglands Way, Renf.	17	M10
Riglaw Pl. G13	18	P8
Rigmuir Rd. G51	33	Q13
Rimsdale St. G40	37	Y13
Ringford St. G21	22	X10
Ripon Dr. G12	20	S9
Risk St. G40	36	X13
Risk St., Clyde.	4	K6
Ristol Rd. G13	19	Q9
Anniesland Rd.		
Ritchie Cres., John.	44	F14
Ritchie Pk., John.	44	E14
Ritchie St. G5	51	V14
River Rd. G32	54	BB16
River Rd. G41	51	U16
Mansionhouse Rd.		
Riverbank St. G43	50	T16
Riverford Rd. G43	50	T16
Riverford Rd. G73	53	Z15
Riversdale Cotts. G14	18	N9
Dumbarton Rd.		
Riversdale La. G14	18	N9
Dumbarton Rd.		
Riverside Ct. G44	63	V19
Riverside Pk. G44	63	V19
Linnpark Av.		
Riverside Pl. G72	67	DD17
Riverside Rd. G43	51	U16
Riverview Av. G5	35	V13
West St.		
Riverview Dr. G5	35	V13
Riverview Gdns. G5	35	V13
Riverview Pl. G5	35	V13
Roaden Av., Pais.	45	G16
Roaden Rd., Pais.	45	G16
Roadside G67	71	PP1
Robb St. G21	22	X10
Robert Burns Av., Clyde.	5	M6
Robert St. G51	34	S12
Robert Templeton Dr. G72	67	CC17
Roberton Av. G41	50	T15
Roberts St., Clyde.	4	K6
Robertson La. G2	35	V12
Robertson St.		
Robertson St. G2	35	V12
Robertson St. G78	59	L18
Robertson Ter. G69	40	FF13
Edinburgh Rd.		
Robin Way G32	55	CC16
Robroyston Av. G33	24	AA10
Robroyston Rd. G33	24	AA9
Robroyston Rd. G64	12	AA7
Robslee Cres. G46	62	S18
Robslee Dr. G46	62	S18
Robslee Rd. G46	62	S19
Robson Gro. G42	51	V15
Rock Dr., John.	42	B15
Rock St. G4	21	V10
Rockall Dr. G44	64	W18
Rockbank Pl. G40	37	Y13
Broad St.		
Rockbank Pl., Clyde.	5	L5
Glasgow Rd.		
Rockbank St. G40	37	Y13
Rockcliffe St. G40	52	X14
Rockfield Pl. G21	23	Z9
Rockfield Rd. G21	23	Z9
Rockmount Av. G46	62	S18
Rockmount Av. G78	59	M19
Rockwell Av., Pais.	46	J16
Rodger Dr. G73	65	Y17
Rodger Pl. G73	65	Y17
Rodil Av. G44	64	W18
Rodney St. G4	35	V11
Roebank Dr. G78	59	M19
Roebank St. G31	37	Y12
Roffey Pk. Rd., Pais.	31	M13
Rogart St. G40	36	X13
Rogerfield Rd. G69	40	FF12
Rokeby Ter. G12	20	T10
Great Western Rd.		
Roman Av. G15	6	P7
Roman Av. G61	7	R5
Roman Ct. G61	7	R5
Roman Dr. G61	7	R5
Roman Gdns. G61	7	R5
Roman Rd. G61	7	R5
Roman Rd., Clyde.	5	L5
Romney Av. G44	64	W17
Rona St. G21	37	Y11
Rona Ter. G72	66	AA18
Ronaldsay Dr. G64	11	Z7
Ronaldsay Pl. G67	70	MM4
Ronaldsay St. G22	22	W8
Ronay St. G22	22	W8
Rooksdell Av., Pais.	46	J15
Rose Cotts. G13	19	R9
Crow Rd.		
Rose Dale G64	23	Y8
Rose Knowe Rd. G42	52	X15
Rose St. G3	35	V12
Rosebank Av. G72	69	GG19
Rosebank Dr. G72	67	CC18
Rosebank Ter. G69	57	GG14
Rosebery Pl., Clyde.	5	L7
Miller St.		
Rosebery St. G5	52	X15
Rosedale Av., Pais.	44	F16
Rosedale Dr. G69	56	EE14
Rosedale Gdns. G20	20	T8
Rosefield Gdns. G71	57	GG16
Roselea Gdns. G13	19	R8
Roselea Pl. G72	68	FF19
Rosemont Meadows G71	69	GG19
Rosemount G68	70	NN1
Rosemount Cres. G21	37	Y11
Rosemount St. G21	36	X11
Rosemount Ter. G51	35	U13
Paisley Rd. W.		
Rosevale Rd. G61	7	R6
Rosevale St. G11	34	S11
Rosewood Av., Pais.	45	H15
Rosewood St. G13	19	R8
Roslea Dr. G31	37	Y12
Roslyn Dr. G69	41	GG13
Rosneath St. G51	34	S12
Ross Av., Renf.	31	L11
Ross Hall Pl., Renf.	17	M10
Ross St. G40	36	W13
Ross St., Pais.	47	L14
Rossendale Rd. G41	50	T16
Rossendale Rd. G43	50	T16
Rosshall Av., Pais.	47	M14
Rosshill Av. G52	32	N13
Rosshill Rd. G52	32	N13
Rossie Cres. G64	23	Z8
Rosslea Dr. G46	62	T19
Rosslyn Av. G73	53	Y16
Rosslyn Rd. G61	6	P5
Rosslyn Ter. G12	20	T10
Horslethill Rd.		
Rostan Rd. G43	62	T17
Rosyth Rd. G5	52	X15
Rosyth St. G5	52	X15
Rotherwick Dr., Pais.	48	N14
Rotherwood Av. G13	7	Q7
Rotherwood Av., Pais.	45	G16
Rotherwood La. G13	7	Q7
Rotherwood Av.		
Rotherwood Pl. G13	19	Q8
Rothes Dr. G23	8	T7
Rothes Pl. G23	8	T7
Rottenrow G4	36	W12
Rottenrow E. G4	36	W12
Roual Ter., Pais.	31	L13
Greenlaw Av.		
Rouken Glen Pk. G46	61	R19
Rouken Glen Rd. G46	61	R19
Roukenburn St. G46	61	R18
Roundhill Dr., John.	45	G14
Rowallan Gdns. G11	20	S10
Rowallan La. G11	20	S10
Churchill Dr.		
Rowallan La. E. G11	20	S10
Churchill Dr.		
Rowallan Rd. G46	61	R19
Rowallan Ter. G33	24	BB10
Rowan Av., Renf.	17	M10
Rowan Cres. G66	13	CC5
Rowan Dr., Clyde.	4	K6
Rowan Gdns. G41	50	S14
Rowan Gdns. G71	69	HH18
Rowan Gate, Pais.	46	K15
Rowan Pl. (Cambuslang) G72	67	CC17
Caledonian Circuit		
Rowan Rd. G41	50	S14
Rowan Rd. G67	71	QQ2
Rowan Rd., Pais.	28	E12
Rowan St., Pais.	46	K15
Rowand Av. G46	62	T19
Rowandale Av. G69	56	EE14
Rowanlea Av., Pais.	45	G16
Rowanlea Dr. G46	62	T18
Rowanpark Dr. G78	59	L17
Rowans, The G64	10	X7
Rowans Gdns. G71	69	HH18
Rowantree Av. G73	65	Y17
Rowantree Gdns. G73	65	Y17
Rowantree Rd., John.	43	D15
Rowchester St. G40	37	Y13
Rowena Av. G13	7	Q7
Roxburgh La. G12	20	T10
Saltoun St.		
Roxburgh Rd., Pais.	44	F16
Roxburgh St. G12	20	T10
Roy St. G21	22	W10
Royal Bk. Pl. G1	36	W12
Buchanan St.		
Royal Cres. G3	35	U11
Royal Cres. G42	51	V15
Royal Ex. Bldgs. G1	36	W12
Royal Ex. Sq.		
Royal Ex. Ct. G1	36	W12
Queen St.		
Royal Ex. Sq. G1	36	W12
Royal Inch Cres., Renf.	17	M9
Campbell St.		
Royal Inch Ter., Renf.	17	M9
Royal Ter. G3	35	U11
Royal Ter. G42	51	V15
Queens Dr.		
Royal Ter. La. G3	35	U11
North Claremont St.		
Royston Rd. G21	36	X11
Royston Rd. G33	24	AA10
Royston Sq. G21	36	X11
Roystonhill G21	36	X11
Rozelle Av. G15	6	P6
Rubislaw Dr. G61	7	R6
Ruby St. G40	53	Y14
Ruchazie Pl. G33	38	AA12
Ruchazie Rd. G32	38	AA13
Ruchazie Rd. G33	38	AA13
Ruchill Pl. G20	21	U9
Ruchill St. G20	21	U9
Ruel St. G44	51	V16
Rufflees Av. G78	59	M18
Rugby Av. G13	18	P8
Rullion Pl. G33	38	AA12
Rumford St. G40	52	X14
Rupert St. G4	35	U11
Rushyhill St. G21	23	Y10
Cockmuir St.		
Ruskin Pl. G12	20	T10
Great Western Rd.		
Ruskin Sq. G64	11	Y7
Ruskin Ter. G12	21	U10
Ruskin Ter. G73	53	Y15
Russell Cres. G69	56	FF14
Russell Dr. G61	7	R5
Russell Gdns. G71	57	HH16

Street	Page	Grid
Russell St. G11	34	S11
Vine St.		
Russell St., John.	44	E14
Russell St., Pais.	30	J12
Rutherford Av. G66	14	EE5
Chryston Rd.		
Rutherford La. G2	35	V12
Hope St.		
Rutherglen Bri. G40	52	X14
Rutherglen Bri. G42	52	X14
Rutherglen Rd. G5	36	W13
Rutherglen Rd. G73	52	W14
Ruthven Av. G46	62	T19
Ruthven La. G12	20	T10
Byres Rd.		
Ruthven Pl. G64	23	Z8
Ruthven St. G12	20	T10
Rutland Cres. G51	35	U13
Rutland La. G51	35	U13
Govan Rd.		
Rutland Pl. G51	35	U13
Ryan Rd. G64	11	Y7
Ryan Way G73	65	Z18
Rye Cres. G21	23	Z9
Rye Rd. G21	23	Z9
Rye Way, Pais.	45	G15
Ryebank Rd. G21	23	Z9
Ryecroft Dr. G69	40	EE13
Ryedale Pl. G15	6	P6
Ryefield Av., John.	43	C15
Ryefield Pl., John.	43	C15
Ryefield Rd. G21	23	Y9
Ryehill Gdns. G21	23	Z9
Ryehill Pl. G21	23	Z9
Ryehill Rd. G21	23	Z9
Ryemount Rd. G21	23	Z9
Ryeside Rd. G21	23	Y9
Rylands Dr. G32	55	DD14
Rylands Gdns. G32	55	DD14
Rylees Cres. G52	32	N12
Rylees Pl. G52	32	N13
Rylees Rd. G52	32	N13
Ryvra Rd. G13	19	Q9

S

Street	Page	Grid
Sackville Av. G13	19	R9
Sackville La. G13	19	R9
Sackville Av.		
Saddell Rd. G15	6	P6
St. Abbs Dr., Pais.	45	H15
St. Andrews Av. G64	10	X7
St. Andrew's Av. G71	69	HH19
St. Andrews Cres. G41	51	U14
St. Andrews Cres., Pais.	30	J11
St. Andrews Cross G41	51	V14
St. Andrews Dr. G41	50	T15
St. Andrews Dr., Pais.	30	K11
St. Andrews Dr. W., Pais.	30	J11
St. Andrews La. G1	36	W13
Gallowgate		
St. Andrews Rd. G41	51	U14
St. Andrews Rd., Renf.	31	M11
St. Andrews Sq. G1	36	W13
St. Andrews St. G1	36	W13
St. Anns Dr. G46	62	T19
St. Blanes Dr. G73	64	X17
St. Boswell's Cres., Pais.	45	H15
St. Brides Rd. G43	50	T16
St. Brides Way G71	69	HH18
St. Catherines Rd. G46	62	T19
St. Clair Av. G46	62	T18
St. Clair St. G20	35	U11
Woodside Rd.		
St. Conval Pl. G43	50	S16
Shawbridge St.		
St. Cyrus Gdns. G64	11	Z7
St. Cyrus Rd. G64	11	Y7
St. Enoch Sq. G1	35	V13
St. Enoch Wynd G2	35	V12
Argyle St.		
St. Fillans Rd. G33	25	CC9
St. Georges Cross G3	35	V11
St. Georges Pl. G20	35	V11
St. Georges Rd.		
St. Georges Rd. G3	35	V11
St. Germains G61	7	R6
St. Helena Cres., Clyde.	5	M5
St. Ives Rd. G69	15	GG6
St. James Av., Pais.	29	H12
St. James Pl., Pais.	30	K13
Love St.		
St. James Rd. G4	36	W12
St. James St., Pais.	30	K13
St. Johns Ct. G41	51	U14
St. Johns Quad. G41	51	U14
St. Johns Rd. G41	51	U14
St. Johns Ter. G12	35	U11
Southpark Av.		
St. Josephs Pl. G40	36	X13
Abercromby St.		
St. Kenneth Dr. G51	33	R12
St. Kilda Dr. G14	19	R10
St. Leonards Dr. G46	62	T18
St. Margarets Pl. G1	36	W13
Bridgegate		
St. Mark Gdns. G32	38	AA13
St. Mark St.		
St. Mark St. G32	38	AA13
St. Marnock St. G40	37	Y13
St. Mary's Gdns. G78	59	M19
St. Marys La. G2	35	V12
West Nile St.		
St. Marys Rd. G64	10	X7
St. Mirren St., Pais.	46	K14
St. Monance St. G21	22	X9
St. Mungo Av. G4	36	W12
St. Mungo Pl. G4	36	W12
St. Mungo St. G64	22	X8
St. Mungo's Rd. G67	70	NN3
St. Ninian St. G5	36	W13
St. Ninians Cres., Pais.	46	K15
Rowan La.		
St. Ninians Rd., Pais.	46	K15
St. Peters La. G2	35	V12
Blythswood St.		
St. Peters St. G4	35	V11
St. Rollox Brae G21	36	X11
St. Ronans Dr. G41	50	T15
St. Ronans Dr. G73	65	Z17
St. Stephens Av. G73	65	Z18
St. Stephens Cres. G73	66	AA18
St. Valleyfield St. G21	22	X10
Ayr St.		
St. Vincent Cres. G3	34	T12
St. Vincent Cres. La. G3	35	U12
Corunna St.		
St. Vincent La. G2	35	V12
Hope St.		
St. Vincent Pl. G1	36	W12
St. Vincent St. G2	35	U12
St. Vincent St. G3	35	U12
St. Vincent Ter. G3	35	U12
Salamanca St. G31	37	Z13
Salen St. G52	33	R13
Salisbury Pl. G12	20	T10
Great Western Rd.		
Salisbury Pl., Clyde.	4	K5
Salisbury St. G5	51	V14
Salkeld St. G5	51	V14
Salmona St. G22	21	V10
Saltaire Av. G71	69	HH17
Salterland Rd. G53	60	N17
Salterland Rd. G78	60	N17
Saltmarket G1	36	W13
Saltmarket Pl. G1	36	W13
King St.		
Saltoun Gdns. G12	20	T10
Roxburgh St.		
Saltoun La. G12	20	T10
Ruthven St.		
Saltoun St. G12	20	T10
Salvia St. G72	66	AA17
Sanda St. G20	21	U10
Sandaig Rd. G33	39	DD13
Sandbank Av. G20	20	T9
Sandbank Dr. G20	20	T8
Sandbank St. G20	20	T9
Sandbank Ter. G20	20	T8
Sandeman St. G11	33	R11
Sandend Rd. G53	48	P16
Sanderling Pl., John.	43	C16
Sandfield St. G20	21	U9
Maryhill Rd.		
Sandford Gdns. G69	56	EE14
Scott St.		
Sandgate Av. G32	55	CC14
Sandhaven Rd. G53	48	P16
Sandholes, Pais.	46	J14
Sandholm Pl. G14	18	N9
Sandholm Ter. G14	18	N9
Sandiefauld St. G5	52	W14
Sandielands Av., Ersk.	16	J8
Sandilands St. G32	38	BB13
Sandmill St. G21	37	Y11
Sandra Rd. G64	11	Z7
Sandringham Dr., John.	44	E16
Glamis Av.		
Sandringham La. G12	20	T10
Kersland St.		
Sandwood Cres. G52	32	P13
Sandwood Rd.		
Sandwood Path G52	32	P13
Sandwood Rd. G52	32	P13
Sandy La. G11	34	S11
Crawford St.		
Sandy Rd. G11	34	S11
Sandy Rd., Renf.	31	M11
Sandyford Pl. G3	35	U12
Sandyford Pl. La. G3	35	U11
Elderslie St.		
Sandyford Rd., Pais.	31	L12
Sandyford St. G3	34	T12
Sandyhills Cres. G32	54	BB14
Sandyhills Dr. G32	54	BB14
Sandyhills Gro. G32	55	CC15
Hamilton Rd.		
Sandyhills Pl. G32	54	BB14
Sandyhills Rd. G32	54	BB14
Sandyknowes Rd. G67	71	PP4
Sanguhar Gdns. G72	68	EE19
Sannox Gdns. G31	37	Y12
Saracen Gdns. G22	22	W9
Saracen Head La. G1	36	W13
Gallowgate		
Saracen St. G22	22	W10
Sardinia La. G12	20	T10
Great George St.		
Sardinia Ter. G12	20	T10
Cecil St.		
Saucel Lonend, Pais.	46	K14
Saucel St., Pais.	46	K14
Saucelhill Ter., Pais.	46	K14
Sauchenhall Rd. G66	15	GG5
Sauchiehall La. G2	35	V12
Sauchiehall St.		
Sauchiehall St. G2	35	U12
Sauchiehall St. G3	35	U12
Saughs Av. G33	24	AA9
Saughs Dr. G33	24	AA9
Saughs Gate G33	24	AA9
Saughs Pl. G33	24	AA9
Saughs Rd. G33	24	AA9
Saughton St. G32	38	AA12
Savoy Arc. G40	52	X14
Main St.		
Savoy St. G40	52	X14
Sawfield Pl. G4	35	V11
Garscube Rd.		
Sawmill Rd. G11	33	R11
South St.		
Sawmillfield St. G4	35	V11
Saxon Rd. G13	19	Q8
Scadlock Rd., Pais.	29	H13
Scalpay Pl. G22	22	W8
Scalpay St. G22	22	W8
Scapa St. G23	21	U8
Scapa St. G40	53	Y14
Springfield Rd.		

Smith St. G14	33	R11	Southerness Dr. G68	71	PP1	Springhill Rd. G78	59	L19
Smith Ter. G73	53	Y15	*Dornoch Way*			Springkell Av. G41	50	T14
Smithhills St., Pais.	30	K13	Southesk Av. G64	10	X7	Springkell Dr. G41	50	S14
Smiths La., Pais.	30	K13	Southesk Gdns. G64	10	X6	Springkell Gdns. G41	50	T15
Smithy Ends G67	71	PP1	Southfield Av., Pais.	46	K16	Springkell Gate G41	50	T15
Smithycroft Rd. G33	38	AA11	Southfield Cres. G53	49	Q16	Springside Pl. G15	6	P6
Snaefell Av. G73	65	Z18	Southfield Rd. G68	70	MM3	Springvale Ter. G21	22	X10
Snaefell Cres. G73	65	Z17	Southinch Av. G14	18	N9	*Hillkirk Pl.*		
Society St. G31	37	Y13	Southinch La. G14	18	N9	Spruce Av., John.	44	E15
Soho St. G40	37	Y13	*Tweedvale Av.*			Spruce Dr. G66	12	BB5
Sollas Pl. G13	18	N8	Southlea Av. G46	62	S18	Spruce Rd. G67	71	QQ2
Solway Pl. G69	26	FF8	Southloch St. G21	22	X10	Spruce St. G22	22	W9
Solway Rd. G64	11	Z7	Southmuir Pl. G20	20	T9	Spynie Pl. G64	11	Z7
Solway St. G40	52	X15	Southpark Av. G12	34	T11	Squire St. G14	33	R11
* Somerford Rd. G61	7	R7	Southpark La. G12	21	U10	Staffa Av., Renf.	31	M11
Somerled Av., Pais.	31	L11	*Glasgow St.*			Staffa Dr., Pais.	46	K16
Somerset Pl. G3	35	U11	Southpark Ter. G12	35	U11	Staffa Rd. G72	66	AA18
Somerset Pl. Meuse G3	35	U11	*Southpark Av.*			Staffa St. G31	37	Y12
Elderslie St.			Southview Ct. G64	22	X8	Staffa Ter. G72	66	AA18
Somervell St. G72	66	AA17	Southview Dr. G61	7	Q5	Staffin Dr. G23	8	T7
Somerville Dr. G42	51	V16	Southview Pl. G69	27	GG9	Staffin St. G23	9	U7
Somerville St., Clyde.	5	L7	Southview Ter. G64	22	X8	Stafford St. G4	36	W11
Sorby St. G31	37	Z13	Southwold Rd., Pais.	32	N13	Stag St. G51	34	T12
Sorn St. G40	53	Y14	Southwood Dr. G44	64	W17	Stair St. G20	21	U10
Souter La., Clyde.	5	M6	Spateston Rd., John.	43	C16	Stamford St. G31	37	Y13
South Annandale St. G42	51	V15	Spean St. G44	51	V16	Stamford St. G40	37	Y13
South Av., Clyde.	5	L7	Speirs Rd., John.	44	E14	Stamperland Gdns. G76	63	U19
South Av., Pais.	46	K16	Speirshall Clo. G14	18	N9	Stanalane St. G46	61	R18
South Av., Renf.	17	M10	Speirshall Ter. G14	18	N9	Standburn Rd. G21	23	Z8
South Bk. St., Clyde.	17	M8	Spence St. G20	20	T8	Stanely Av., Pais.	45	H15
South Brook St., Clyde.	4	K6	Spencer Dr., Pais.	44	F16	Stanely Ct., Pais.	45	H15
South Campbell St.	46	K14	Spencer St. G13	19	R8	Stanely Cres., Pais.	45	H16
Pais.			Spencer St., Clyde.	5	L6	Stanely Dr., Pais.	46	J15
South Carbrain Rd. G67	71	PP4	Spey Av., Pais.	45	G15	Stanely Rd., Pais.	46	J15
South Chester St. G32	38	BB13	Spey Dr., Renf.	32	N11	Stanford St., Clyde.	5	M7
South Cotts. G14	33	R11	*Almond Av.*			Stanhope Dr. G73	65	Z17
Curle St.			Spey Pl., John.	43	C16	Stanley Dr. G64	11	Y6
South Cft. St., Pais.	30	K13	Spey Rd. G61	7	Q7	Stanley Pl. G72	68	FF19
Lawn St.			Spey St. G33	38	AA12	Stanley St. G41	35	U13
South Crosshill Rd. G64	11	Y7	Spiers Gro. G46	61	R18	Stanley St. La. G41	35	U13
South Deanpark Av. G71	69	HH19	Spiers Pl., Pais.	28	E12	*Milnpark St.*		
South Douglas St., Clyde.	17	M8	Spiers Rd. G61	8	S6	Stanmore Rd. G42	51	V16
South Dr., Pais.	28	E13	Spiersbridge Av. G46	61	R18	Stark Av., Clyde.	4	K5
South Elgin Pl., Clyde.	17	M8	Spiersbridge La. G46	61	R18	Startpoint St. G33	38	BB12
South Elgin St.			Spiersbridge Rd. G46	61	R19	Station Rd. G20	20	T8
South Elgin St., Clyde.	17	M8	Spiersbridge Ter. G46	61	R18	Station Rd. G33	24	BB9
South Erskine Pk. G61	7	Q5	Spiersfield Gdns., Pais.	46	K14	Station Rd.	25	CC9
South Ex. Ct. G1	36	W12	Spindlehowe Rd. G71	69	GG17	(Stepps) G33		
Queen St.			Spinner Gdns., Pais.	45	H14	Station Rd. G46	62	T18
South Frederick St. G1	36	W12	Spinners Row, John.	43	C15	*Fenwick Rd.*		
South Hill Av. G73	65	Z17	Spittal Rd. G73	64	X18	Station Rd. G61	7	Q6
South Moraine La. G15	7	Q7	Spittal Ter. G72	68	EE19	Station Rd.	56	FF14
Moraine Av.			Spoutmouth G1	36	W13	(Baillieston) G69		
South Muirhead Rd. G67	71	PP3	Spring La. G5	52	W14	Station Rd.	26	FF9
South Pk. Dr., Pais.	46	K15	*Lawmoor St.*			(Muirhead) G69		
South Portland St. G5	35	V13	Springbank Rd., Pais.	30	J12	Station Rd.	69	HH19
South Scott St. G69	56	EE14	Springbank St. G20	21	U10	(Bothwell) G71		
South Spiers Wf. G4	35	V11	Springbank Ter., Pais.	30	J12	Station Rd.	69	GG17
South St. G11	33	Q11	Springboig Av. G32	39	CC13	(Uddingston) G71		
South St. G14	18	P10	Springboig Rd. G32	39	CC12	Station Rd. G72	69	GG19
South Vesalius St. G32	38	BB13	Springburn Rd. G21	22	X9	Station Rd., John.	42	B15
South Vw. G66	13	CC7	Springburn Rd. G64	22	X9	Station Rd., Pais.	45	H14
Gadloch Av.			Springburn Way G21	22	X10	Station Rd., Renf.	17	M10
South Vw. G72	68	FF19	Springcroft Av. G69	40	EE13	Station Way G71	69	HH17
South Vw., Clyde.	4	K6	Springcroft Dr. G69	40	EE13	*Mansefield Dr.*		
South Wardpark Ct. G67	71	QQ1	Springcroft Rd. G69	40	EE13	Station Wynd, John.	42	B15
South Wardpark Pl. G67	71	QQ1	Springfield Av. G64	23	Y8	Steel St. G1	36	W13
South William St., John.	43	D15	Springfield Av. G71	69	GG17	Steeple St., John.	42	B14
South Woodside Rd. G4	35	U11	Springfield Av., Pais.	47	M14	Stenton St. G32	38	AA12
South Woodside Rd. G20	21	U10	Springfield Ct. G1	36	W12	Stepford Path G33	40	EE12
Southampton Dr. G12	20	S9	Springfield Cres. G64	23	Y8	*Stepford Rd.*		
Southbank St. G31	37	Z13	Springfield Cres. G71	69	GG17	Stepford Pl. G33	39	DD12
Sorby St.			Springfield Dr. G78	60	N19	Stepford Rd. G33	39	DD12
Southbar Av. G13	18	P8	Springfield Pk., John.	44	E15	Stephen Cres. G69	39	DD13
Southbrae Dr. G13	19	Q9	Springfield Pk. Rd. G73	65	Z17	Stephenson St. G52	32	N12
Southbrae La. G13	19	R9	Springfield Quay G5	35	U13	Stepps Rd. G33	39	CC11
Milner Rd.			Springfield Rd. G31	53	Z14	Stepps Rd. G66	13	DD7
Southcroft Rd. G73	52	X15	Springfield Rd. G40	53	Y14	Steppshill Terr. G33	25	CC9
Southcroft St. G51	34	S12	Springfield Rd. G64	11	Y7	Stevbrae G66	13	DD5
Southdeen Av. G15	6	P6	Springfield Rd. G67	71	PP2	Stevenson St. G40	36	X13
Southdeen Rd. G15	6	P6	Springfield Rd. G78	23	Y8	Stevenson St., Clyde.	4	K6
Southend Rd., Clyde.	5	L5	Springhill Gdns. G41	51	U15	Stevenson St., Pais.	46	K14
Southern Av. G73	65	Y17	Springhill Rd. G69	39	DD13	Stewart Av., Renf.	31	L11

Stewart Ct. G78	59	M18
Stewart St.		
Stewart Dr. G69	41	HH13
Coatbridge Rd.		
Stewart Dr., Clyde.	5	L5
Stewart Rd., Pais.	46	K16
Stewart St. G4	35	V11
Stewart St. G78	59	M18
Stewart St., Clyde.	4	K6
Stewarton Dr. G72	66	AA17
Stewarton Rd. G46	61	R19
Stewartville St. G11	34	S11
Stirling Av. G61	7	R7
Stirling Dr. G61	7	Q5
Stirling Dr. G64	10	X6
Stirling Dr. G73	65	Y17
Stirling Dr., John.	43	C15
Stirling Dr., Pais.	28	E13
Stirling Fauld Pl. G5	35	V13
Stirling Gdns. G64	10	X6
Stirling Rd. G4	36	W12
Stirling St. G67	71	PP2
Stirling Way, Renf.	31	M11
York Way		
Stirrat St. G20	20	T9
Stirrat St., Pais.	29	H12
Stobcross Rd. G3	35	U12
Stobhill Rd. G21	22	X8
Stobs Dr. G78	59	L17
Stobs Pl. G34	40	FF11
Stock Av., Pais.	46	K15
Stock St., Pais.	46	K15
Stockholm Cres., Pais.	46	K14
Stockwell Pl. G1	36	W13
Stockwell St. G1	36	W13
Stoddard Sq., John.	44	F14
Glenpatrick Rd.		
Stonefield Av. G12	20	T9
Stonefield Av., Pais.	46	K15
Stonefield Cres., Pais.	46	K15
Stonefield Dr., Pais.	46	K15
Stonefield Grn., Pais.	46	K15
Stonelaw Dr. G73	53	Y16
Stonelaw Rd. G73	53	Y16
Stoneside Dr. G43	62	S17
Stoneside Sq. G43	62	S17
Stoney Brae, Pais.	30	K13
Stoneyetts Cotts. G69	15	GG6
Stoneyetts Rd. G69	15	GG7
Stony Brae, Pais.	46	K16
Stonyhurst St. G22	21	V10
Stonylee Rd. G67	71	PP3
Storie St., Pais.	46	K14
Stormyland Way G78	59	M19
Stornoway St. G22	22	W8
Stow Brae, Pais.	46	K14
Stow St., Pais.	46	K14
Strachur St. G22	21	V8
Straiton St. G32	38	AA12
Stranka Av., Pais.	46	J14
Stranraer Dr. G15	7	Q7
Moraine Av.		
Stratford St. G20	21	U9
Strathallan La. G12	34	T11
Highburgh Rd.		
Strathallan Ter. G12	34	T11
Caledon St.		
Strathallon Pl. G73	65	Z18
Ranald Gdns.		
Strathbran St. G31	53	Z14
Strathcarron Pl. G20	20	T9
Glenfinnan Rd.		
Strathcarron Rd., Pais.	47	L15
Strathclyde Dr. G73	53	Y16
Strathclyde Path G71	69	GG13
Strathclyde St. G40	53	Y15
Strathclyde Vw. G71	69	HH19
Strathcona Dr. G13	19	R8
Strathcona Gdns. G13	20	S8
Strathcona Pl. G73	65	Z18
Strathcona St. G13	19	R9
Strathdee Av., Clyde.	5	L5
Strathdee Rd. G44	63	U19

Strathdon Av. G44	63	U19
Strathdon Av., Pais.	46	J15
Strathdon Dr. G44	63	U19
Strathendrick Dr. G44	63	U18
Strathkelvin Retail Pk. G64	11	Z6
Strathmore Av. G72	68	FF19
Strathmore Av., Pais.	47	M14
Strathmore Gdns. G12	35	U11
Gibson St.		
Strathmore Gdns. G73	65	Z18
Strathmore Rd. G22	21	V8
Strathord Pl. G69	15	HH6
Strathord St. G32	54	BB14
Strathtay Av. G44	63	U19
Strathview Gdns. G61	7	Q6
Strathview Gro. G44	63	U19
Strathview Pk. G44	63	U19
Strathy Pl. G20	20	T9
Glenfinnan Rd.		
Strathyre Gdns. G61	8	S5
Strathyre Gdns. G69	15	HH7
Heathfield Av.		
Strathyre St. G41	51	U16
Stratton Dr. G46	62	S19
Strauss Av., Clyde.	6	N7
Stravanan Av. G45	64	W19
Stravanan Rd. G45	64	W19
Stravanan St. G45	64	W19
Strenabey Av. G73	65	Z18
Striven Gdns. G20	21	U10
Stroma St. G21	37	Y11
Stromness St. G5	51	V14
Strone Rd. G33	38	BB12
Stronend St. G22	21	V9
Stronsay Pl. G64	11	Z7
Stronsay St. G21	37	Y11
Stronvar Dr. G14	18	P10
Stronvar La. G14	18	P10
Larchfield Av.		
Strowan Cres. G32	54	BB14
Strowan St. G32	54	BB14
Struan Av. G46	62	S18
Struan Gdns. G44	63	V17
Struan Rd. G44	63	V17
Struie St. G34	40	EE12
Stuart Av. G73	65	Y17
Stuart Dr. G64	22	X8
Succoth St. G13	19	R8
Suffolk St. G40	36	X13
Kent St.		
Sugworth Av. G69	40	EE13
Sumburgh St. G33	38	AA12
Summer St. G40	36	X13
Summerfield Cotts. G14	33	R11
Smith St.		
Summerfield Pl. G40	53	Y14
Ardenlea St.		
Summerfield St. G40	53	Y15
Summerhill Rd. G15	6	P6
Summerlee Rd. G46	61	R18
Summerlee St. G33	39	CC12
Summertown Rd. G51	34	S12
Sunart Av., Renf.	17	L10
Sunart Gdns. G64	11	Y7
Sunart Rd. G52	33	R13
Sunart Rd. G64	11	Y7
Sunningdale Rd. G23	20	T8
Sunningdale Wynd G71	69	GG18
Sunnybank St. G40	53	Y14
Sunnylaw Dr., Pais.	45	H15
Sunnylaw St. G22	21	V10
Sunnyside Av. G71	69	GG17
Sunnyside Dr. G15	6	P7
Sunnyside Dr. G69	41	GG13
Sunnyside Pl. G15	6	P7
Sunnyside Pl. G78	59	L19
Sunnyside Rd., Pais.	46	J15
Surrey La. G5	51	V14
Pollokshaws Rd.		
Sussex St. G41	35	U13
Sutcliffe Rd. G13	19	R8
Sutherland Av. G41	50	T14
Sutherland Dr. G46	62	T19

Sutherland Rd., Clyde.	5	L7
Sutherland St., Pais.	30	J13
Swan La. G4	36	W11
Swan Pl., John.	43	C16
Swan St. G4	36	W11
Swan St., Clyde.	4	K6
Swanston St. G40	53	Y15
Sween Dr. G44	63	V18
Sweethope Pl. G71	69	HH18
Swift Pl., John.	43	C16
Swindon St., Clyde.	4	K6
Swinton Av. G69	40	FF13
Swinton Cres. G69	40	FF13
Swinton Cres., Coat.	57	HH14
Swinton Dr. G52	32	P13
Swinton Gdns. G69	40	FF13
Swinton Av.		
Swinton Pl. G52	32	P13
Swinton Rd. G69	40	EE13
Swinton Vw. G69	40	FF13
Swinton Av.		
Switchback Rd. G61	7	R7
Sword St. G31	36	X13
Swordale Path G34	40	EE12
Swordale Pl.		
Swordale Pl. G34	40	EE12
Sycamore Av. G66	13	CC5
Sycamore Av., John.	44	E15
Sycamore Dr., Clyde.	5	L6
Sydenham La. G12	20	S10
Crown Rd. S.		
Sydenham Rd. G12	20	T10
Sydney Ct. G2	35	V12
Argyle St.		
Sydney St. G31	36	X13
Sydney St., Clyde.	4	J6
Sylvania Way, Clyde.	5	L7
Sylvania Way S., Clyde.	5	L7
Symington Dr., Clyde.	5	L7
Syriam Pl. G21	22	X10
Syriam St.		
Syriam St. G21	22	X10

T

Tabard Pl. G13	19	Q8
Tabard Pl. N. G13	19	Q8
Tabard Rd.		
Tabard Pl. S. G13	19	Q8
Tabard Rd.		
Tabard Rd. G13	19	Q8
Tabernacle La. G72	66	BB17
Tabernacle St. G72	66	BB17
Tain Pl. G34	40	FF12
Tait Av. G78	59	M18
Talbot Dr. G13	18	P9
Talbot Pl. G13	18	P9
Talbot Ter. G13	18	P9
Talbot Ter. G71	57	GG16
Talisman Rd. G13	19	Q9
Talisman Rd., Pais.	45	G16
Talla Rd. G52	32	P13
Tallant Rd. G15	6	P6
Tallant Ter. G15	7	Q6
Tallisman, Clyde.	5	M7
Onslow Dr.		
Tambowie St. G13	19	R8
Tamshill St. G20	21	U9
Tamworth St. G40	37	Y13
Rimsdale St.		
Tanar Av., Renf.	32	N11
Tanar Way, Renf.	32	N11
Tandlehill Rd., John.	42	B15
Tanera Av. G44	64	W18
Tanfield Av. G32	39	CC12
Tanfield Pl. G32	39	CC12
Tanfield Av.		
Tankerland Rd. G44	63	V17
Tanna Dr. G52	49	R14
Tannadice Av. G52	49	Q14
Tannahall Rd., Pais.	29	H13
Tannahall Ter., Pais.	29	H13
Tannahill Cres., John.	43	D15

Street	Map	Grid
Tannahill Rd. G43	63	U17
Tannoch Dr. G67	71	PP4
Tannoch Pl. G67	71	PP4
Tannock St. G22	21	V10
Tantallon Dr., Pais.	45	H15
Tantallon Rd. G41	51	U16
Tantallon Rd. G69	56	EE14
Tanzieknowe Av. G72	66	BB18
Tanzieknowe Dr. G72	66	BB18
Tanzieknowe Pl. G72	66	BB18
Tanzieknowe Rd. G72	66	BB18
Taransay St. G51	34	S12
Tarbert Av. G72	68	FF19
Tarbolton Dr., Clyde.	5	M6
Tarbolton Rd. G43	62	T17
Tarbolton Rd. G67	71	PP3
Tarbolton Sq., Clyde.	5	M6
Tarbolton Dr.		
Tarfside Av. G52	49	Q14
Tarfside Gdns. G52	49	Q14
Tarfside Oval G52	49	Q14
Tarland St. G51	33	R13
Tarras Dr., Renf.	32	N11
Tarras Pl. G72	67	CC17
Tassie St. G41	50	T16
Tattershall Rd. G33	39	CC11
Tavistock Dr. G43	62	T17
Tay Av., Pais.	45	G15
Tay Av., Renf.	18	N10
Tay Cres. G33	38	AA11
Tay Cres. G64	11	Y7
Tay Pl., John.	43	C16
Tay Rd. G61	7	Q7
Tay Rd. G64	11	Y7
Taylor Av., John.	42	A14
Taylor Pl. G4	36	W12
Taylor St. G4	36	W12
Taylor St., Clyde.	17	M8
Taymouth St. G32	54	BB14
Taynish Dr. G44	64	W18
Tealing Av. G52	49	Q14
Tealing Cres. G52	49	Q14
Teasel Av. G53	60	P18
Teith Av., Renf.	32	N11
Teith Dr. G61	7	Q6
Teith Pl. G72	67	CC17
Teith St. G33	38	AA11
Telford Pl. G67	71	PP4
Telford Rd. G67	71	PP4
Templar Av. G13	7	Q7
Temple Gdns. G13	19	R8
Temple Pl. G13	19	R8
Temple Rd. G13	20	S8
Templeland Av. G53	49	Q15
Templeland Rd. G53	49	Q15
Templeton St. G40	36	X13
Tennant Rd., Pais.	29	H13
Tennant St., Renf.	17	M10
Tennyson Dr. G31	54	AA14
Tern Pl., John.	43	C16
Terrace Pl. G72	67	DD17
Terregles Av. G41	50	T15
Terregles Cres. G41	50	T15
Terregles Dr. G41	50	T15
Teviot Av. G64	11	Y6
Teviot Av., Pais.	45	G16
Teviot Cres. G61	7	Q7
Teviot St. G3	34	T12
Teviot Ter. G20	21	U10
Sanda St.		
Teviot Ter., John.	43	C16
Thane Rd. G13	19	Q9
Thanes Gate G71	69	GG17
Castle Gate		
Tharsis St. G21	36	X11
Third Av. G33	24	BB9
Third Av. G44	51	V16
Third Av. G66	13	CC7
Third Av., Renf.	31	M11
Third Gdns. G41	50	S14
Third St. G71	57	GG16
Thirdpart Cres. G13	18	N8
Thistle Bk. G66	13	CC6
Thistle Cotts. G13	19	R9
Crow Rd.		
Thistle St. G5	51	V14
Thistle St., Pais.	46	J15
Thomas Muir Av. G64	23	Y8
Thomas St., Pais.	45	H14
Thomson Av., John.	43	D14
Thomson Dr. G61	7	R5
Thomson Gro. G72	54	BB16
Thomson Pl., Clyde.	5	M5
Thomson St. G31	37	Y13
Thomson St., John.	43	D15
Thomson St., Renf.	31	M11
Thorn Brae, John.	44	E14
Thorn Dr. G61	7	Q5
Thorn Dr. G73	65	Z18
Thorn Rd. G46	62	S17
Thorn Rd. G61	7	Q5
Thorn St. G11	34	S11
Dumbarton Rd.		
Thornbank St. G3	34	T11
Yorkhill Par.		
Thornbridge Av. G12	20	T9
Thornbridge Av. G69	40	EE13
Balcarres Av.		
Thornbridge Av. G69	40	EE13
Bannercross Dr.		
Thornbridge Gdns. G69	40	EE13
Thornbridge Rd. G69	40	EE13
Thorncliffe Gdns. G41	51	U15
Thorncliffe La. G41	51	U14
Thorncroft Dr. G44	64	W18
Thornden Cotts. G14	18	N9
Dumbarton Rd.		
Thornden La. G14	18	N9
Dumbarton Rd.		
Thorndene, John.	44	E14
Thornhill, John.	44	E15
Thornhill Av., John.	44	E15
Thornhill Dr., John.	44	E15
Thornhill Path G31	37	Z13
Grier Path		
Thorniewood Gdns. G71	57	HH16
Thorniewood Rd. G71	57	GG16
Thornlea Dr. G46	62	T18
Thornley Av. G13	18	P9
Thornliebank Rd. G43	62	S17
Thornliebank Rd. G46	62	S18
Thornliebank Rd. (Deaconsbank) G46	61	Q19
Thornly Pk. Av., Pais.	46	K16
Thornly Pk. Dr., Pais.	46	K16
Thornly Pk. Rd., Pais.	46	K16
Thornside Rd., John.	44	E14
Thornton La. G20	21	U8
Thornton St. G20	21	U8
Thorntree Way G71	69	HH18
Thornwood Av. G11	34	S11
Thornwood Av. G66	12	BB5
Thornwood Cres. G11	19	R10
Thornwood Dr.		
Thornwood Dr. G11	33	R11
Thornwood Dr., Pais.	45	H15
Thornwood Gdns. G11	34	S11
Thornwood Pl. G11	20	S10
Thornwood Quad. G11	19	R10
Thornwood Dr.		
Thornwood Rd. G11	33	R11
Thornwood Ter. G11	33	R11
Thornyburn Dr. G69	56	FF14
Thornyburn Pl. G69	56	FF14
Three Ell Rd. G51	34	T12
Govan Rd.		
Threestonehill Av. G32	38	BB13
Thrums Av. G64	11	Z7
Thrums Gdns. G64	11	Z7
Thrush Pl., John.	43	C16
Thrushcraig Cres., Pais.	46	K15
Thurso St. G11	34	T11
Dumbarton Rd.		
Thurston Rd. G52	32	P13
Tibbermore Rd. G11	20	S10
Tillet Oval, Pais.	30	J12
Tillie St. G20	21	U10
Tillycairn Dr. G33	39	CC11
Tillycairn Rd. G33	39	DD11
Tilt St. G33	38	AA11
Tintagel Gdns. G69	15	GG6
Tinto Dr. G78	59	L19
Tinto Rd. G43	62	T17
Tinto Rd. G61	6	P5
Tinto Rd. G64	11	Z7
Fintry Cres.		
Tinto Sq., Renf.	31	L11
Ochil Rd.		
Tinwald Av. G52	32	N13
Tinwald Path G52	32	P13
Tiree Av., Pais.	46	J16
Tiree Av., Renf.	31	M11
Tiree Ct. G67	70	MM4
Tiree Dr. G67	70	MM4
Tiree Gdns. G61	6	P5
Tiree Rd. G67	70	MM4
Tiree St. G21	37	Z11
Tirry Way, Renf.	32	N11
Morriston Cres.		
Titwood Rd. G41	50	T15
Tiverton Av. G32	55	CC14
Tobago Pl. G40	36	X13
Tobago St. G40	36	X13
Tobermory Rd. G73	65	Z18
Todburn Dr., Pais.	46	K16
Todd St. G31	37	Z12
Todholm Rd., Pais.	47	L15
Todholm Ter., Pais.	47	L15
Tofthill Av. G64	10	X7
Tofthill Gdns. G64	10	X7
Toll La. G51	34	T13
Paisley Rd. W.		
Tollcross Rd. G31	37	Z13
Tollcross Rd. G32	37	Z13
Tolsta St. G23	9	U7
Tontine La. G1	36	W13
Bell St.		
Tontine Pl. G73	66	AA18
Toppersfield, John.	43	C16
Torbreck St. G52	33	R13
Torbrex Rd. G67	71	PP3
Torburn Av. G46	62	S18
Tordene Path G68	70	MM2
Torgyle St. G23	8	T7
Tormore St. G51	33	Q13
Tormusk Dr. G45	65	Y18
Tormusk Gdns. G45	65	Y18
Tormusk Rd. G45	65	Y18
Torness St. G11	34	T11
Torogay Pl. G22	22	X8
Torogay St. G22	22	W8
Torogay Ter. G22	22	W8
Toronto Wk. G32	55	CC16
Torphin Cres. G32	38	BB13
Torphin Wk. G32	38	BB13
Torr Rd. G64	11	Z7
Torr St. G22	22	W10
Torran Rd. G33	39	DD12
Torrance Rd. G64	11	Z5
Torrance St. G21	22	X10
Torridon Av. G41	50	S14
Torrin Rd. G23	8	T7
Torrington Av. G46	62	S19
Torrington Cres. G32	55	CC14
Torrisdale St. G42	51	U15
Torryburn Rd. G21	23	Z10
Torwood La. G69	15	HH7
Burnbrae Av.		
Torylgen Rd. G73	52	X16
Toryglen St. G5	52	W15
Toward Ct. G72	69	GG19
Toward Rd. G33	39	CC12
Tower Av. G78	59	M18
Tower Cres., Renf.	31	L11
Tower Dr., Renf.	31	L11
Tower Pl. G20	20	T9
Glenfinnan Dr.		
Tower Pl., John.	44	E15
Tower Rd., John.	43	D15
Tower St. G41	35	U13

Waldemar Rd. G13	19	Q8
Waldo St. G13	19	R8
Walker Ct. G11	34	S11
Walker St.		
Walker Dr., John.	44	E15
Walker Path G71	57	HH15
Walker Sq. G20	20	T8
Bantaskin St.		
Walker St. G11	34	S11
Walker St., Pais.	46	J14
Walkerburn Rd. G52	48	P14
Walkinshaw Cres., Pais.	29	H13
Ferguslie Pk. Av.		
Walkinshaw Rd., Renf.	16	J10
Walkinshaw St. G40	53	Y14
Walkinshaw St., John.	43	D14
Walkinshaw Way, Pais.	30	J12
Broomdyke Way		
Wallace Av., John.	44	F15
Wallace Pl. G72	69	GG19
Wallace Rd., Renf.	31	L11
Wallace St. G5	35	V13
Wallace St. G73	53	Y16
Wallace St., Clyde.	17	L8
Wallace St., Pais.	30	K13
Wallacewell Cres. G21	23	Y9
Wallacewell Pl. G21	23	Y9
Wallacewell Quad. G21	23	Z9
Wallacewell Rd. G21	23	Y9
Wallbrae Rd. G67	71	PP4
Wallneuk, Pais.	30	K13
Incle St.		
Wallneuk Rd., Pais.	30	K13
Walls St. G1	36	W12
Walmer Cres. G51	34	T13
Walmer Ter. G51	34	T13
Paisley Rd. W.		
Walnut Cres. G22	22	W9
Walnut Cres., John.	44	E15
Walnut Dr. G66	12	BB5
Walnut Pl. G22	22	W9
Walnut Rd. G22	22	W9
Walter St. G31	37	Z12
Walton St. G41	51	U16
Walton St. G78	59	M18
Wamba Av. G13	19	R8
Wamba Pl. G13	19	R8
Wandilla Av., Clyde.	5	M7
Warden Rd. G13	19	Q8
Wardhill Rd. G21	23	Y9
Wardhouse Rd., Pais.	46	J16
Wardie Path G33	39	DD12
Wardie Pl. G33	40	EE12
Wardie Rd. G33	40	EE12
Wardie Rd. G34	40	EE12
Wardlaw Av. G73	53	Y16
Wardlaw Dr. G73	53	Y16
Wardlaw Rd. G61	7	R7
Wardpark Rd. G67	71	QQ1
Wardrop St. G51	34	S12
Wardrop St., Pais.	46	K14
Ware Path G34	40	EE12
Ware Rd. G34	39	DD12
Warilda Av., Clyde.	5	M7
Warp La. G3	35	U12
Argyle St.		
Warren St. G42	51	V15
Warriston Cres. G33	37	Z12
Warriston Pl. G32	38	BB12
Warriston St. G33	37	Z12
Warroch St. G3	35	U12
Washington Rd., Pais.	30	K12
Washington St. G3	35	V13
Water Brae, Pais.	46	K14
Forbes Pl.		
Water Rd. G78	59	M18
Water Row G51	34	S12
Waterfoot Av. G53	49	Q16
Waterford Rd. G46	62	S18
Waterloo La. G2	35	V12
Waterloo St.		
Waterloo St. G2	35	V12
Watermill Av. G66	13	CC6
Waterside La., John.	43	C15
Kilbarchan Rd.		
Waterside St. G5	52	W14
Waterside Ter., John.	43	C15
Kilbarchan Rd.		
Watling St. G71	57	GG16
Watson Av. G73	52	X16
Watson Av., Pais.	28	E13
Watson St. G1	36	W13
Watson St. G71	69	GG17
Watt Low Av. G73	64	X17
Watt Rd. G52	32	N12
Watt St. G5	35	U13
Waukglen Av. G53	60	P19
Waukglen Cres. G53	61	Q18
Waukglen Dr. G53	60	P18
Waukglen Gdns. G53	60	P19
Waukglen Path G53	60	P18
Waukglen Dr.		
Waukglen Rd. G53	60	P18
Waulkmill Av. G78	59	M18
Waulkmill St. G46	61	R18
Waverley, Clyde.	5	M7
Onslow Rd.		
Waverley Ct. G71	69	HH19
Waverley Cres. G67	70	MM4
Waverley Dr. G73	53	Z16
Waverley Gdns. G41	51	U15
Waverley Gdns., John.	44	F15
Waverley Rd., Pais.	45	G16
Waverley St. G41	51	U15
Waverley Ter. G31	37	Y13
Whitevale St.		
Waverley Way, Pais.	45	G16
Waverley Rd.		
Weardale La. G33	39	CC12
Weardale St. G33	39	CC12
Weaver La., John.	42	B14
Glentyan Av.		
Weaver St. G4	36	W12
Weaver Ter., Pais.	47	L14
Weavers Av., Pais.	45	H14
Weavers Gate, Pais.	45	H14
Weavers Rd., Pais.	45	H14
Webster St. G40	53	Y14
Webster St., Clyde.	18	N8
Wedderlea Dr. G52	32	P13
Weensmoor Pl. G53	60	P18
Weensmoor Rd. G53	60	P17
Weeple Dr., Pais.	28	E13
Weighhouse Clo., Pais.	46	J14
Weir Av. G78	59	M19
Weir Rd., Pais.	28	E12
Weir St., Pais.	30	K13
Weirwood Av. G69	55	DD14
Weirwood Gdns. G69	55	DD14
Welbeck Rd. G53	60	P17
Welfare Av. G72	67	CC18
Well Grn. G43	50	T16
Well Rd., John.	42	B14
Well St. G40	36	X13
Well St., Pais.	30	J13
Wellbank Pl. G71	69	GG17
Church St.		
Wellbrae Ter. G69	15	GG7
Wellcroft Pl. G5	51	V14
Wellfield Av. G46	62	S18
Wellfield St. G21	22	X10
Wellhouse Cres. G33	39	DD12
Wellhouse Path G34	39	DD12
Wellhouse Rd. G33	39	DD12
Wellington La. G2	35	V12
West Campbell St.		
Wellington Pl., Clyde.	4	J6
Wellington Rd. G64	11	Z6
Wellington St. G2	35	V12
Wellington St., Pais.	30	J13
Caledonia St.		
Wellington St. E. G31	37	Z13
Wellington Way, Renf.	31	M11
Tiree Av.		
Wellmeadow Rd. G43	62	S17
Wellmeadow St., Pais.	46	J14
Wellpark St. G31	36	X12
Wells St., Clyde.	4	K6
Wellshot Dr. G72	66	AA17
Wellshot Rd. G32	54	AA14
Wellside Dr. G72	67	CC18
Wemyss Gdns. G69	56	EE14
Wendur Way, Pais.	30	J12
Abbotsburn Way		
Wenlock Rd., Pais.	46	K15
Wentworth Dr. G23	9	U7
West Av. G33	25	CC9
West Av. G71	69	HH17
West Av., Renf.	17	M10
West Brae, Pais.	46	J14
West Campbell St. G2	35	V12
West Campbell St., Pais.	45	H14
West Chapelton Av. G61	7	R6
West Chapelton Cres. G61	7	R6
West Chapelton Dr. G61	7	R6
West Chapelton La. G61	7	R6
West Chapelton Av.		
West Coats Rd. G72	66	AA18
West Cotts. G69	26	EE10
West Ct., Clyde.	4	K6
Little Holm		
West George La. G2	35	V12
West Campbell St.		
West George St. G2	35	V12
West Graham St. G4	35	V11
West Greenhill Pl. G3	35	U12
West La., Pais.	45	H14
West Lo. Rd., Renf.	17	L10
West Nile St. G1	35	V12
West Princes St. G4	35	U11
West Regent La. G2	35	V12
Renfield St.		
West Regent St. G2	35	V12
West Rd., John.	42	B14
West St. G5	51	V14
West St., Clyde.	18	N8
West St., Pais.	46	J14
West Thomson St., Clyde.	5	L6
West Whitby St. G31	53	Z14
Westbank La. G12	35	U11
Gibson St.		
Westbank Quad. G12	35	U11
Gibson St.		
Westbank Ter. G12	35	U11
Gibson St.		
Westbourne Cres. G61	7	Q5
Westbourne Dr. G61	7	Q5
Westbourne Gdns. La. G12	20	T10
Lorraine Rd.		
Westbourne Gdns. N. G12	20	T10
Westbourne Gdns. S. G12	20	T10
Westbourne Gdns. W. G12	20	T10
Westbourne Rd. G12	20	S10
Westbourne Ter. La. G12	20	S10
Westbourne Rd.		
Westbrae Dr. G14	19	R10
Westburn G72	67	DD17
Westburn Av. G72	67	CC17
Westburn Av., Pais.	29	H13
Westburn Cres. G73	52	X16
Westburn Dr. G72	66	BB17
Westburn Fm. Rd. G72	66	BB17
Westburn Rd. G72	68	EE17
Westclyffe St. G41	51	U15
Westend G61	8	S7
Maryhill Rd.		
Westend Pk. St. G3	35	U11
Wester Cleddens Rd. G64	11	Y7
Wester Common Dr. G22	21	V10
Wester Common Rd. G22	21	V10
Wester Common Ter. G22	21	V10
Wester Rd. G32	55	CC14

Woodhead Rd. G53	60	N17	Woodside Av. G73	53	Z16	Wyvis Quad. G13	18	N8
Woodhead Rd. G69	26	EE9	Woodside Cres. G3	35	U11			
Woodhead Ter. G69	26	EE8	Woodside Cres. G78	59	M19	**Y**		
Woodhill Rd. G21	23	Y9	Woodside Cres., Pais.	46	J14			
Woodhill Rd. G64	11	Y7	*William St.*			Yair Dr. G52	32	P13
Woodholm Av. G44	64	W17	Woodside Pl. G3	35	U11	Yarrow Ct. G72	67	DD17
Woodhouse St. G13	19	R8	Woodside Pl. La. G3	35	U11	Yarrow Gdns. G20	21	U10
Woodilee Cotts. G66	13	DD5	*Elderslie St.*			Yarrow Gdns. La. G20	21	U10
Woodilee Rd. G66	13	DD5	Woodside Rd. G20	21	U10	*Yarrow Gdns.*		
Woodland Av. G69	27	GG8	Woodside Ter. G3	35	U11	Yarrow Rd. G64	11	Y6
Woodland Av., Pais.	46	K16	Woodside Ter. G64	10	W6	Yate St. G31	37	Y13
Woodland Cres. G72	66	BB18	Woodside Ter. La. G3	35	U11	Yetholm St. G14	18	N9
Woodland Vw. G67	71	PP2	*Woodlands Rd.*			Yew Dr. G21	23	Y10
Braehead Rd.			Woodstock Av. G41	50	T15	*Foresthall Dr.*		
Woodland Way G67	71	PP2	Woodstock Av., Pais.	45	G16	Yew Pl., John.	44	E15
Woodlands Av. G71	69	HH18	Woodvale Av. G61	8	S7	Yoker Ferry Rd. G14	18	N9
Woodlands Ct. G46	61	R19	Woodvale Dr., Pais.	29	H13	Yoker Mill Gdns. G13	18	N8
Woodlands Rd.			Woodville St. G51	34	S13	Yoker Mill Rd. G13	18	N8
Woodlands Cres. G46	61	R18	Wordsworth Way G71	69	HH18	Yokerburn Ter., Clyde.	17	M8
Woodlands Cres. G71	69	HH18	Works Av. G72	67	DD17	York Dr. G73	65	Z17
Woodlands Dr. G4 •	35	U11	Wraes Av. G78	59	M18	York La. G2	35	V12 .
Woodlands Gdns. G71	69	GG18	Wraes Vw. G78	58	K19	*York St.*		
Woodlands Gate G3	35	U11	Wren Pl., John.	43	C16	York St. G2	35	V13
Woodlands Gate G46	61	R18	Wright Av. G78	59	L19	York St., Clyde.	5	M7
Woodlands Pk. G46	61	R19	Wright St., Renf.	31	L11	York Way, Renf.	31	M11
Woodlands Rd. G3	35	U11	Wrightlands Cres., Ersk.	16	K8	Yorkhill La. G3	34	T12
Woodlands Rd. G46	61	R19	Wykeham Pl. G13	19	Q9	*Yorkhill St.*		
Woodlands Ter. G3	35	U11	Wykeham Rd. G13	19	Q9	Yorkhill Par. G3	34	T11
Woodlands Ter. G71	69	HH18	Wynd, The G67	71	PP1	Yorkhill Quay G3	34	S12
Woodlea Dr. G46	62	T18	Wyndford Dr. G20	20	T9	Yorkhill St. G3	34	T12
Woodlinn Av. G44	63	V17	Wyndford Pl. G20	20	T9	Young Pl. G71	57	HH15
Woodneuk Rd. G53	60	P17	*Wyndford Rd.*			Young St., Clyde.	5	L6
Woodneuk Rd. G69	27	GG9	Wyndford Rd. G20	20	T9	Young Ter. G21	23	Y10
Woodneuk Ter. G69	27	GG9	Wyndham St. G12	20	T10			
Woodrow Circ. G41	50	T14	Wynford Ter. G71	57	HH16	**Z**		
Woodrow Pl. G41	50	T14	*Myrtle Rd.*					
Maxwell Dr.			Wyper Pl. G40	37	Y13	Zambesi Dr. G72	68	FF19
Woodrow Rd. G41	50	T14	*Gallowgate*			Zena Cres. G33	23	Z10
Woods La., Renf.	17	M10	Wyvil Av. G13	7	R7	Zena Pl. G33	23	Z10
Woodside Av. G46	62	S18	Wyvis Av. G13	18	N8	Zena St. G33	23	Z10
Woodside Av. G66	13	CC5	Wyvis Pl. G13	18	N8	Zetland Rd. G52	32	N12